The Ascent
to Truth

# THE
# ASCENT
# TO
# TRUTH

## Thomas Merton

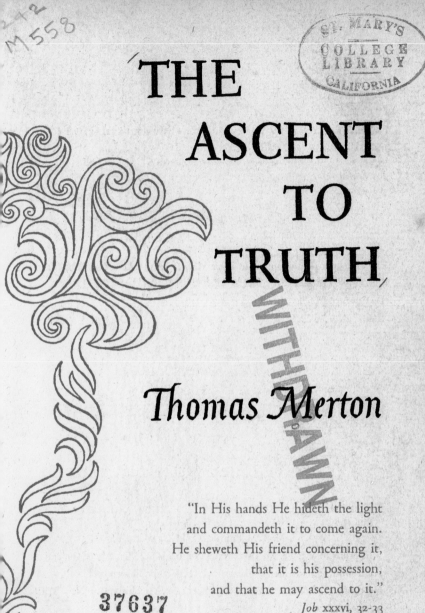

"In His hands He hideth the light
and commandeth it to come again.
He sheweth His friend concerning it,
that it is his possession,
and that he may ascend to it."
*Job* xxxvi, 32-33

Harcourt, Brace and Company, New York

The endpaper photograph, showing a view from the Abbey of Saint Martin
du Canigou in southern France, was taken by Yvonne Sauvageot.

Ex Parte Ordinis

Nihil Obstat: Fr. M. Maurice Malloy, O.C.S.O.
Fr. M. Paul Bourne, O.C.S.O.

Imprimi Potest: Fr. M. Dominique Nogues, O.C.S.O., Abbot General

Nihil Obstat: John M. A. Fearns, S.T.D., Censor librorum

Imprimatur: ✠ FRANCIS CARDINAL SPELLMAN, Archbishop of New York

The *Nihil Obstat* and *Imprimatur* are official declarations that a book or pamphlet is
free of doctrinal or moral error. No implication is contained therein that those who
have granted the *Nihil Obstat* and *Imprimatur* agree with the contents, opinions or
statements expressed.

To Our Lady of Mount Carmel

# Contents

viii CONTENTS

# Author's Note

As soon as the reader has penetrated to the substance of this book, he will understand why it is dedicated to Our Lady of Mount Carmel. It is chiefly concerned with the doctrine of the Carmelite theologian, Saint John of the Cross. Then again, under her title (among others) of Our Lady of Mount Carmel the Blessed Virgin is venerated as patroness of contemplatives and, above all, of those who try to share with others the fruits of their contemplation. The whole aim of the Order founded in her honor is to enable its members to reach the height of contemplation under her guidance and to bring others to that same end, aided by her intercession.

There is no member of the Church who does not owe something to Carmel. But there are few who owe more to the saints of Carmel and to its Queen than does the author. Above all, this book was written, so to speak, under her direction and tutelage. Difficult technical problems and other obstacles which had delayed its writing for two years suddenly vanished after the feast of Saint John of the Cross in 1951 when, among other graces, the author came by a precious relic of the great Mystic of Carmel. From then on, it was relatively smooth sailing, and the author is left with the impression that his finished manuscript reached the publication stage in a manner totally unexpected, not because of his abilities but rather in spite of his limitations.

The dedication of this book is also a special expression of gratitude and of brotherly affection for all those Discalced Carmelites with whom the author is united by bonds of friendship, including Father François de Sainte Marie, Friar of Avon in France, and all the members of three Carmels in particular—the convents in Louisville, San Francisco, and New York. That these have been singled out does not imply exclusion of other Carmelites, both

Regular and Tertiaries; for all are one with the author in the pursuit of Divine Union. May their prayers make up for the defects of this book, which is intended for the glory of Christ, through Our Lady, and ensure that it does not fall short of her desires.

To end here would perhaps leave the reader with the impression that the book was solely inspired from on high and that the author owed nothing to any human instructor. This would be a false impression and quite contrary to the spirit of Catholicism, besides being an injustice to living writers to whom I am much indebted. The first of these is Jacques Maritain who, in his longest and greatest work, *Degrees of Knowledge,* has given us an orderly and luminous treatment of the whole ascent to truth. I refer the reader to everything that has been said by Jacques Maritain, here and elsewhere, about scientific and philosophical knowledge. It forms the necessary groundwork for the doctrine which I here propose: I am particularly indebted to Part Two of the *Degrees of Knowledge* and to the little book, *Prayer and Intelligence.* Another excellent book, which gives a simple but lucid outline of the questions which have most exercised me in the present work, is *The Dark Knowledge of God* by Monsignor Charles Journet of the University of Fribourg.

Needless to say, I am also in everlasting debt for the aid given me by the friendship, inspiration, and prayers of Jacques and Raïssa Maritain. I cannot omit my indebtedness in this same regard to my friends, Dr. Daniel C. Walsh and Sister M. Thérèse, S.D.S. Finally, of course, I express my gratitude to Professor E. Allison Peers of the University of Liverpool, the translator of Saint John of the Cross, whose translation I have quoted even more extensively here than elsewhere.

It gives me great joy to feel that by virtue of the present book, whatever may be its failings, the charity of Christ has united me with these and numberless other guides, advisers, and friends, under the peaceful shadow of Our Lady's mantle.

FR. M. LOUIS MERTON, O.C.S.O.

*Abbey of Our Lady of Gethsemani*

# The Ascent
# to Truth

# Mysticism in Man's Life

The only thing that can save the world from complete moral collapse is a spiritual revolution. Christianity, by its very nature, demands such a revolution. If Christians would all live up to what they profess to believe, the revolution would happen. The desire for unworldliness, detachment, and union with God is the most fundamental expression of this revolutionary spirit. The one thing that remains is for Christians to affirm their Christianity by that full and unequivocal rejection of the world which their Baptismal vocation demands of them. This will certainly not incapacitate them for social action in the world, since it is the one essential condition for a really fruitful Christian apostolate.

The human race is facing the greatest crisis in its history, because religion itself is being weighed in the balance. The present unrest in five continents, with everyone fearful of being destroyed, has brought many men to their knees. This should not lead us into the illusion that the world is necessarily about to return to God. Nevertheless, the exposure of the nineteenth-century myths—"unlimited progress" and the "omnipotence" of physical science—has thrown the world into confusion. Many are spontaneously turning to the only evident hope for spiritual and moral integration—an order based on philosophical and theological truth, one which allows free expression to the fundamental religious instinct of man. So vast is this movement that a psychoanalyst as important as Carl Jung can make the following declaration:

I have treated many hundreds of patients, the larger number being Protestants, a smaller number Jews and not more than five or six believing Catholics. Among all my patients in the second half of my life . . . there has not been one whose problem in the last resort was not that of finding a religious outlook on life. It is safe to say that every one of them fell ill because he had lost that which the living religions of every age have given their followers and none of them has really been healed who did not regain his religious outlook.[1]

The big problem that confronts Christianity is not Christ's enemies. Persecution has never done much harm to the inner life of the Church as such. The real religious problem exists in the souls of those of us who in their hearts believe in God, and who recognize their obligation to love Him and serve Him—yet do not!

The world we live in is dry ground for the seed of God's Truth. A modern American city is not altogether a propitious place in which to try to love God. You cannot love Him unless you know Him. And you cannot come to know Him unless you have a little time and a little peace in which to pray and think about Him and study His truth. Time and peace are not easily come by in this civilization of ours. And so those who profess to serve God are often forced to get along without either, and to sacrifice their hopes of an interior life. But how far can one go in this sacrifice before it ceases to be a sacrifice and becomes a prevarication? The truth is, we are simply not permitted to devote ourselves to God without at the same time leading an interior life.

The reason for this is plain. Everything we do in the service of God has to be vitalized by the supernatural power of His grace. But grace is granted us in proportion as we dispose ourselves to receive it by the interior activity of the theological virtues: faith, hope, charity. These virtues demand the full and constant exercise of our intelligence and will. But this exercise is frequently obstructed by exterior influences which blind us with passion and draw us away from our supernatural objective. This cannot be avoided, but it must be fought against by a constant discipline of recollection, meditation, prayer, study, mortification of the desires, and at least some measure of solitude and retirement.

It is certainly not possible, or even desirable, that every Christian should leave the world and enter a Trappist monastery. Nevertheless, the sudden interest of Americans in the contemplative life seems to prove one thing quite clearly: that contemplation, asceticism, mental prayer, and unworldliness are elements that most need to be rediscovered by Christians of our time. There is little danger that we will neglect apostolic labor and exterior activity. Pope Pius XII in a recent exhortation drew attention to the fact that external activity had perhaps been overstressed in some quarters, and reminded Catholics that their personal sanctity and union with Christ in a deep interior life were the most important things of all. His Holiness writes:

We cannot abstain from expressing our preoccupation and our anxiety for those who, on account of the special circumstances of the moment, have become so engulfed in the vortex of external activity that they neglect the chief duty [of the Christian]: his own sanctification. We have already stated publicly in writing that those who presume that the world can be saved by what has rightly been called the "heresy of action" must be made to exercise better judgment.[2]

The fact that the Communists used to be in revolt against everything "bourgeois" imposed on every serious Communist the obligation to practice a strict and almost religious asceticism with regard to practically everything that is valued by the society he hates. I say that this *used to be* the case, because it is clear that the Stalinist empire has rapidly reached a cultural level in which everything that was basest in bourgeois materialism has become the Stalinist ideal. If Christianity is to prove itself in open rebellion against the standards of the materialist society in which it is fighting for survival, Christians must show more definite signs of that *agere contra,* that positive "resistance," which is the heart of the Christian ascetic "revolution." The true knowledge of God can be bought only at the price of this resistance.

We, who live in what we ourselves have called the Atomic Age, have acquired a peculiar facility for standing back and reflecting on our own history as if it were a phenomenon that took place five thousand years ago. We like to talk about our time as if we had no part in it. We view it as objectively as if it existed outside ourselves, in a glass case. If you are looking for the Atomic Age, look inside yourself: because you are it. And so, alas, am I.

The evil that is in the modern world ought to be sufficient indication that we do not know as much as we think we do. It is a strange paradox indeed that modern man should know so much and still know practically nothing. The paradox is most strange because men in other times, who have known less than we know, have in fact known more.

True, in all times there has been wickedness and great blindness in this world of men. There is nothing new under the sun, not even the H-bomb (which was invented by our Father Adam). And it is also true that the ages of greatest despair have sometimes ended up by being ages of triumph and of hope. There would be little point in writing a book about the Ascent to Truth if there were no hope for the sanity of the human race. Now that we have awakened to our fundamental barbarism, it seems to me that there is once again a hope for civilization, because men of good will want more than ever to be civilized. And now that we have our tremendous capacities for evil staring us in the face, there is more incentive than ever for men to become saints. For man is naturally inclined to good, and not to evil. Besides our nature, we have what is infinitely greater—the grace of God, which draws us powerfully upward to the infinite Truth and is refused to no one who desires it.

The whole happiness of man and even his sanity depend on his moral condition. And since society does not exist all by itself in a void, but is made up of the individuals who compose it, the problems of society cannot ultimately be solved except in terms of the moral life of individuals. If the citizens are sane, the city will be sane. If the citizens are wild animals, the city will be a jungle.

But morality is not an end in itself. Virtue, for a Chris-

tian, is not its own reward. God is our reward. The moral
life leads to something beyond itself—to the experience
of union with God, and to our transformation in Him.
This transformation is perfected in another life, and in
the light of glory. Yet even on earth man may be granted
a foretaste of heaven in mystical contemplation. And
whether he experiences it or not, the man of faith, by
virtue of his faith, is already living in heaven. *Conversatio
nostra in coelis!*

The fact that contemplation is actually the lot of very
few men does not mean that it has no importance for
mankind as a whole.

If the salvation of society depends, in the long run,
on the moral and spiritual health of individuals, the subject of contemplation becomes a vastly important one,
since contemplation is one of the indications of spiritual
maturity. It is closely allied to sanctity. You cannot save
the world merely with a system. You cannot have peace
without charity. You cannot have order without saints.

2

Our nature imposes on us a certain pattern of development which we must follow if we are to fulfill our best
capacities and achieve at least the partial happiness of
being human. This pattern must be properly understood
and it must be worked out in all its essential elements.
Otherwise, we fail. But it can be stated very simply, in
a single sentence: *We must know the truth, and we must
love the truth we know, and we must act according to
the measure of our love.*

What are the elements of this "pattern" I speak of?

*First,* and most important of all: I must adapt myself to objective reality. *Second,* this adaptation is achieved by the work of my highest spiritual faculties—intelligence and will. *Third,* it demands expression when my whole being, commanded by my will, produces actions which, by their moral vitality and fruitfulness, show that I am living in harmony with the true order of things.

These are the bare essentials of the pattern. They represent a psychological necessity without which man cannot preserve his mental and spiritual health.

I have only stated these fundamentals of our nature in order to build on them. Contemplation reproduces the same essential outline of this pattern, but on a much higher level. For contemplation is a work of grace. The Truth to which it unites us is not an abstraction but Reality and Life itself. The love by which it unites us to this Truth is a gift of God and can only be produced within us by the direct action of God. The activity which is its final and most perfect fruit is a charity so supreme that it gathers itself into a timeless self-oblation in which there is no motion, for all its perfection is held within the boundless radius of a moment that is eternal.

These are difficult matters. To return to our simple sentence: When I say that we must know the truth and love the truth we know, I am not talking primarily about the truth of individual facts and statements but about Truth as such. Truth is reality itself, considered as the object of the intellect. The Truth man needs to know is the transcendent reality, of which particular truths are merely a partial manifestation. Since we ourselves are real, this Truth is not so far distant from us as one might imagine.

Our ordinary waking life is a bare existence in which, most of the time, we seem to be absent from ourselves and from reality because we are involved in the vain pre-occupations which dog the steps of every living man. But there are times when we seem suddenly to awake and discover the full meaning of our own present reality. Such discoveries are not capable of being contained in formulas or definitions. They are a matter of personal experience, of uncommunicable intuition. In the light of such an experience it is easy to see the futility of all the trifles that occupy our minds. We recapture something of the calm and the balance that ought always to be ours, and we understand that life is far too great a gift to be squandered on anything less than perfection.

In the lives of those who are cast adrift in the modern world, with nothing to rely on but their own resources, these moments of understanding are short-lived and barren. For, though man may get a glimpse of the natural value of his spirit, nature alone is incapable of fulfilling his spiritual aspirations.

The Truth man needs is not a philosopher's abstraction, but God Himself. The paradox of contemplation is that God is never really known unless He is also loved. And we cannot love Him unless we do His will. This explains why modern man, who knows so much, is nevertheless ignorant. Because he is without love, modern man fails to see the only Truth that matters and on which all else depends.

God becomes present in a very special way and manifests Himself in the world wherever He is known and loved by men. His glory shines in an ineffable manner through those whom He has united to Himself. Those who as yet know nothing of God have a perfect right to expect that we who *do* pretend to know Him should give evidence of the fact, not only by "satisfying every one that asketh us a reason of that hope which is in us," [3] but above all by the testimony of our own lives. For Christ said, in His priestly prayer:

> The glory which thou hast given me I have given them,
> that they may be one as we also are one: I in them
> and thou in me, that they may be made perfect in one:
> and the *world may know that thou hast sent me, and hast
> loved them as thou hast also loved me.*[4]

It is useless to study truths about God and lead a life that has nothing in it of the Cross of Christ. No one can do such a thing without, in fact, displaying complete ignorance of the meaning of Christianity. For the Christian economy is by no means a mere philosophy or an ethical system, still less a social theory.

Christ was not a wise man who came to teach a doctrine. He is God, Who became incarnate in order to effect a mystical transformation of mankind. He did, of course, bring with Him a doctrine greater than any that was ever preached before or since. But that doctrine does not end with moral ideas and precepts of asceticism. The teaching of Christ is the seed of a new life. Reception of the word of God by faith initiates man's transformation. It elevates him above this world and above his own nature and transports his acts of thought and of desire to a supernatural level. He becomes a partaker of the divine nature, a Son of God, and Christ is living in him. From that moment forward, the door to eternity stands open in the

depths of his soul and he is capable of becoming a contemplative. Then he can watch at the frontier of an abyss
of light so bright that it is darkness. Then he will burn
with desire to see the fullness of Light and will cry out
to God, like Moses in the cloud on Sinai: "Show me
Thy face!"

3

The function of this book is to define the nature of the
contemplative experience, to show something of the necessary interior ascesis which leads up to it, and to give a
brief sketch of mature contemplation. When faith opens
out into a deep spiritual understanding and advances
beyond the range of concepts into a darkness which can
only be enlightened by the fire of love, man truly begins
to know God in the only way that can satisfy his soul.

Concepts tells us the truth about God, but their light
is so far from being perfect that the man who is fully
content with conceptual knowledge of God, and does not
burn to possess Him by love, has never really known
Him. But if the contemplative experience of God goes
beyond concepts, is it purely subjective? Does it imply a
complete rejection of scientific truth? Does it evade the
reach of every authority? Is the mystic a kind of religious
genius who lives in an atmosphere entirely his own and
whose inspiration is nobody else's business? Perhaps the
reason why William James admitted the validity of mystical experience was precisely because it could be fitted into
the context of his pragmatism by an absolutely affirmative
answer to these questions.

All these problems furnish the subject matter of the
present volume. My solutions can be condensed as follows.

First of all, the contemplative life demands detachment from the senses, but it is not therefore a complete rejection of sense experience. It rises above the level of reasoning; yet reason plays an essential part in the interior ascesis without which we cannot safely travel the path of mysticism. Mystical prayer rises above the natural operation of the intelligence, yet it is always essentially intelligent. Ultimately, the highest function of the human spirit is the work of the supernaturally transformed intelligence, in the beatific vision of God. Nevertheless, the will plays an integral part in all contemplation since there is, in fact, no contemplation without love. Love is both the starting point of contemplation and its fruition.

Furthermore, contemplation presupposes ascetic action. By this interrelation of the work of intelligence, will, and the rest of our being, contemplation immolates our entire self to God. God is the principal agent in this sublime work. Contemplation is His gift, and He is free to dispose of it as He sees fit. It can never, strictly speaking, be merited by any generosity of ours. However, in actual fact, God usually grants this gift to those who are most generous in emptying themselves of every attachment to satisfactions that fall outside the periphery of pure faith.

Finally, mystical contemplation comes to us, like every other grace, through Christ. Contemplation is the fullness of the Christ-life in the soul, and it consists above all in the supernatural penetration of the mysteries of Christ. This work is performed in us by the Holy Ghost substantially present in our soul by grace, along with the other two Divine Persons. The highest peak of contemplation is a mystical union with God in which the soul and its faculties are said to be "transformed" in God, and enter into a full conscious participation in the hidden life of the Trinity of Persons in Unity of Nature.

My chief preoccupation in this work has been not to describe or account for the highest levels of mystical experience, but only to settle certain fundamental questions which refer more properly to the ascetical preparation for graces of mystical prayer. The chief of these questions concerns the relations of the intellect and will in contemplation.

The reason I have insisted on this is that we stand in very great danger of a wave of false mysticism. When the world is in greatest confusion, visionaries become oracles. Panic, like every other passion, blinds the intelligence of man, and he is glad of an excuse to take refuge from everything that bewilders him by giving it a "supernatural" interpretation. Therefore it must be made quite clear that traditional Christian mysticism, although it is certainly not intellectualistic in the same sense as the mystical philosophy of Plato and his followers, is nevertheless neither antirational nor anti-intellectualistic.

There is absolutely no enmity between Christian mysticism, on the one hand, and physical science, natural philosophy, metaphysics, and dogmatic theology on the other. Contemplation is suprarational, without in the least despising the light of reason. The modern popes have insisted on the fundamental harmony between "acquired" or speculative wisdom and the "infused" wisdom which is a gift of the Holy Ghost and is true contemplation. Pope Pius XI, in holding up Saint Thomas Aquinas as a model for priests and theologians, pointed out that the sanctity of the Angelic Doctor consisted above all in the marvelous union of speculative science and infused contemplation which combined to feed the pure flame of his perfect love for God, in such a way that the whole theology of Saint Thomas has but one end: to bring us to intimate union with God.[5]

Pius XII, in his encyclical *Humani Generis,* insisted on the perfect conformity that exists between theological science and the "connatural" knowledge of God by love in mystical contemplation, while at the same time reproving loose philosophical statements which confused the action of the intelligence and the will in the speculative knowledge of divine things.

All this reminds us that the intelligence has a vitally important part to play in Christian sanctity, and that no one can pretend to love God while rejecting all desire to know Him better and to study His perfections in the truths He has revealed to us about Himself. Nevertheless, love remains the very essence of Christian perfection and sanctity, since it unites us to God directly and without medium even in this life. Love also, which is the fruit of our vision of Him in heaven, will be our purest joy in heaven because by it we will be able not merely to receive of His infinite bounty but also to repay Him out of the treasury of His own unbounded perfections.

The traditional teaching of the Church, which has been so strongly emphasized by the encyclicals of recent popes and which is the very heart of the *Summa Theologica,* refuses to divide man against himself. The sanity of Catholic theology will never permit the ascetic to wander off into bypaths of angelism or gnosticism. The Church does not seek to sanctify men by destroying their humanity, but by elevating it, with all its faculties and gifts, to the supreme perfection which the Greek Fathers called "deification." At the same time, the Church does not leave man under any illusion about himself. She clearly shows him the powerlessness of his natural faculties to achieve Divine Union by their own efforts.

There are, then, two extremes to be avoided. On the one hand, false mysticism ascribes to human nature the power and the right to acquire supernatural illuminations by the effort of our own intelligence. On the other hand, false mysticism darkens the intelligence altogether in a formal rejection of truth in order to seek Divine Union in an ecstasy of blind love which takes no account of the intelligence, and which accepts deification as a gift so pure that no effort is required on the part of the one who receives it.

But what is the true nature of mystical contemplation? It is first of all a supernatural experience of God as He is in Himself. This experience is a free gift of God in a more special sense than are all the other graces required for our sanctification, although it forms part of the normal supernatural organism by which we are sanctified. Essentially, mystical experience is a vivid, conscious participation of our soul and of its faculties in the life, knowledge, and love of God Himself. This participation is ontologically possible only because sanctifying grace is imparted to us as a new "being" superadded to our nature and giving it the power to elicit acts which are entirely beyond its own capacity.

More particularly, however, the mystical experience is directly caused by special inspirations of the Holy Ghost substantially present within the soul itself and already obscurely identified with it by grace. The effect of these inspirations is to enable the soul to "see" and appreciate, in a manner totally new and unexpected, the full reality of the truths contained in hitherto "untasted" conceptual statements about God. But above all, this experience gives us a deep penetration into the truth of our identification with God by grace. Contemplative experience in the strict sense of the word is always an experience of God Who is apprehended not as an abstraction, not as a distant and alien Being, but as intimately and immediately present to the soul in His infinite Reality and Essence.

This is the substance of Catholic mysticism. I propose to study this substance as it is expounded in the works of the Church's "safest" mystical theologian, the sixteenth-century Spanish Carmelite, Saint John of the Cross.

This great servant of God, who joined Saint Teresa of Ávila in the work of restoring the purity of Carmelite life and of teaching his world the ways of mystical prayer, stands at the culminating point of the mystical tradition which used to be ascribed to the Pseudo-Dionysius. Saint John of the Cross is the leader of the "apophatic" theologians, the teachers of the "dark" knowledge of God. He completes and fulfills the tradition of the greatest contemplatives among the Greek Fathers—Saint Gregory of Nyssa, who really founded the apophatic school; Evagrius Ponticus, and Saint Maximus. But what is much more important, he avoids all the ambiguities and exaggerations inherent in Patristic mysticism, and he does so by basing his whole doctrine upon the solid foundation of Thomism, which he acquired at the University of Salamanca.

The doctrine of Saint John of the Cross is so clear, so solid, and so universal that Pope Pius XI could say without hesitation that he "points out to souls the way of perfection as though illumined by light from on high, in his limpidly clear analysis of mystical experience." The Pontiff adds: "And although [the works of Saint John of the Cross] deal with difficult and hidden matters, they are nevertheless replete with such lofty spiritual doctrine and are so well adapted to the understanding of those who study them that they can rightly be called a guide and handbook for the man of faith who proposes to embrace a life of perfection." [6]

The proper Mass of Saint John of the Cross approved by the Church for the Discalced Carmelites is filled with the Scriptural images which he used to illustrate his mystical theology. The Preface of that Mass is a brief but eloquent summary of his doctrine of renunciation and of "Night" as the sure path to Divine Union.

Testimony such as this gives evidence of the great importance which the Holy See attributes to the teaching and intercession of so great a saint. The development of interest in his theology, and especially the studies in which Dominican theologians have illustrated the fundamental harmony of the mysticism of Saint John of the Cross with the dogmatic theology of Saint Thomas, lead us to expect, in all confidence, that someday Saint John of the Cross will assume his rightful place as the *doctor communis* of Catholic Mystical Theology. In the Apostolic Letter from which I quoted above, Pope Pius XI concludes that present-day theologians can turn to Saint John of the Cross and verify for themselves his greatness as a master of the spiritual life by "drawing from his doctrine and writings the limpid purity of all the spiritual teaching that has ever poured forth from the fountain-head of Christian thought and from the spirit of the Church."

PART ONE

# THE CLOUD AND THE FIRE

# CHAPTER I

# Vision
# and Illusion

The earthly desires men cherish are shadows. There is no true happiness in fulfilling them. Why, then, do we continue to pursue joys without substance? Because *the pursuit itself* has become our only substitute for joy. Unable to rest in anything we achieve, we determine to forget our discontent in a ceaseless quest for new satisfactions. In this pursuit, desire itself becomes our chief satisfaction. The goods that so disappoint us when they are in our grasp can still stimulate our interest when they elude us in the present or in the past.

Few men have so clearly outlined this subtle psychology of illusion as Blaise Pascal, who writes:

A man can pass his whole life without boredom, merely by gambling each day with a modest sum. Give him, each morning, the amount of money he might be able to win in a day, on condition that he must not gamble: you will make him miserable! You may say that what he seeks is the amusement of gaming, not the winnings. All right, let him play for nothing. There will be no excitement. He will be bored to death!

So it is not just amusement that he seeks. An amusement that is tame, without passion, only bores him. He wants to get worked up and to delude himself that he is going to be happy if he wins a sum that he would actually refuse if it were given him on condition that he must not gamble. He needs to create an object for his passions, and to direct upon that object his desire, his anger and his fear—like children who scare themselves with their own painted faces.[1]

A life based on desires is like a spider's web, says Saint Gregory of Nyssa. Woven about us by the father of lies, the Devil, the enemy of our souls, it is a frail tissue of vanities without substance, and yet it can catch us and hold us fast, delivering us up to him as his prisoner. Nevertheless, the illusion is only an illusion, nothing more. It should be as easy for us to break through this tissue of lies as it is for us to destroy a spider's web with a movement of the hand. Saint Gregory says:

All that man pursues in this life has no existence except in his mind, not in reality: opinion, honor, dignities, glory, fortune: all these are the work of this life's spiders. . . . But those who rise to the heights escape, with the flick of a wing, from the spiders of this world. Only those who, like flies, are heavy and without energy remain caught in the glue of this world and are taken and bound, as though in nets, by honors, pleasures, praise and manifold desires, and thus they become the prey of the beast that seeks to capture them.[2]

The fundamental theme of *Ecclesiastes* is the paradox that, although there is "nothing new under the sun," each new generation of mankind is condemned by nature to wear itself out in the pursuit of "novelties" that do not exist. This concept, tragic as the Oriental notion of *karma* which it resembles so closely, contains in itself the one great enigma of paganism. Only Christ, only the Incarnation, by which God emerged from His eternity to enter into time and consecrate it to Himself, could save time from being an endless circle of frustrations. Only Christianity can, in Saint Paul's phrase, "redeem the times." Other

religions can break out of the wheel of time as though
from a prison: but they can make nothing of time itself.

Saint Gregory of Nyssa, pursuing his meditations on
the psychology of attachment and illusion, vision and detachment, which constitute his commentary on *Ecclesiastes*, observes how time weaves about us this web of
illusion. It is not enough to say that the man who is
attached to this world has bound himself to it, once and
for all, by a wrong choice. No: he spins a whole net of
falsities around his spirit by the repeated consecration of
his whole self to values that do not exist. He exhausts
himself in the pursuit of mirages that ever fade and are
renewed as fast as they have faded, drawing him further
and further into the wilderness where he must die of
thirst. A life immersed in matter and in sense cannot help
but reproduce the fancied torments which Greek mythology displays in Hades—Tantalus starving to death with
food an inch from his lips, Sysiphus rolling his boulder
uphill though he knows it must escape him and roll down
to the bottom again, just as he is reaching the summit.

And so, that "vanity of vanities" which so exercised
the Ancient Preacher of *Ecclesiastes* and his commentator
is a life not merely of deluded thoughts and aspirations,
but above all a life of ceaseless and sterile activity. What
is more, in such a life the measure of illusion is the very
intensity of activity itself. The less you have, the more
you do. The final delusion is movement, change, and
variety for their own sakes alone.

All the preoccupation of men with the things of this life [writes
Saint Gregory], is but the game of children on the sands. For
children take delight in the activity of their play and as soon as

they have finished building what they build, their pleasure ends. For as soon as their labor is completed, the sand falls down and nothing is left of their buildings.[3]

This profound idea often finds echoes in the pages of Pascal. It might well have provided a foundation for his famous theory of "distraction"—*divertissement*.[4] Pascal knew that the philosophers, who laughed at men for running all day long after a hare that they would probably not have accepted as a present, had not plumbed the full depths of man's inanity. Men who call themselves civilized do not hunt foxes because they want to catch a fox. Neither do they, for that matter, always study philosophy or science because they want to know the truth. No: they are condemned to physical or spiritual movement because it is unbearable for them to sit still. As Pascal says:

We look for rest, and overcome obstacles to obtain it. But if we overcome these obstacles, rest becomes intolerable, for we begin at once to think either of the misfortunes that are ours, or of those that threaten to descend upon us.[5]

Man was made for the highest activity, which is, in fact, his rest. That activity, which is contemplation, is immanent and it transcends the level of sense and of discourse. Man's guilty sense of his incapacity for this one deep activity which is the reason for his very existence, is precisely what drives him to seek oblivion in exterior motion and desire. Incapable of the divine activity which alone can satisfy his soul, fallen man flings himself upon exterior things, not so much for their own sake as for the sake of the agitation which keeps his spirit pleasantly numb. He has but to remain busy with trifles; his preoccupation will serve as a dope. It will not deaden all the pain of thinking; but it will at least do something to blur his sense of who he is and of his utter insufficiency.

Pascal sums up his observations with the remark: "Distraction is the only thing that consoles us for our miseries and yet it is, itself, the greatest of our miseries." [6]

Why? Because it "diverts" us, turns us aside from the one thing that can help us to begin our ascent to truth. That one thing is the sense of our own emptiness, our poverty, our limitations, and of the inability of created things to satisfy our profound need for reality and for truth.

What is the conclusion of all this? We imprison ourselves in falsity by our love for the feeble, flickering light of illusion and desire. We cannot find the true light unless this false light be darkened. We cannot find true happiness unless we deprive ourselves of the *ersatz* happiness of empty diversion. Peace, true peace, is only to be found through suffering, and we must seek the light in darkness.

2

There are, in Christian tradition, a theology of light and a theology of darkness. On these two lines travel two mystical trends. There are the great theologians of light: Origen, Saint Augustine, Saint Bernard, Saint Thomas Aquinas. And there are the great theologians of darkness: Saint Gregory of Nyssa, Pseudo-Dionysius, Saint John of the Cross. The two lines travel side by side. Modern theologians of genius have found no difficulty in uniting the two, in synthesizing Saint Thomas Aquinas and Saint John of the Cross. Some of the greatest mystics—Ruysbroeck, Saint Teresa of Ávila, and Saint John of the Cross himself—describe both aspects of contemplation, "light" and "darkness."

There are pages in the works of Saint Gregory of Nyssa —as there are also in those of Saint John of the Cross— which might easily fit into a context of Zen Buddhism of Patanjali's Yoga. But we must remember that when a Christian mystic speaks of the created world as an illusion and as "nothingness," he is only using a figure of speech. The words are never to be taken literally and they are not ontological. The world is metaphysically real. Creatures can lead us efficaciously to the knowledge and love of their Creator and ours. But since the created world is present to our senses, and God as He is in Himself is infinitely beyond the reach both of sense and of intelligence, and since the disorder of sin gives us a tendency to prefer sensible goods before all others, we have a way of seeking the good things of this life as if they were our last end.

When Creation appears to us in the false light of concupiscence, it becomes illusion. The supreme value that cupidity seeks in created things does not exist in them. A man who takes a tree for a ghost is in illusion. The tree is objectively real: but in his mind it is something that it is not. A man who takes a cigar coupon for a ten-dollar bill is also in illusion. It is a real cigar coupon, and yet, considered as a ten-dollar bill, it is a pure illusion. When we live as if the multiplicity of the phenomenal universe were the criterion of all truth, and treat the world about us as if its shifting scale of values were the only measure of our ultimate good, the world becomes an illusion. It is real in itself, but it is no longer real to us because it is not what we think it is.

Many Christian mystics look at the world only from the subjective standpoint of fallen man. Do not be surprised, then, if they say that the world is empty, that it is nothingness, and offer no explanation. But Saint Gregory of Nyssa, together with many of the Greek Fathers, not to mention those of the West, sees all sides of the question.

The contemplation of God in nature, which the Greek Fathers called *theoria physica,* has both a positive and a negative aspect. On the one hand, *theoria physica* is a positive recognition of God as He is manifested in the essences (*logoi*) of all things. It is not a speculative science of nature but rather a habit of religious awareness which endows the soul with a kind of intuitive perception of God as He is reflected in His creation. This instinctive religious view of things is not acquired by study so much as by ascetic detachment. And that implies that the positive and negative elements in this "contemplation of nature" are really inseparable. The negative aspect of *theoria physica* is an equally instinctive realization of the vanity and illusion of all things as soon as they are considered apart from their right order and reference to God their Creator. Saint Gregory of Nyssa's commentary on *Ecclesiastes,* from which we have quoted, is a tract on the "contemplation of nature" in its twofold aspect, as vanity and as symbol.

Does all this mean that the *theoria physica* of the Greek Fathers was a kind of perpetual dialectic between the two terms *vision* and *illusion?* No. In the Christian platonism of the Fathers, dialectic is no longer as important as it was in Plato and Plotinus. The Christian contemplation of nature does not consist in an intellectual tennis game between these two contrary aspects of nature. It consists rather in the ascetic gift of a discernment which, in one penetrating glance, apprehends what creatures are, and what they are not. This is the intellectual counterpoise of detachment in the will. Discernment and detachment (*krisis* and *apatheia*) are two characters of the mature Christian soul. They are not yet the mark of a mystic, but they bear witness that one is traveling the right way to mystical contemplation, and that the stage of beginners is passed.

The presence of discernment and detachment is manifested by a spontaneous thirst for what is good—charity, union with the will of God—and an equally spontaneous repugnance for what is evil. The man who has this virtue no longer needs to be exhorted by promises to do what is right, or deterred from evil by threat of punishment.[7]

So great is the power of man's intelligence that it can start out from the least of all beings and arrive at the greatest. The mind of man is, by its very nature, a participation in the intelligence of God, Whose light illumines the conclusions of rational discourse. Words can be sadly mistreated and misused; but they could not be false unless they could also be true. Language may become a suspicious instrument on the tongues of fools or charlatans, but language as such retains its power to signify and communicate the Truth.

Faith, without depending on reason for the slightest shred of justification, never contradicts reason and remains ever reasonable. Faith does not destroy reason, but fulfills it. Nevertheless, there must always remain a delicate balance between the two. Two extremes are to be avoided: credulity and skepticism; superstition and rationalism.

If this balance is upset, if man relies too much on his five senses and on his reason when faith should be his teacher, then he enters into illusion. Or when, in defiance of reason, he gives the assent of his faith to a fallible authority, then too he falls into illusion. Reason is in fact the path to faith, and faith takes over when reason can say no more.

# CHAPTER II

# The Problem
# of Unbelief

It is absolutely impossible for a man to live without some kind of faith. Faith, in the broadest sense, is the acceptance of truth on the evidence of another. The essence of all faith is the submission of our judgment to the authority of someone else, on whose word we accept a truth that is not intrinsically evident to our own minds. Human or *natural faith* is the acceptance of truths on the authority of other men. *Supernatural faith* is the belief in truths revealed by God, on the testimony of God, and because of the authority of God Who reveals these truths to us.

One of the paradoxes of our age, which has so far not distinguished itself as an Age of Faith, is that millions of men who have found it impossible to believe in God have blindly submitted themselves in human faith to every charlatan who has access to a printing press, a movie screen, or a microphone. Men who cannot believe in the revealed word of God swallow everything they read in the newspapers. Men who think it absurd that the Church should be able, by virtue of the guidance and protection of the Holy Ghost, to make infallible pronouncements as to what has or has not been revealed by God concerning doctrine or morality, will believe the most fantastic claims of political propaganda, even though the dishonesty of propagandists has become, by now, proverbial.

They find it impossible to believe the Pope when, with the extreme caution and reserve which is characteristic of Rome, he makes one of his rare and guarded *ex cathedra* pronouncements within the very narrow field of "faith and morals" concerning which, as the Vicar of Christ on earth, he might be expected to know something. And yet if some movie star or other celebrity, who stalled for three years in the eighth grade and finally gave up all hope of high school, makes a dogmatic declaration on anything from marriage to astrophysics, they will regard it as "authoritative."

The final irony of the situation is this: that most men have no intellectual right to their theological unbelief. Strictly speaking, of course, no man has an intellectual right to unbelief because theological faith is eminently reasonable. The intelligence has no right to be consciously unintelligent. But there do nevertheless exist a few men who, in all sincerity, have arrived by their own research at the error that theological faith is unacceptable. We cannot respect their error, but at least we have to admit that they worked hard to reach it. Their ignorance is invincible. They are in "good faith" in having no faith, because they think they have evidence against the validity of faith as such. This supposes (at least in theory) that if they saw the evidence in favor of faith, they would instantly change their view.

But no: the paradox is this. While one or two men hold, as a result of false reasoning, that theological faith is unacceptable, millions of others reject the notion of faith by an act not of reason but of blind faith. Here is evi-

dence of the supreme intellectual indigence of our civilization: our very refusal to believe is based on faith.

There is still a greater enormity in our unbelief. We
disbelieve God on the testimony of man. We reject the
word of God because we are told to do so by men who, in
their turn, were told to do so by men. The only real reason
why most unbelievers cannot yield to the infallible authority of God is that they have already submitted to the
fallible authority of men.

Now, reason shows that the only one who can tell us
anything about God is God Himself. Men know nothing
of His inner life or of His plans for them. Men can only
command belief in their statements about Him when it is
reasonable to hold that their statements are not theirs but
His—when they speak as His representatives. "The things
that are of God no man knoweth, but the Spirit of God."
(I Cor. 2:4.)

God, being Pure Actuality, Pure Intelligence, not only
sees all truth but is all Truth. Every truth, every being, is
simply a reflection of Him. Truths are only true in Him,
and because of Him. The light of reason is a natural participation in His Truth. Reason itself draws its authority
from Him. That is why reason, if it be allowed to light
our way, will bring us, without prejudice, to faith.

But men without theological faith, reasoning from false
premises which they receive, on faith, from the fallible
authority of other men, use the God-given light of reason
to argue against God, against faith and even against reason
itself.

This issue is generally misunderstood, because faith has
so often been proposed as alien to reason and even as contrary to it. According to this view, faith is an entirely sub-

jective experience which can neither be communicated nor explained. It is something emotional. It either happens to you or it does not. If it happens, you "have faith." The fact that you "have faith" does not necessarily have any effect on your reasoning, because your "faith" is an emotional thing beyond the pale of reason. You cannot explain it to yourself or to anybody else. But if faith has no intellectual reference whatever, it is hardly possible to see how "having faith" can contribute much to your outlook on life or to your behavior. It does not seem to be much more important than having red hair or a wooden leg. It is just something that happened to you, but did not happen to your next-door neighbor.

This false idea of faith is the last refuge of religious compromise with rationalism. Fearing that domestic peace is no longer possible, faith barricades itself in the attic, and leaves the rest of the house to reason. Actually, faith and reason are meant to get along happily together. They were not meant to live alone, in divorce or in separation.

2

In all faith, whether natural or supernatural, we must have some rational assurance that the person on whose word we accept a truth really speaks with authority. The relations of the average layman with his doctor demand a large amount of human faith. We expect our doctor to know quite a lot about a subject of which we ourselves are ignorant. We take the medicines he prescribes, trusting in his skill, on his authority. But it is not rational to trust every man who calls himself a doctor. We are unreasonable if we place ourselves in the hands of someone whose pa-

tients spend more and more money for esoteric treatments
and strange operations without ever getting well.

The fact remains that not a few such doctors have become rich. And the funniest thing about it is that often
they have fattened on the faith of agnostics and of atheists!

It is easy to see the rational basis for human "faith" in
something like penicillin. What is not clear to most people is that it is just as rational to believe in miracles as it is
to believe in penicillin. But here again, the issue is vastly
confused. Some seem to think that belief in miracles somehow implies that the believer will normally expect to be
cured of pneumonia by a miracle rather than by penicillin.

Actually, the situation is quite otherwise. The experience of doctors shows that most pneumonia patients (but
certainly not all of them) profit by the use of penicillin.
The experience of doctors also shows that men have been
cured of seemingly incurable diseases in an altogether extraordinary fashion for which they offer no explanation but
the direct intervention of God. The believing Christian is
well aware that in any event the cure is attributable to God,
that God can cure me of pneumonia through the instrumentality of a doctor pumping me full of penicillin, or
by means of a drop of Lourdes water on the tip of my
tongue. God, Who made the laws of nature, can also
suspend them as He pleases. Nevertheless, the believing Christian is bound, under pain of sin, to take ordinary, reasonable means to preserve his life and even his
bodily health. He is never bound to drink Lourdes water.
He would even be guilty of sin if he sought a miraculous
cure while culpably neglecting ordinary means to preserve
his life!

The Catholic is obliged to believe that God is able to work miracles. But this truth is also evident to reason, for we have just pointed out that God, the author of nature, can do what He pleases with its laws. But no Catholic is obliged to believe in the concrete proposition "miracles take place daily at Lourdes." In fact, this proposition cannot be believed with theological faith, since it has nowhere been revealed by God that miracles are to take place precisely at Lourdes.

The hundreds of genuine miracles which have happened at Lourdes and which are registered there in the Medical Bureau for anyone to examine are no more the object of theological faith than are the cures that have followed from the use of penicillin. It must be made quite clear that the miracles at Lourdes—or any other miracles recorded outside the deposit of divine revelation—are simply proposed to believers and unbelievers alike as historical facts. They are to be examined and tested in the same way as any other historical fact, by rational investigation.

The miracles of Lourdes can be accepted without any previous theological faith, merely on the testimony of medical men. The only reason why this objective testimony is so often rejected by unbelievers is that they hold, *a priori*, that miracles cannot happen, and they hold this as an *article of faith!*

Hence the paradox: when a miraculous cure is reported —for instance as evidence of the intercessory power of a saint in heaven—the average agnostic rejects the miracle, *a priori* on faith, while the Church, if she does anything about it at all, proceeds to a slow and careful *a posteriori* rational investigation of the facts, to discover whether or not a miracle has taken place.

Now I ask you: Who is the more rational, the Church or the rationalist who "cannot believe"?

# 3

The "problem of unbelief" in modern times is clearly not a problem of faithlessness but of irrationality. Most men of our time do not have enough brains or training to be capable of a formal sin against the theological virtue of faith. The faithlessness that is so prevalent in a country like America is not formal unbelief but crass ignorance. It is the confusion of well-meaning people who are lost in a fog, who do not know their left hands from their right. The agnosticism and atheism which benight the spirits of men in the world spring less from a formal, deliberate and studied rejection of revealed truth than from an inability to think.

It is because men are not able to think for themselves that they are so often incapable either of belief or of unbelief. They are lucky if they rise high enough to be able to rehearse clearly in their minds the propositions that have been fed to them over the radio. No one can expect them to have any means of judging the truth or falsity of the things they read in the papers when their best efforts are devoted to spelling out the words. If they cannot keep pace with the thought of another, how can they think for themselves?

The first step in bringing men to faith is taken on the level not of theology but of philosophy. It is not a matter of faith but of reason. It is impossible to ask anyone to believe in truths revealed by God unless he first understand that there is a God and that He can reveal Truth.

But in converting adults to the Catholic faith, the Church does not ask them to sacrifice their reason in order to believe in God. She tries to convince them, by philosophical arguments, of a truth which ought, by the very nature of things, to be practically inescapable.

It would be useless to deny that the traditional Catholic proofs for the existence of God—the five ways of Saint Thomas—sometimes fail to convince men who do not fall under the category I was speaking of a moment ago. These men do have minds. They rate, in fact, as intellectuals; they are able to think. In their case, the inability to accept the Thomist proofs for God's existence generally springs from the complete philosophical confusion that prevails outside the Church. One of the symptoms of this confusion is that secular philosophers seem unable to make up their minds whether or not there are such things as a law of contradiction or of causality, although they live in the midst of scientific developments that bear witness to both these fundamental principles of thought.

And so, even in the case of intellectuals who really have some claim to that title, the inability to accept the existence of God springs from powerlessness to think. Not that they do not have brilliant or well-trained minds, but in their approach to ultimate metaphysical problems their minds are all but paralyzed by a philosophical equipment that is worse than ineffectual: it leaves them in doubt as to the nature of being, of truth, and even sometimes of their own existence. It is not for these that we raise the question of unbelief. Even our intellectuals are not sufficiently implemented to sin against faith!

That is why it is a mistake to situate the problem of unbelief on the mere level of proofs for God's existence.

On that level we are not dealing with faith, but with the
rational preambles to faith. Pascal saw this clearly. He
also saw the paradox that philosophers like Descartes, who
had in fact reduced theology to the level of philosophy
and tended to shift the problem of belief into the area of
his "clear ideas" of God, had obscured and falsified the
whole issue. Pascal predicted correctly that the influence
of Descartes on theology would be a watering down of
faith by specious philosophizing.

The problem of unbelief cannot arise until a man has
found his way to God. True, since the existence of God
is an article of faith as well as a truth accessible to reason,
any denial of His existence is materially a sin against
faith. But there is so much invincible ignorance of the
rational preambles to faith that it would be misleading
to suppose that the godlessness of most men presents a
real problem of unbelief.

# 4

It has been said that the multitudes are faithless because
of their faith in a few. With the unbelief of these few
we touch upon the real problem.

Three classes of men concern us, in their unbelief.

First, there is the atheist who, having once believed in
God, has formally rejected Him. And having rejected
God, he strives to stamp out the idea of God and of revelation. He even goes to the trouble of organizing and sys-
tematizing his attack on God so that his atheism becomes
a kind of religion turned inside out. Extreme atheism is
a perversion of faith in which every aspect of divine revelation is *dis*believed precisely because of its claim to divine

authority. Everything in religion that appeals to our love
for God, by that very fact arouses the atheist's hatred.
Atheism in its fullest development is religion gone hay-
wire. Its extreme form can only be explained as a variety of
psychosis.

The second class of unbelievers presents the most cogent
problem, as we shall see. It consists of those who, while
intellectually accepting the existence of God and the fact
of revelation as at least credible, still find themselves paralyzed, "unable to believe."

The third class is the least recognized and the hardest
to talk about. It consists of those who, while remaining
nominal members of the Church and even occasionally
receiving the Sacraments as a matter of form, have almost
entirely lost their faith. They retain a certain loyalty to
their Catholic antecedents, to the Catholic society of
which they may form a part. But this is a purely human
and social loyalty that has lost all theological foundation.
They retain the name of Catholics but their faith is dead
because it never finds expression in any Christian activity.
As far as they are concerned, God and the will of God
might as well not exist. They lead lives which are frankly
and openly ungodly. They even descend appreciably below
the level of some of the relatively virtuous unbelievers in
the world around them. The unbelief of those who are
still, in some exterior sense, religious men, is one of the
deepest mysteries in the world. Who can say what is
really going on in such souls? Who can dare to account
for them, still less condemn them? Only God can plumb
the depths of the darkness in which these men live without concern. Sometimes He works in them some miracle of

grace at the last moment—and this they accept calmly as their due, as if they had been depending on it all along!

These three classes of men present different problems. That of the frank atheist, however difficult it may be, is certainly not subtle. The atheist has mobilized his mind and his will and his whole being against God and against religion. The third group—those who still cling to the outward forms of religion without a living faith in God —are a mystery indeed: their wills do not belong to God, since they have no scruple in disobeying Him. What do they think about Him? Perhaps very little. They are skeptics in practice. The thought of God, even the question of His existence, has ceased to have any immediate practical value to them. They do not even bother to deny Him. And in this sense they are perhaps worse off than the atheist, who still finds the thought of God a source of positive excitement.

But the real problem of unbelief is, to my mind, centered in those who to some extent *know* God but cannot *believe in* Him. They are often involved in the most acute spiritual anguish because of this ambivalence. They recognize the existence and the value of faith. They often wish they had some of it. They sincerely envy those who can believe, who can accept the teaching authority of the Church and enter fully into Catholic life, with all its privileges and obligations. They are able to appreciate the happiness of truly religious men. They find the claims of Catholicism entirely reasonable. They are not in the least perplexed at the thought that God speaks to men through Christ and that Christ has handed on His ruling, teaching, and sanctifying power to His Mystical Body, which prolongs His Incarnation and keeps Him visibly present in the world of men. And yet they cannot *believe*.

I wonder how many millions of such men there are in the world today! Perhaps the problem has not quite formulated itself in them all: but it could easily do so. They all obscurely want peace in God; but they are morally paralyzed. They cannot bring themselves to make a move to obtain it. To my mind, these are the men we should be trying hardest to help. And I have no doubt that these, in practice, are the ones that most priests actually find it hard to deal with, in so-called "convert work." Yet I know, too, that their problem is often satisfactorily solved. How? By the recognition that their difficulty is not simply intellectual.

If we sometimes fail to meet this problem of unbelief in those who would "like to believe but cannot," it is generally because we are merely apologetes when we ought to be Apostles. We have been trained to feed men not with Christ, the Bread of Life, but rather with apologetic arguments. The reason for this is, perhaps, that we have been brought up on the technique of grappling with the Church's strongest and most vocal opponents: the atheists and skeptics. But actually, these are seldom the ones we are called upon to convert. Even when someone with a genuine desire to believe comes to a priest with difficulties and with questions drawn from the enemies of the Church, the chances are that these questions are not really his difficulties at all. He thinks he needs them as a pretext for talking—or he hopes to use them as an excuse for not committing himself to any moral action!

Cardinal Newman long ago saw the distinction between *intellectual difficulties* and *theological doubt*. I think that, as soon as this distinction is explained to some of those who recognize the rationality of faith without being able to believe, their difficulties will vanish. For they do not realize that the virtue of faith has, for its material object, truths which are so profound and which so far exceed our intelligence that they are called—and are in the highest sense—mysteries. It is quite obvious that these truths are not easy to understand and that they present tremendous intellectual difficulties. However, it is not at all true to say that the mysteries of faith are of themselves unintelligible or that their intelligibility does not matter. Of themselves, the mysteries of faith are supremely intelligible, for they are all deeply immersed in the eternal Truth and infinite Intelligence of God. For that very reason we are incapable of penetrating their depths by the mere light of our reason.

To be unable to *understand* the mysteries of faith is by no means to be unable to *believe* them. And yet, as I have said, faith is in no way the blind acceptance of a truth which we have no hope of understanding. Although we can never comprehend the full meaning of these mysteries, yet faith is the key to a relative understanding of them. It is after the initial act of belief that the believer begins to see. Only then can the intellectual difficulties presented by these mysteries be dealt with in a way that is in some sense satisfactory.

The motives of credibility always need to be made clear. But their clarification alone will do nothing to solve a problem that is essentially concerned not with credibility but with *faith*. Information, reasoning, sympathetic explanation of truths usually do not suffice. There is a subtle distinction between merely "instructing converts" and preaching the word of God. Saint Paul has already antici-pated the arguments of those who, when they have dealt out all the arguments in the textbook of fundamental theology, find themselves in a blind alley and attribute their lack of success to the fact that perhaps God has somehow failed to give the prospective convert enough grace to believe. The man has accepted all their arguments. He knows that revelation is credible. He wants to believe in God, in Christ, in the Church. He even sees that he ought to believe in them. He has a fair idea of all there is to believe, and it all sounds rational. But after that— he is inarticulate. He cannot go one step further and for-mally accept the faith. He cannot "believe."

What shall he do? Fold his hands and wait for grace to descend on him from heaven? Saint Paul says:

The justice which is of faith, speaketh thus: Say not in thy heart, who shall ascend into heaven? that is, to bring Christ down. Or who shall descend into the deep, that is to bring up Christ again from the dead. But what saith the Scripture? The word is nigh thee, even in thy mouth and in thy heart. This is the word of faith, which we preach. (Rom. 10:6-8.)

For Saint Paul, the problem of justification is not a matter of proving the truth of this or that doctrine, but of making Christ live in our hearts by faith (Eph. 3:17). An Apostle is one who engenders "new beings" in Christ, by the word of God. "For," says Paul to the Corinthians, "if you have ten thousand instructors in Christ, yet not many fathers. For in Christ Jesus, by the gospel, I have begotten you." (I Cor. 4:15.)

The word of faith is what begets spiritual life in the believer. The word, says Saint Paul, is very near to us, once it has been "planted" like the mustard seed in our heart. This planting starts an interior activity which results in a "new birth," or the fundamental spiritual transformation from which emerges a new interior self, a "new creature," united with Christ by faith. This supernatural transformation is precipitated by the "word of faith." Our spiritual generation as "new men in Christ" depends entirely on our reaction to this "word." The problem of the catechumen who wants to believe and cannot do so will be resolved as soon as he finds out what to make of the "word" that has been planted in him. Saint Paul sums up his solution in two statements:

With the heart we believe unto justice: with the mouth confession is made unto salvation. (Rom. 10:10.)

This is old-fashioned language. It is not the sort of thing that will suddenly leave the modern unbeliever flooded with light! Nevertheless these words contain the crux of the problem of unbelief, if we can but draw it out of them.

Saint Thomas Aquinas helps us to do so. Commenting on the words "with the heart we believe unto justice" he says:

This means that it is with the *will* that we believe. For other things, which pertain to the exterior worship of God, can be done by a man unwillingly. But no one can believe unless he wills to do so (*Nemo credere potest nisi volens*). For the intellect of the believer is not determined to assent to truth by the force of argument (*ex necessitate rationis*) as is the mind of one who knows. That is why justification [i.e. supernatural life] is *not a matter of knowing but of believing, since justification takes place in the will.*[1]

This movement of the will, by which the intellect accepts the truth of God on faith, is inevitably conditioned by the further action of the will which will be demanded as a consequence of faith. Faith will sooner or later have to be "confessed unto salvation." This means that the truth which we believe must take possession of our entire being, in such a way that faith will "work by charity" and our words and actions will outwardly express the change of life that has taken place within us. If necessary, we must even speak loud our faith into the face of death.

Unbelief that really presents a problem is centered not in the mind but in the *will*. And Saint Augustine long ago made it quite plain that one of the main reasons why the will refuses to go into action and embrace the faith is that it fears to pay the price of faith. Faith without works is dead (Jas. 2:17 *ff.*). The works by which faith demands expression, and by which it lives, demand the sacrifice of things to which the will is attached. Anyone who is sincerely drawn to belief in God realizes, even though obscurely, that this belief is, by its very nature, associated with the love of God, with submission to His will, with the desire to please Him. The same activity of grace which attracts him to the faith warns him that his acceptance of faith will demand a transformation of his whole spiritual life. He will have to "die" and be "reborn" as a new person. He will not only have to change his whole outlook on life, but he will have to break loose from old habits which have taken firm possession of his being. He will have to be uprooted and transplanted. He will have to be cut off from an old tree and grafted into the new tree, the Mystical Body of Christ—and there live by an entirely new life principle. Faith means war.

The man who has no real intellectual difficulties about faith and yet "cannot believe" is sometimes one who cannot face the prospect of this interior revolution. He earnestly desires peace: but not at the price of battle. He wants Christ to be a sign for the salvation of his spirit without being a sign of contradiction. Convinced of the credibility of revelation, hungry for a life of faith, he needs only to make an act of will. But that act of will is so tremendous, so sweeping in its consequences! No wonder the poor man is paralyzed.

This moral paralysis often obscures the intellectual issue. A person who has no real difficulties with Catholic truth can suddenly find himself beset with "problems" which are nothing but the transference of his moral impotence into an intellectual sphere. A week ago, a month ago, he was able to grasp quite clearly the outlines of Catholic doctrine: but now, under "instruction" he becomes bewildered, he can no longer see. His mind has been darkened by the hesitation of his will. He is subconsciously diverting himself from the truth which he is afraid to embrace in its entirety.

Yet it is not necessary to imagine that all who hesitate on the threshold of the faith are held captive, like Saint Augustine, by great sins. There are men of high and sincere spirituality who come close to the Church but cannot quite accept the faith. They understand some aspects of Catholic theology as well as, if not better than, some of the priests who might undertake to instruct them. They have gone deep into the mystical writings of saints of whom many of the clergy have never even heard. They have high spiritual ideals and are even, to some extent, ascetics. Perhaps they have reached a certain proficiency in mental prayer.

What is more, they are often sincere and humble men.

They are capable of a certain spiritual modesty and tact which many of us might envy. It would be shameful to declare, offhand, that their inability to accept the faith was due to spiritual pride. And yet, perhaps, there is a certain generic, unconscious tendency to pride in their whole attitude toward faith. It is not the sort of pride for which they are individually responsible, but rather an expression of the original sin that has left the whole race in confusion. The curious result of all this is that their very gifts, their natural spirituality, lead them to behave, unconsciously, as if some kind of special experience were due to them before they could break down and believe.

They realize, at least abstractly, that faith is a gift. They realize that it will involve them in the gift of themselves to God. But they feel that this gift of themselves should be preceded by some sign, some spiritual experience, some fitting consolation.

It is not for anyone to say how or when God is to dispense His gifts of grace. But it seems to me probable that anyone who sees the credibility of the Catholic faith and feels at some time or other a definite desire to embrace it, has already received sufficient grace to do so. There is no need to wait about for a star to appear in the heavens or for an angel to tell him to get baptized or for him to see Our Lord surrounded by a great light.

If he does not know for sure whether he has the grace to accept the faith, let him start accepting it anyway, and he will soon find out that he has been given not only sufficient but efficacious grace to do so. Let him make the act of will which he thinks is impossible: he will find out, after he has done it, that it was possible. In so doing he will commit himself to embrace all the apparently severe moral consequences of Christian faith. But he can be morally certain that, if he has enough grace to start the journey, he will also receive all the grace he needs to continue it and to reach the end.

It is only when faith, by the action of the will in charity, takes full possession of our being that the so-called "light of faith" becomes what one might classify as an "experience." In the order of faith, light is only procured by the mediation of the will. The intellect cannot find the way alone because in this particular case it is determined by the will. Only after it has been led over the path by the will can it reflect back on its experience and realize what has happened.

This same law applies all the way from the first act of faith to the highest degree of mystical contemplation. The whole road is ordinarily traveled in darkness. We receive enlightenment only in proportion as we give ourselves more and more completely to God by humble submission and love. We do not first see, then act: we act, then see. It is only by the free submission of our judgment in dark faith that we can advance to the light of understanding: *credo ut intelligam*. And that is why the man who waits to see clearly, before he will believe, never starts on the journey.

# CHAPTER III

# On a Dark Night

We learn from Pascal's gambler, described in the first chapter, that the tragedy of man's state on earth is not simply that he has passions. On the contrary: that is no tragedy. If you have no passions, you are not human. (And that is why it is pointless for preachers to rant about desires, which are a basic natural good, as if passion were synonymous with sin and the mere fact of having a body were an almost irreparable evil!) Nor is the essence of our tragedy to be found in the fact that our passions are a source of illusion. For we have reason. And reason is essentially sufficient to break through the web of illusion woven around us by passion.

Our tragedy consists in this: that although our reason may be capable of showing us clearly the futility of what we desire, we continue to desire it *for the sake of* the desire. Passion itself is our pleasure. Reason then becomes the instrument of passion. Its perverted function is to create idols—that is, fictions—to which we can dedicate the worship of love and hatred, joy and anguish, hope and fear.

From this servitude there is no natural deliverance. Reason itself, which has the power to free itself from passion, has in fact devoted itself in advance to the service of passion: and that is what we call original sin. It takes faith and grace, it takes the irruption into our life of the supernatural order, for the web of passion to be finally broken by our reason.

The spiritual life, for Saint Gregory of Nyssa, is a journey from darkness to light and from light to darkness. It is a transition from a light which is darkness to a darkness which is light. The ascent from falsity to Truth begins when the false light of error (which is darkness) is exchanged for the true but insufficient light of elementary and too-human notions of God. Then this light must itself be darkened, he says. The mind must detach itself from sensible appearances and seek God in those invisible realities which the intellect alone can apprehend. And this is what we have been talking about as *theoria*—an intellectual form of contemplation. This darkening of the senses is like a cloud in which the soul becomes accustomed to traveling blind, without relying on the appearances of changing things or on the emotional import of experience in its judgments of truth and falsity, of good and evil. Before the spirit can see the Living God, it must be blind even to the highest perceptions and judgments of its natural intelligence. It must enter into pure darkness. But this darkness is pure light—because it is the infinite Light of God Himself. And the mere fact that His Light is infinite means that it is darkness to our finite minds.

These degrees of the ascent to God were symbolized, thought Saint Gregory, in the degrees of illumination and darkness through which Moses journeyed to God. Moses first saw God in the burning bush. Then he was led by God across the desert in a pillar of cloud. Finally he ascended Sinai, where God spoke to him "face to face" but in the divine darkness.

To the great Moses God first appeared in light. Afterwards God spoke to him through a cloud. Finally, when he had ascended to greater and more perfect heights, Moses saw God in darkness. All this signifies that our passage from false and errant notions of God is a passage from darkness to light. A closer consideration of hidden things through things which can be seen leads the soul to that nature which cannot be seen: and this is like a cloud over-shadowing all that has outward appearances, in order to lead the soul on and accustom it to the dark. The soul that thus climbs into the heights, leaving behind everything that human nature can attain by itself, enters into the sanctuary of the knowledge of God, surrounded on every side by the divine darkness. And there, everything that can be seen or understood having been left out-side, nothing is left for the soul to see but that which is invisible and incomprehensible. And therein God is hidden, for Scripture says, of the Lawgiver: "Moses entered into the darkness where God was." (Exod. 24:18.)[1]

Now, this voyage in darkness is not accomplished without anguish. Our spirits were made for light, not for darkness. But the fall of Adam has turned us inside out, and the light we now love is darkness. The only way to true life is a kind of death. The man who feels the attraction of the Divine Truth and who realizes that he is being drawn out of this visible world into an unknown realm of cloud and darkness, stands like one whose head spins at the edge of a precipice. This intellectual dizziness, *spiritus vertiginis,* is the concrete experience of man's interior division against himself by virtue of the fact that his mind, made for the invisible God, is nevertheless dependent for all its clear knowledge on the appearances of exterior things.[2] And this vertigo, which reminds us of the dark fear that pervades the pages of the Danish mystic Sören

Kierkegaard, is also one of the aspects of that *theoria physica* of which we have spoken. It is the metaphysical anguish that seizes a soul for whom the "nothingness" of visible things is no longer merely a matter of discourse but of experience!

All this brings to mind the classical pages which Saint John of the Cross wrote on the two nights: the Night of Sense and the Night of the Spirit. There is a clear correspondence between Saint Gregory of Nyssa's degrees of obscurity and the Nights of Saint John of the Cross.

Just as Saint Gregory of Nyssa takes Moses through three stages in his ascent to God, so Saint John of the Cross divides his night into three: [3]

These three parts of the night are all one night; but like night itself, it has three parts. For the first part, which is that of sense, is comparable to the beginning of night, the point at which things begin to fade from sight. And the second part, which is faith, is comparable to midnight, which is total darkness. And the third part is like the close of night: which is God, the part which is near to the light of day.

Saint John of the Cross is a remarkably lucid and simple writer. If some find him difficult, it certainly cannot be because he is obscure. He is almost brutally clear. And that is the trouble. His simplicity is too radical. He never wastes time attempting to compromise.

He sums up his asceticism in lines which have proved to be a terror and a scandal to many Christians:

In order to have pleasure in everything
Desire to have pleasure in nothing.
In order to arrive at possessing everything
Desire to possess nothing.

In order to arrive at being everything
Desire to be nothing.
In order to arrive at knowing everything
Desire to know nothing.
In order to arrive at that wherein thou hast no pleasure
Thou must go by a way in which thou hast no pleasure.
In order to arrive at that which thou knowest not
Thou must go by a way that thou knowest not.
In order to arrive at that which thou possessest not
Thou must go by a way that thou possessest not.
In order to arrive at that which thou art not
Thou must go through that which thou art not.[4]

*Todo y Nada.* All and nothing. The two words contain
the theology of Saint John of the Cross. Todo—all—is
God, Who contains in Himself eminently the perfections
of all things. For Him we are made. In Him we possess
all things. But in order to possess Him Who is all, we
must renounce the possession of anything that is less than
God. But everything that can be seen, known, enjoyed,
possessed in a finite manner, is less than God. Every
desire for knowledge, possession, being, that falls short
of God must be blacked out. *Nada!*

But be careful! Saint John of the Cross does not waste
words. Therefore every word in his writings is important.
And the key word in each of his rules for entering into
the ascetic night is the word "desire." He does not say:
"In order to arrive at the knowledge of everything, *know*
nothing," but *"desire to know* nothing." It is not pleasure,
knowledge, possession or being as such that must be "darkened" and "mortified," but only the passion of desire for
these things.

Far from seeking to deprive the soul of pleasure, knowledge, and the rest, Saint John of the Cross wants us to arrive at the purest of pleasure and the highest knowledge —"pleasure in everything," "knowledge of all," "possession of All. . . ." His motive in prescribing this blackout of desire is the deep psychological fact with which Pascal and Gregory of Nyssa have already made us familiar. Desire, considered as a passion, is necessarily directed to a finite object. Therefore all desire imposes a *limit* to our knowledge, possession, existence. Now, in order to escape from every limitation, we must cast off that which ties us down. There are a thousand passions which involve us in what is finite and contingent. Each one of them causes us to be occupied with sensible things. And this occupation (Pascal's "diversion") narrows and closes the soul, imprisons it within its own limitations, and makes it incapable of perfect communion with the Infinite.

All the passions can be reduced to four: joy, hope, fear, and grief. These four are so closely connected that, when one is controlled, the others all obey. Consequently they can be reduced to one: joy. And desire is the movement of the soul seeking joy. Therefore the secret of ascetic liberation is the "darkening" of all desire.[5]

Saint John of the Cross, in his usual matter-of-fact way, explains that this black-out of desire is necessary if we are to arrive at a literal fulfillment of the First Commandment! That sounds like a shattering statement. However, we must remember that Saint John of the Cross regarded the First Commandment as a summary of the entire ascetic and mystical life, up to and including Transforming Union. He tells us in fact that his works are simply an explanation of what is contained in the commandment to "love the Lord thy God with all thy heart and with all thy soul and with all thy strength."

Herein is contained all that the spiritual man ought to do, and all that I have here to teach him, so that he may truly attain to God, through union of the will, by means of charity. For herein man is commanded to employ all his faculties and desires and operations and affections of his soul in God so that all the ability and strength of his soul may serve for no more than this.[6]

He also tells us in another place that this complete mortification of desire is simply the imitation of Christ. For if we wish to conform ourselves to Christ, "Who in His life had no other pleasure . . . than to do the will of His Father," we must "renounce and completely reject every pleasure that presents itself to the senses, if it be not purely for the honor and glory of God." [7]

In other words, the *nada* of Saint John of the Cross is simply a drastically literal application of the Gospel. "If any one of you renounce not all that he possesses, he cannot be my disciple." (Luke 14:33.)

2

In the first book of *The Ascent of Mount Carmel* Saint John of the Cross gives a most exhaustive analysis of the effects of inordinate desire upon the soul. Every Christian is aware that when desire reaches a certain measure of disorder, called mortal sin, the soul is entirely deprived of the supernatural presence and light of God. Everyone who takes his religion seriously fears this obvious danger. But it is not what most concerns Saint John of the Cross. He probes into the soul that is apparently healthy and full of life, in order to show the great harm done by the infec-

tion of desires that scarcely anyone fears. Before he does
so, he is careful to explain that no harm can be done in the
soul by desires which receive no consent from the will.
Involuntary movements of passion can never be suppressed
on this earth and it would be extremely harmful to attempt to do so by violence. Saint John of the Cross is in
no sense trying to root out the instinctive movements of
the flesh or to destroy human nature. But he does pay close
attention to the effects of conscious, deliberate venial sins
and imperfections, for there is much that we can and
should do to get rid of them. Much, he says, but not all.
For in the end only God can wash the soul clean of these
things, in passive or mystical purifications.

This is not the place to go into all the details of Saint
John's psychology of desire. But one chapter is important
for us here. It will help to clear up the false idea that,
because Saint John of the Cross is constantly talking of
"darkness," he is fundamentally irrational and anti-intellectual.

We have already seen that Saint John of the Cross is
trying to bring the soul to the knowledge of all truth in
the Truth of God. If there is a knowledge with which he
is not content, it is one that is fragmentary, illusory and
incomplete. This is what must be darkened, in order that
through darkness we may come to the light of truth.

Everybody knows that passion blinds the intelligence.
Prejudice is the fruit of inordinate desire. When the truth
is not what we want it to be, we twist its image out of
shape in our own mind to fit the pattern of our desires.
In so doing, we do not hurt the truth itself: we ruin our
own spirit. Saint John of the Cross says:

Even as vapors darken the air and allow not the bright sun to shine; or as a mirror that is clouded over cannot receive in itself a clear image; or as water defiled by mud reflects not the image of one that looks therein; even so the soul that is clouded by desires is darkened in the understanding and allows neither the sun of natural reason nor that of the supernatural wisdom of God to shine upon it and illumine it clearly.[8]

Clear as Saint John of the Cross may be, he is so drastic that many people are convinced he is preaching a kind of Manichaean dualism, as if nature were evil in itself, as if creatures could never be anything but obstacles to union with God. But the strict logic of Saint John is unimpeach-able. On the one hand he affirms, without reservation, that the desire of creatures as ends in themselves cannot coexist with the desire of God as our true end. We cannot serve God and Mammon. And when our minds and wills are involved in the desire of illusory values (the vanity of *Ecclesiastes*) we become darkened by error, tormented and exhausted by frustration. In this state we can know neither God nor creatures as they are. We do not rest in God and we do not find true joy in His creation. Every-thing becomes "vanity and vexation of spirit."

On the other hand, as soon as we are liberated from the slavery of desire we become capable of serene knowledge, incorruptible joy. This knowledge and joy are fulfilled in God, true enough: but in Him they also find and know and enjoy all creation. That is why the saint can love God's creation. In fact, only the saint can know and enjoy this world and the creatures in it "according to their reality" and "as they are."

Speaking of the man who is "spiritual" and detached from created things, Saint John of the Cross says:

He will find greater joy and recreation in creatures through his detachment from them, for he cannot rejoice in them if he look upon them with attachment to them as his own. Attachment is an anxiety that, like a bond, ties the spirit down to the earth and allows it no enlargement of heart. He will also acquire in his detachment from things *a clear conception of them,* so that he can well understand the truths relating to them, both naturally and supernaturally. He will therefore enjoy them after a very different fashion from that of one who is attached to them. . . . For while *he enjoys them according to their truth* the other enjoys them according to their deceptiveness; the one appreciates the best side of them, the other the worst; the one rejoices in their substance, the other, whose sense is bound to them, in their accident. For sense cannot attain to more than the accident, but the spirit, purged of the clouds and species of accident, penetrates the truth and worth of things.[9]

Far from teaching us to hate this world, John of the Cross is telling us the way to love it and understand it. His message could not be more plain. His is an ignorance that ignores nothing but error, and is therefore the surest path to truth.

# CHAPTER IV

# False Mysticism

The "ignorance" of the true mystic is not unintelligence but superintelligence. Though contemplation sometimes seems to be a denial of speculative thought it is really its fulfillment. All philosophy, all theology that is vitally aware of its place in the true order of things, aspires to enter the cloud around the mountaintop where man may hope to meet the Living God. All true learning should therefore be alive with the sense of its own limitations and with the instinct for a vital experience of reality which speculation alone cannot provide.

Just as there is a Pharisaism of knowledge, so also there is a Pharisaism of studied ignorance, for one perverse instinct can feed on everything under the sun. The man who is proud of an abstruse and technical doctrine, difficult to acquire and acquired by few, may be proud in the same way as another man who is pleased with a sweet religious ignorance that makes him feel complacently superior to all learning. Each of these two men is proud of the same thing. Each thinks he has reached a peak of secret wisdom which is closed to all but a few. But the ignorant Pharisee is perhaps more obnoxious than the other, since he is proud of what he conceives to be his humility, and this is a great perversion.

We are living in a time when false mysticism is a much

greater danger than rationalism. It has now become much
easier to play on men's emotions with a political terminology that sounds religious than with one that sounds
scientific. This is all the more true in an age in which the
religious instincts of millions of men have never received
their proper fulfillment. A nation that is starved with the
need to worship something will turn to the first false god
that is presented to it.

Hitler showed the world what could be done with an
*ersatz* mysticism of "Race" and "Blood." The mythology
of Communism, while pretending to be objective and
unemotional, is no less romantic in its broad outlines.
Marx's vision of a dialectic between economic forces that
was to end in the emergence of the proletariat and the
establishment of a classless society was a nineteenth-century adaptation of Old Testament themes—the Promised
Land, the Chosen People, the Messiah. *Das Kapital* owed
much to the subconscious heritage of the Jew. Stalinist
imperialism is a new expression of an old Tsarist ideal—the
"salvation" of the world by Holy Russia.

There is always a danger that the darkness of faith,
which is meant to perfect man's intelligence on a level
that transcends man's nature, may be exploited—as it has
been exploited for instance by Fascists—to bring man's
intelligence into subjection to powers below his nature.
There are many Dark Nights of the soul, only one of
which is a purification. All the others are a defilement of
man's spirit. And their impurity is all the greater when
they seem to be the real thing.

False mysticism is often viciously anti-intellectual. It
promises man a fierce joy in the immolation of his intelligence. It calls him to throw his spirit into the hands of

some blind life-force, considered sometimes as beyond man, sometimes as within himself. Sometimes this mysticism is political, sometimes religious. It almost always exalts emotion above thought, and its reply to intellectual argument is sometimes a program of systematic violence—the suppression of schools, the destruction of books, and the imprisonment of learned men. Why all this? Because the intelligence itself is regarded with suspicion.

False mysticism depends on a psychology in which man is divided against himself. Intellect and will form two camps within him. There is a power within him, and it is a dark power, struggling for emancipation. It is held down by frail chains forged by reason—norms of thought and action sanctioned by intelligence. The false mystic tends to despise all the norms and laws of reason in themselves, precisely because they are reasonable. For reason itself is regarded as a usurper. The intellect has to be discredited. A typical way of doing so is to argue that the "light of reason" is really only a complexity of psychophysical reactions to environment, conditioned by one's social heritage. Reason is then renounced in order that other and supposedly more "vital" and "fundamental" impulses may find expression. This is how one arrives at the fake mysticism of sexuality which has absorbed not a few writers in our time.

Strictly speaking, there is no such thing as mysticism in politics, philosophy, art, or music, still less in other more bodily expressions of man's psychic life. Since the Romantic Revival, the term mysticism has been usurped by literary critics and historians and applied to anyone who has sought to liberate the emotional and affective life of man from the restraint of conventional or reactionary norms of thought. In fact, any political or artistic dreamer who could bring tears to your eyes or smother you with sensations of unutterable *Weltschmerz* was considered a "mystic."

2

The experience of the artist and the experience of the mystic are completely distinct. Although it is quite possible for a man to be both an artist and a mystic at the same time, his art and his mysticism must always remain two essentially different things. The mystical experience can, on reflection, become the subject of an esthetic experience. Saint John of the Cross could convey, in poetry, something of his experience of God in prayer. But there always remained an unpassable abyss between his poetry and his prayer. He would never have been tempted to suppose that the composition of a poem was an act of contemplation.

Saint Catherine of Siena played a crucially important part in the political life of the fourteenth century, and she only did so because she was a mystic and an instrument of God. Nevertheless her mysticism was not political, her politics were not mysticism. Mysticism is the "hidden" or "secret" knowledge of God which is granted to the soul that is united with Him by love. Mysticism embraces the whole interior experience of a soul immersed in the Absolute. Therefore, to speak of "political mysticism" is quite absurd because it implies that "political action" is a sort of emanation of the Divine Nature and that to be immersed in politics is to be immersed in the Absolute! Saint Catherine of Siena had no such conception either of the mystical life or of politics. Her mysticism was her experience of union with God, in Christ, whose Kingdom is "not of this world." Her politics were simply the working out of God's will, in the temporal affairs of men and above all of the Church, in such a way that the greatest possible number of souls should enter the City of God, which is irrevocably opposed to the city of this world because it belongs to an entirely different order of being.

In the present volume, we cannot delay to discuss anything but mysticism in the strict sense of the word. The only true mysticism is religious mysticism. I therefore take it for granted that all nonreligious mysticism is "false mysticism" and proceed to a brief discussion of true and false *religious* mysticism.

At this point, however, it is necessary to warn the reader that mysticism has nothing to do with occultism. Mysticism is not magic. It is not divination. It is not spiritualism. It has nothing to do with magnetism. Not one of these things can be called "mystical" because not one of them is religious. On the contrary, these practices all involve man's spirit in sins against religion. They are all fundamentally irreligious. Religion is the virtue by which man gives expression to his complete dependence on God. But the characteristic feature of all occult practices and of the inordinate use of magnetism is that they claim to give man a natural command of the supernatural world. They pretend to put him in control of supernatural effects which are somehow "independent" of God. They all tend to deaden the religious instinct of man and to replace it by a morbid obsession with preternatural phenomena. The fundamental human need to worship God and to find the fullest expression of his spiritual capacities in the supernatural

experience of His Goodness and His Truth is thus frustrated and forced to content itself with weird manifestations of "the beyond." All occult practices end in an ob-
scene caricature of religion and of mysticism.

Closely allied with occultism is theosophy, which, in its
roots, is more or less religious. Theosophy is a degraded
Western popularization of oriental religions. It has in it the
traces of what can rightly claim the name of mysticism in
a less strict sense than that used by Catholic theologians.
The religions of the Orient, upon which theosophy is
based, have earned the respect of great minds because of
the natural perfection to which their moral and ascetic
codes are capable of elevating certain specially endowed
souls. But the confused amalgam of spiritualism and theosophy which has managed to fascinate the minds of so
many thousands in the decadent bourgeois culture of the
West—and especially in the United States—is worthy of
no respect whatever. The dreary vulgarity of its manifestations ought to be enough to warn us against it. It is surprising that anything so stupid should have to be formally
condemned by the Church. One would think that man's
inborn common sense would be enough to deliver him
from its banal attractions.

The danger of these pseudoreligions does not lie merely
in their doctrinal haziness and in their practice of superstition. The Church does not condemn them merely because they are stupid. There is a real and mysterious power
at work behind the screen of idiot doctrines. That power
belongs to a spirit that is above our nature and yet is not
God. It is the power of an angelic intelligence and will
which is capable of all-too-disastrous an interference in
the life of man's world. This particular intelligence is

commonly known as the Devil. His chief and most characteristic work is the perversion of what is best in the spiritual order, and therefore he specializes in false mysticism.

On the other hand, it would be naïve as well as absurd to attribute all false mysticism to the Devil, although it is true that this spirit can directly or indirectly pervert the work of true mystical grace in the soul.

And this brings us to the problem that is our main concern: false mystical experiences in a truly religious soul. False mysticism is most dangerous when it is a deviation of grace. And, since grace is given us by God to bring us to the high supernatural perfection which He has planned to bestow upon our nature, false mysticism ends also in a perversion even of nature.

By nature we seek truth. God's grace can give us an intimate experience of Him Who is infinite Truth. False mysticism turns us aside from the true path to that end. It leads us away after a mirage and leaves us to die in the desert, locked in the embrace of an illusion. This can happen in many different ways, but they all follow a few characteristic patterns. That is why it is quite easy to talk about false mysticism in the abstract. And yet, in concrete cases, the discovery of illusion is sometimes extremely difficult, often impossible.

### 3

In the abstract, false mysticism can fall under two characteristic headings. Both of these situate the private mystical experience in an incorrect relation to the Truth which God has revealed publicly to the Church. One of these

incorrect definitions says that the mystic has no need whatever of any conceptual knowledge of God, revealed or
otherwise. In order to enter into "contemplative union"
with God the "spiritual man" must cease from every form
of spiritual activity, empty his soul of all thought and
affection. As soon as the soul is empty, it automatically
and naturally becomes filled with "acquired" contemplation, in which it "knows" God without experiencing the
fact that it knows anything at all. Since this is supposed
to be the nature of true contemplation, it follows that
theological knowledge of God is by its very nature an
obstacle to contemplation and that the theologian is pro-
fessionally ill equipped to become a mystic, while an ignorant man is naturally best disposed for contemplation.
Such were the errors of Quietism condemned by the
Church in the seventeenth century. The danger of these
errors is speculative rather than practical, because in actual
fact it is very laborious to empty your mind of all thought,
and few there are who will be disposed to attempt it. However, this is the error that most concerns us here because it
resembles, in some superficial respects, the true doctrine
which we are going to draw from the pages of Saint John
of the Cross.

The errors of Quietism with respect to the knowledge of
God consist in a formal rejection of theology, a deprecia-
tion of God's revelation of Himself to man in Christ the
Incarnate Word, in the complete rejection of formal prayer
and meditation, and in the theory that supernatural contemplation can be "acquired" by the mere cessation of
mental activity. These errors, as we shall see, actually
make true contemplation impossible.

I should like to point out, parenthetically, that Oriental

mysticism at large has no more in common with the Quietism of Molinos than does the mysticism of Saint John of
the Cross. It is a very great mistake to think that Yoga
seeks absorption in the Absolute by a mere relaxation of
the mind and stoppage of activity. The techniques and
disciplines of meditation practiced in the Orient are far
more laborious and exacting than anything known in the
West. The Oriental contemplative is no more indifferent
to conceptual knowledge than his Christian counterpart.
Divine "revelation" plays a part in Oriental mysticism,
and "knowledge" is one of the foundation stones of Yoga.
Oriental mysticism is far more intellectual and speculative
than the mysticism of the West, and this is, in fact, one
of its deficiencies. It is *too* intellectual. It tends to depend
too exclusively on the work of man's own intelligence and
on human techniques, leaves too little place for love, and
has only a hesitant, uncertain knowledge of the supreme
work of God's grace in mystical prayer.

I said that false mysticism came under two headings.
I have described the first kind of false mysticism, which
literally substitutes ignorance for knowledge. The second
kind of false mysticism is much more common: it claims
to arrive at special supernatural knowledge by means other
than those normally ordained by God. This kind of thing
is of course extremely flattering to human nature. Fallen
man loves to elevate himself above his fellows and soar
aloft on wings borrowed from the angels. The most common illusion of well-meaning religious souls is to imagine
that they hear heavenly voices, see visions, fall into ecstasies and swoon away with rapture when in actual fact they
are fabricating these experiences by the work of their own
imagination. However, a distinction must be made. Locu-

tions, visions, ecstasies, and other extraordinary experiences can quite easily be supernatural. Such things can and do come from God, although not every vision is from heaven. The important thing to remember is that even when they are supernatural, these experiences are not of the essence of true mysticism. They are only accidental to it. This means that mystical contemplation in the strict sense is an experience of God which is directly achieved, under the inspiration of grace, without the medium of anything that is seen or heard or "understood." In mystical contemplation God is known to the soul without the medium of any species or image, whether of the mind or of the senses. And therefore it follows that all visions and locutions are in a certain sense opposed to true contemplation, at least in so far as they diminish its purity and its perfection. According to the language of the Christian apohatic theologians, in the tradition of Saint Gregory of Nyssa and the Pseudo-Dionysius, if you have a vision in which you think you see God clearly, you have not seen God. Saint John of the Cross devotes a large part of *The Ascent of Mount Carmel* to proving the thesis that visions and locutions and other experiences which purport to give us a precise supernatural knowledge of the divinity should never be either sought after or positively accepted, since no created and visible thing, no clear idea, can convey to us the full reality of God as He is in Himself.

An objection immediately occurs to everyone who is familiar with the lives of the saints, and especially with the famous apparitions of the Blessed Virgin in modern times. What about these? To say that the visions of the saints, the prophecies of enlightened souls, the apparitions of Our Lady all fall outside the area of contemplation

in the strict sense is not to question the reality and moral
value of such visions as have been approved by the Church.
Such approval in no way affects our present thesis.

No theologian would assert that all visions, as such, are
illusory. Saint John of the Cross certainly does not do so.
He himself had visions and other experiences and directed
souls who also had them, and he was well aware that such
experiences often come from God. However, concerned
as he was with the practical problems of spiritual direction, he knew how difficult it was to distinguish between
a vision that came from God and one that came from the
Devil.

What is the reason for this difficulty? Distinct visions
of supernatural things are produced by pictures in the
imagination or at least by ideas formed in the intelligence.
Such pictures and ideas can be formed or at least suggested
by agents outside ourselves. Just as in ordinary conversation I can arouse images and ideas in your mind by speaking of things which you know or remember, so a hypnotist, without using words, can cause you to form such
images and ideas by means of magnetic suggestion. These
*natural* operations provide an analogy for the much more
subtle and powerful work of spiritual agents. The Devil,
far more adroitly than any hypnotist, has the power to
make you see things and think things as he wants you to
see and think them. The natural mode of converse between spiritual beings is by the direct communication of
ideas. The Devil, being a spirit, can so act upon the souls
of men.

It is quite evident that God can make use of other intelli-
gences—His angels—to act in the same way upon the
minds of men and make them see visions. Much more

so is He able to produce images and ideas in the human spirit by His own direct action. The only limitation on this power of God is that He can never produce in man anything of falsity or of delusion.

But true contemplation is not produced by images or ideas formed in the soul. It is the experience of an immediate spiritual union with God, a union which can only be effected by God and which is essentially a union of supernatural charity. Needless to say, no spirit other than God Himself can unite himself immediately to the soul, and no one but God can infuse supernatural charity into the soul. True contemplation is, then, the experience of a union that is so purely and perfectly supernatural that no created nature could possibly bring it about. Indeed, no spirit less than the Spirit of God can possibly produce even a plausible imitation of true mystical union. Imitations are of course foisted upon souls, and sometimes with great success. But, as Saint Teresa somewhere says, anyone who has experienced true mystical union can see at once the infinite distance that lies between it and the false article produced by the Devil or by our own imagination.

No such clear division between truth and error exists in the case of imaginary visions, locutions, and other such "distinct" experiences of the supernatural. That is why Saint John of the Cross advises contemplatives to remain negative toward them all, without even bothering to discover whether they come from God or from the Devil. They are all, indiscriminately, to be refused.

It is significant that the opinion of Saint John of the Cross, the greatest of Catholic mystical theologians, is far more cautious than that of most authorities. Catholic theologians commonly agree that no contemplative soul should ordinarily be allowed, still less encouraged, to seek after visions, locutions, and other such experiences. Incidentally, they also agree that one who shows signs of sufficient spiritual advancement and of proper dispositions should normally be allowed to aspire to true contemplation and to mystical union, and even encouraged to do so, if mystical union be understood first of all as a union with God in perfect charity. However, many theologians are much more tolerant than Saint John of the Cross in allowing souls to *accept* visions, locutions, and the rest, once they are given.

The mind of the Church on this point can best be judged from a semiofficial declaration made by the Assessor of the Holy Office, Monsignor Ottaviani.[1] Reproving the unwholesome credulity with which many Catholics have allowed themselves, in recent years, to be attracted to the scene of supposed miracles and apparitions, Monsignor Ottaviani explicitly warned the faithful of the probable falsity of manifestations at various places which he named in France, Italy, Belgium, Germany, and the United States. He declared that the Church wished to protect her faithful against a superstitious popular passion for marvels and wonders, and that in general the thronging of Catholics in large numbers to the scene of supposed miracles was to viewed with disfavor.

At the same time, however, the apparitions of Our Lady at Fatima have been accorded, by the Holy See, a place of extraordinary prominence in the Catholic life of our time. But this was only after a long and careful investigation.

What are we to conclude? Visions, apparitions, locutions, prophetic inspirations may be, in particular cases, true or false, supernatural, preternatural, or natural. Each

case must be judged on its own merits. Such experiences
cannot be classified, in general, as being essentially true or
essentially false. False mysticism comes in where there is
an inordinate appetite for these experiences and an undue
emphasis upon them. It is not false mysticism to have
visions, but it *is* false to make mysticism consist essentially
in visions. It is also false mysticism to attribute greater
importance to visions, locutions, and private revelations
than to the truths revealed by God to the Church, which
are the object of theological faith. It is certainly false
mysticism to follow a road that leads to spectacular experiences rather than to obscure union with God, as if
spiritual perfection consisted in having such experiences
and as if no one could become a saint without them.

To sum up: our abstract considerations of false mysticism have shown us that all false mysticism misconceives
the proper roles of knowledge and love in contemplation,
as well as the essence of contemplation itself. It either dis-
cards all knowledge of God or else aspires to a "marvelous"
knowledge of Him which falls outside the orbit of faith
and is actually no knowledge of Him at all. False mysticism tends to treat contemplation either as if it were all
love and no knowledge, or all knowledge and no love.
Finally, false mysticism turns us away from our true end
and seeks the enjoyment of flattering and glorious experiences rather than the perfect gift of our whole being to
God alone.

In this chapter I have only been trying to sketch the
broad outlines of an abstract treatment of false mysticism.
I have not touched upon the concrete and practical signs
by which false mysticism is to be detected in a determinate
case. But the principles suggested here, as well as others

which will be laid down in later chapters of this book, will give a general id a of what these signs might be. Clearly, a prominent place among them must be assigned to a contumacious rejection of reason, of philosophy, of theological truth, and of the dogmatic authority of the teaching Church.

# CHAPTER V

# Knowledge and Unknowing in Saint John of the Cross

Saint John of the Cross comments on Saint Paul's words: "If any man among you seem to be wise in this world, let him become ignorant that he may be wise." (I Cor. 3:18-19.) We have already seen something of what it means to be "wise in this world." And we now know that there are very important qualifications to be applied to this "unknowing" which leads to true wisdom. Even then, there seems to be a devastating absoluteness about Saint John's remarks on this subject:

In order to come to union with the wisdom of God the soul has to proceed rather by unknowing than by knowing. . . . Any soul that makes account of all its knowledge and ability in order to come to union with the wisdom of God, is supremely ignorant in the eyes of God and will remain far removed from that wisdom . . . for ignorance [in the bad sense] knows not what wisdom is. . . . Those alone gain the wisdom of God who are like ignorant [in the good sense] children and, laying aside their knowledge, walk in His service with love.[1]

This is all quite true, and it is moreover in the direct line of Christian mystical tradition. Saint John of the Cross bases his doctrine in this one paragraph on the clear teaching of Saint Paul. But is there no difference between this and Quietism? It might seem hard to see where that difference lies when the two doctrines are presented in a few scattered quotations taken out of context.

First of all, Saint John of the Cross is here talking about mystical wisdom: the experiential knowledge of God that is received by the soul in contemplation. Saint Thomas Aquinas interprets the passages of Saint Paul in this same sense also.

Both Saint John of the Cross and Saint Thomas clearly distinguish between *acquired wisdom,* which is the fruit of man's own study and of his thought, and *infused wisdom or contemplation,* which is a gift of God. In this particular passage, Saint John of the Cross is contrasting the two. Man's "knowledge and ability"—acquired wisdom—can do nothing to bring a man to "Divine Union with God." The apparent redundancy of this term should not be overlooked. It is only apparent, for Saint John of the Cross uses the word "divine" here as synonymous with "mystical." All through *The Ascent of Mount Carmel* and *The Dark Night of the Soul,* this "Divine Union with God" is proposed as the summit of the ascent, the end of the soul's journey. It is the "perfection" toward which the beginner aspires when he undertakes the active mortification ("night") of the senses, and which the progressive approaches in the "passive nights" of the senses and of the spirit.[2] Neither beginners nor progressives have attained this "Divine Union." It is the reward of the "perfect." Yet progressives are already contemplatives, which is to say, in Saint John of the Cross's language, mystics. Beginners, however, are already ascending the mountain. They are on the spiritual way that leads to this "Divine Union with God." It is their vocation, and if they are faithful, it will be their destiny.

Now, in the light of this, what is the meaning of Saint John's statement about the importance of "unknowing"? It is this. Man's knowledge and ability, that is to say, theological learning or acquired wisdom, cannot bridge the distance that lies between the state of a beginner and the state of "Divine Union." Mystical union is a gift of God. It cannot be acquired by any ascetic technique. It cannot be merited (*de condigno*) in the strict sense by any man, however holy he may be. No system of meditations, of interior discipline, of self-emptying, of recollection and absorption can bring a man to union with God, without a free gift on the part of God Himself. Still less can a man arrive at mystical union with God by an effort of the intellect on his own natural level. Mystical vision cannot be produced by study. The knowledge of God in mystical contemplation is so different in its essence from the knowledge of God gained by theological study that Saint John of the Cross calls them in a certain sense "contraries." That is why the man who thinks the power of his intellect, his learning and capacity to learn, will bring him to the supreme goal of all theology, which is contemplation, is blinded by an attachment, a source of illusion which makes his soul "pure darkness in the eyes of God" so that it "has no capacity for being enlightened or possessed by the pure light of God." [8]

Pursuing the same line of thought, Saint John of the Cross returns to what is, in fact, the theme of *The Ascent of Mount Carmel:* that the whole ascetical and mystical life is a reproduction of the life of Christ on earth because it completely empties and "annihilates" the soul in order to unite it to God. For Saint John of the Cross, the imitation of Christ means one thing only: absolute self-renunciation. The only way to make any progress in the ways of the spirit is to advance in this imitation of Christ, for "no man comes to the Father but by Him." [4]

"Christ is the Way, and this Way is death to our natural selves in things both of sense and of spirit." [5] Even those who have embraced a hard life for the love of Christ, and who consider themselves His friends, know Him too little, says the Carmelite saint, because they look rather for spiritual consolations than for a share in His Cross. And if those who are apparently the "friends of Christ" do not know Him, how much more true is this of others. Saint John gives us a few examples of what he means by these others: "Those who live far away, withdrawn from Him, great men of letters and of influence and all others who live yonder, with the world, and are eager about their ambitions and their prelacies, may be said not to know Christ." [6]

The *grandes letrados,* rendered in the translation as "great men of letters," were not secular writers—poets like Garcilaso de la Vega, who exercised a marked influence on Saint John of the Cross himself. They were evidently men learned in Sacred Sciences. The context tells us so. God has set them up as "guides by reason of their learning and position." Damaging as this text may seem to be, it cannot be advanced as an argument that Saint John of the Cross is against theological learning as such. He is clearly talking about men who have abused their learning by making it an instrument of unworthy ambitions. They have perverted a gift which God has given them for their own spiritual advantage and for the sanctification of other men. No other sense can be drawn from the notion that God had set them up as "guides."

In any case, it must be remembered that the great
Discalced Carmelite mystics of the sixteenth century had
a very healthy respect for learning and for *letrados*. There
is a famous saying of Saint Teresa of Ávila: *buen letrado
nunca me engañó*. It can be translated: "I have never
known a good theologian to let me down." Saint Teresa
insisted that her nuns should receive spiritual direction, if
possible, from good theologians. Not that learning was the
first qualification she demanded in a director of contemplatives. There were two others that came before this: prudence ("sound understanding") and experience. Nevertheless she added that all three of these qualifications were
necessary. "If a spiritual director have no learning," she
says, "it will be a great inconvenience." [7] Inconvenience is
too mild a word for the suffering she herself had to undergo
at the hands of stupid directors. Yet she did not hesitate
to say that even if a learned theologian had no experience
of the ways of mystical prayer, his learning might suffice
to make him a competent director of contemplatives. Here
are some of her statements:

My opinion has always been and always will be that every
Christian should try to consult some learned person, if he can,
and the more learned the person the better. Those who walk in
the way of prayer have the greater need of learning; and the
more spiritual they are, the greater is their need. Let us not make
the mistake of saying that learned men who do not practice prayer
(by this she means contemplative prayer) are not suitable directors for those who do. I have consulted many such. . . . I have
always got on well with them, for though some of them have no
experience [i.e. in contemplative prayer] they are not averse from
spirituality nor are they averse from its nature, for they study
Holy Scripture where the truth about it can always be found.
I believe, myself, that if the person who practices prayer consults

learned men, the devil will not deceive him with illusions except by his own desire; for I think the devils are very much afraid of learned men who are humble and virtuous, knowing these will find them out and defeat them.[8]

There is no reason to believe that Saint John of the Cross would have disagreed with this. In fact, his reproof of learned men who do *not* fulfill their function as guides contains an implicit assertion of the same truth. They fail because of their lack of humility. In any case, Saint John of the Cross himself has much to say about bad directors. In *The Living Flame of Love* he demands the same three qualities in a confessor of contemplatives that Saint Teresa has just set down for us. The spiritual guide must, says Saint John of the Cross, be wise, discreet and experienced. For in order to be a spiritual director, although the fundamental qualification is knowledge and discretion [*saber y discreción*], if one does not also have experience of the higher reaches of prayer, he will not be able to set the soul on the right road to them when God grants it such a gift.[9]

Saint John of the Cross was himself one of Saint Teresa's directors, and we know that she was delighted with his wisdom.

As for directors who do not know their business, Saint Teresa has something more to say about them. She hated to see a contemplative fall into the hands of such a one, with no chance to consult anyone else: "For directors who cannot understand spirituality, afflict their penitents both in soul and in body and prevent them from making progress."[10] She advised all those who could choose their own director to take full advantage of their freedom. And she expressed her sympathy for those who had no recourse to any but one unenlightened guide who, besides laying down the law about the spiritual life in a way that made prayer a great burden, also arrogated to himself a tyrannical command over the soul.

It is interesting to see what she gives as an example of stupid direction. A married woman is attracted to a life of prayer. Her confessor, instead of telling her how to carry out her household duties in a spirit of prayer, tells her to drop her work and to pray when she ought to be doing the dishes. Her life of prayer at once becomes an obstacle to her happiness as a wife, and her marriage, at the same time, erects a barrier between herself and God.

So much for spiritual directors. But to return to the real issue. In what sense does Saint John of the Cross mean that man cannot arrive at union with God by "his own knowledge and ability"?

Remember his division of spiritual men into three classes: beginners, progressives, and the perfect. If the saint prescribes a course of "unknowing" and "unlearning," is it for all these three classes? Is it for some and not for others? Do the three groups pass through different kinds and different degree of "night"?

Saint John of the Cross does not demand that a spiritual man abandon all intellectual and affective activity from the very beginning of his spiritual life. This is one of the big differences between Saint John and the Quietist Molinos. Saint John of the Cross insists that the beginner must meditate on spiritual truths. He must put his mind to work in order to grasp spiritual and even philosophical principles. Over and over again, in *The Ascent of Mount Carmel,* the Spanish saint presents his reader with basic axioms from scholastic philosophy. More numerous still are the thoughts taken from Scripture and theology and offered to the one ascending the mountain with an explicit injunction that he must *meditate* on these things in order to arrive at detachment.[11]

Clearly, for Saint John of the Cross, there is a stage in the ascent to Divine Union in which one must acquire a clear knowledge of principles and think clearly and coherently about them. Above all, one must meditate on the life of Christ in order to imitate His renunciation.[12] This is the foundation of the whole spiritual life for Saint John of the Cross, as it is for all Christian mystics. For those called to be priests and spiritual directors, all this necessarily implies a thorough knowledge of philosophy and theology. Such knowledge cannot be acquired without a long course of study. It demands, in fact, the rudiments of an intellectual life.

The beginner thinks, studies, and meditates. Now, in his prayer, he begins to approach the borderline of infused contemplation. What does this mean? That he has a vision? No. Saint John of the Cross, who treats visions, revelations, and interior locutions as an unimportant by-path of the mystical life, gives a deep and subtle analysis of the beginnings of mystical prayer in what he calls the "night of the senses." I do not mean to discuss his treatment of the subject in detail here.

One thing concerns us. It is the fact that mystical, or infused, prayer tends to inhibit the free and natural play of thought and imagination. The man who has been used to deep and fruitful insights into spiritual truths is now distressed to find that he cannot pray and meditate as he used to. Clear and precise notions of God tend to be fogged over and the usual discursive way of reaching God through notions heavily charged with meaning and affectivity no longer satisfies him. The very effort to think about God is wearisome—but so is the effort to think about anything else. He has lost his taste for ideas and for affections. He wants to keep quiet. He feels himself somehow imprisoned in a baffled silence which, crippling though it may be, offers an inscrutable promise of satisfaction and of deliverance.

It is here that the desire for intellectual activity begins to present a serious problem.

Infused contemplation raises the spirit of man to union with God without the medium of any created species, image, or idea. There is much discussion among theologians as to whether, in mystical prayer, the intellect can be said to be in immediate contact with the essence of God. I do not mean to enter into this discussion. It is enough to say that there is a real immediacy of union between the soul and God in infused contemplation.

It does not have to be an immediacy of intuition, or an immediate intellectual union of the soul with God: theologians are much more willing to agree on the fact that in mystical prayer there is an immediate union of the soul and God in love, that is, there is an immediate union or "contact" of wills, which serves as the basis for a mystical experience of God. Saint John of the Cross says that when this union is produced by infused love the intellect tends to be absorbed in a general, obscure attention to God, not as reflected in a clear, definite idea, but simply to God, unlimited by any idea, yet somehow realized as a "presence." In mystical experience, God is "apprehended" as unknown. He is realized, "sensed" in His immanence and transcendence. He becomes present not in a finite concept but in His infinite reality which overflows every analogical notion we can utter of Him.

Now, the mind of man naturally acquires knowledge only in concepts, ideas, and judgments. The mystical knowledge of God is a judgment, but it is above concepts. It is a knowledge that registers itself in the soul passively *without an idea*. This sounds strange. The testimony of those who experience such things assures us, however, that there is nothing essentially disturbing about this knowledge of God in lucid "darkness," for it brings with it a deep and inexpressible peace.

But it is easy to see that the desire for conceptual knowledge or ideas will become a problem for one who is called to mystical prayer. Saint John of the Cross expresses it in these terms:

No thing, created or imagined, can serve the understanding as a proper means of union with God. All that the understanding can attain serves rather as an impediment [to this union] than as a means, if [the soul] should desire to cling to it. . . .

Among all created things, and things that belong to the understanding, there is no ladder whereby the understanding can attain to this High Lord. Rather it is necessary to know that if the understanding should seek to profit by all of these things or by any of them as a proximate means to such union, they would be not only a hindrance but even an occasion of numerous errors and delusions in the ascent of this mount.[13]

And then, having described the state of a soul united to God in contemplation, in which it receives a supernaturally infused light in "passive understanding," he goes on to explain how active knowledge interferes with this union:

Although in this condition the will freely receives this general and confused knowledge of God, it is needful, in order that it may receive this divine light more simply and abundantly, only that it should take care not to interpose other lights which are more palpable, whether forms or ideas or figures having to do with any kind of meditation; for none of these things is similar to that pure and serene light. Wherefore if at this time the will desires to understand and consider particular things, however spiritual they be, this would obstruct the pure and simple general light of the spirit by setting those clouds in the way; even as a man might set something before his eyes which impeded his vision and kept from him both the light and the sight of things in front of him.[14]

2

The desire to have a clear knowledge and understanding of truths about God is necessary for beginners in the way of prayer. It stimulates their appetite for reading and meditation and prayer. God answers this desire in the gift of contemplation. But contemplation obscures the clear knowledge of divine things. It hides them in a "cloud of unknowing." In this cloud, God communicates Himself to the soul, as Saint John of the Cross says, passively and in darkness.

This does not satisfy the natural desire of the intellect. The intelligence, by its very nature, needs light. It wants to see, to penetrate the essence of things. It wants to understand. But man's instinct to analyze and to rationalize his experience does not prove to be a useful servant in moments of contemplative prayer! If infused contemplation is really being given to the soul, this instinctive hunger for clear ideas can only fill the mind with obstacles to contemplation. It tends to replace the real thing with a series of fabricated and human illusions. Even though the ideas and judgments may, in themselves, be philosophically and theologically sound, they still only detract from the pure light of contemplation. Unfortunately, imaginative and intellectual minds do not realize the harm that is being done by this substitution of the human for the divine, the limited for the infinite.

Saint John of the Cross does not hesitate to apply his principles to every kind of "clear knowledge" about God, even if it should come to the soul in the form of a vision or revelation. All these experiences are less perfect than the union of the soul with God in "pure faith," that is to say, in the "night" of contemplation.

The second book of *The Ascent of Mount Carmel* methodically proceeds from one supernatural "experience" to another and sweeps every kind of revelation, vision, and locution from the house of pure contemplation. Saint John of the Cross is inexorable. He spares practically nothing that popular piety designates by the term of "mysticism." He does not deny that visions may at times be genuine: he simply says that they cannot serve the soul as "proximate means of union with God." The only proximate means of union with God is faith. No vision, no revelation, however sublime, is worth the smallest act of faith, in his eyes.

Speaking of bodily visions, appearances of saints, angels, "supernatural lights and the perception of ethereal perfumes," he says:

Although all these things may happen to the bodily senses in the way of God, we must never rely on them or admit them but we must always fly from them without trying to ascertain whether they be good or evil. . . . The more completely exterior and corporeal they are, the less certainly they are of God. . . . He that esteems such things errs greatly and places himself in great peril of deception; and at best he will have in himself a complete impediment to the attainment of spirituality.[15]

He goes on to say that these things tend to diminish the faith of those who receive them. Pure faith is a stony and arid path. Spiritual experiences stimulate and refresh the soul, and a spirit that has been long in dryness is all the more likely to cling to the sweetness that these things bring. No doubt God sends him such things because he needs them. But who cannot see the temptation that lies in them? What man, seeing the saints and God Himself in visions, is not likely to imagine that his vision is something greater than faith? Saint John of the Cross is always there to remind him that this is an illusion.

To resume these texts: here is their burden. They all say that any knowledge that pretends to offer us a "clear" and "precise" concept of God is inferior to the "obscure" experience of Him in the union produced by infused love. The temptation to prefer any clear knowledge, whether natural or supernatural, to this dark knowledge of God puts the soul in danger of abandoning a reality for an illusion.

What is the conclusion? Many readers might be tempted to argue from such evidence that the mysticism of Saint John of the Cross is completely anti-intellectual and antirational. If this be so, then the saint would have to be considered essentially alien to the intellectual climate of Catholic theology.

The teaching authority of the Church, constantly proposing Saint Thomas Aquinas as the guide and model of Catholic theologians, frowns on anti-intellectualism. The theological structure of Catholicism culminates in a mystical contemplation that is supported not by agnosticism but by a speculative theology and philosophy which show the greatest respect for the light of human reason. Catholic mysticism is in no sense a refuge to which the saints have fled from an unintelligible universe: it is the crown and glory of the human spirit. It fulfills the highest aspirations of a theology, a metaphysics and a cosmology which find the world transparently intelligible because it is "charged with the grandeur of God."

My task is to point out the true significance of Saint John of the Cross's doctrine of "unknowing." What does it mean, and what does it not mean?

In the first place, Saint John of the Cross is not trying to say that the intellect is incapable of knowing any truth. There is not one word in any book of Saint John of the Cross to indicate that he despises the power of the intellect to arrive at scientific, philosophical, or theological conclusions. He nowhere suggests that science, philosophy, and theology are of themselves useless or baneful. Saint John of the Cross is not concerned with general problems of epistemology. He is not scrutinizing the validity of human knowledge, either of created things or of God. In fact, we have seen that his whole teaching is based on solid principles of scholastic philosophy and theology. The mysticism of Saint John of the Cross is built on the epistemology of the Schools.

What is the place of intellectual knowledge in Saint John of the Cross? Knowledge that is acquired by the intelligence, working in its own human mode, whether on the level of reason alone or in the order of grace, where reason deals with the revealed truths of faith, has, for Saint John of the Cross, all the validity it has for Saint Thomas Aquinas. It penetrates, in some sense, all being.

It arrives at a valid univocal knowledge of created being, and it can truly know the Supreme Being of God through the medium of created analogies.

We not only can, but we must, use the means offered by this knowledge to bring us to God. We shall see that even the dark mystical knowledge of God which is beyond concepts nevertheless depends upon the existence of concepts. They are its starting point, the diving board from which it springs into the abyss of God.

Therefore—and this is extremely important—conceptual knowledge presents no problem to Saint John of the Cross in the merely natural order. For Oriental mystics, for idealists and others in the West, the "cloud of unknowing" can descend upon philosophers. The reality of the world itself is brought into question, and therefore it becomes part of the wisdom of a philosopher to ignore what is thought to be essentially an illusion. Not so for Saint John of the Cross. Knowing and "unknowing" do not come into conflict, in his doctrine, until the soul has actually entered mystical prayer.

Remember, therefore, that Saint John of the Cross does not offer us his doctrine of unknowing as a philosophical approach to the universe. It is in no sense a substitute for cosmology. It is not a prescription for the annihilation of physical science, or a technique of entering into a quasi-magical relation with cosmic forces so as to gain control over what seems to be a world. The only cosmology that underlies the doctrine of the Carmelite saint is the cosmology of Saint Thomas Aquinas.

Saint John's "Night" of unknowing concerns only the knowledge of God. Now, even speculative theology can become absorbed in apophatism, considering the names of God in so far as they tell us rather what He is not than what He is. This is not the approach of Saint John of the Cross. His is not a speculative theology. He is concerned with the practical problems of mysticism and of experience. However, his practical doctrine is based on the speculations of Saint Thomas and Pseudo-Dionysius.

Three clear statements will show the exact function of "unknowing" in the doctrine of Saint John of the Cross.

1. Acquired, conceptual knowledge of God should not be discarded as long as it helps a man toward Divine Union. And it continues to help a man toward Divine Union as long as it does not interfere with the infused, passive, mystical experience of God in obscurity.

2. It is not so much the presence of concepts in the mind that interferes with the "obscure" mystical illumination of the soul, as the *desire to reach God through concepts*. There is therefore no question of rejecting all conceptual knowledge of God (as we shall see later on) but of *ceasing to rely on concepts as a proximate means of union with Him*.

3. You are not supposed to renounce this desire of clear, conceptual knowledge of God unless you are actually receiving infused prayer—or unless you are so advanced in the mystical life that you can enter into the presence of God without active thought of Him.

Saint John of the Cross not only says that progressives, who have begun to receive graces of mystical contemplation, should return to active meditation whenever they "see that the soul is not occupied in repose and (mystical) knowledge." [16] He adds that meditation is *an ordinary means of disposing oneself* for mystical prayer. "In order to reach this state, [the soul] will frequently need to make use of meditation, quietly and in moderation." [17]

The reason for all this is clearly that the theology of Saint John of the Cross is not purely negative—any more than is the theology of any other Christian saint. It has a strongly positive element. Light and darkness succeed one another, and they work together. If meditation, if concepts cannot bring us to immediate union with God, they nevertheless have a very definite function in preparing us for that union. And this is what we must now attempt to understand.

# CHAPTER VI

# Concepts
# and Contemplation

Catholic mysticism is based on Catholic dogma. And
Catholic dogma has, as its servant, scholastic philosophy.
Scholastic philosophy teaches us precisely how human
words can be said to make sense when they are applied
to God. The mysticism of Saint John of the Cross is articu-
lated in a thought that relies heavily on the scholastic
doctrine of analogy.

Failure to understand just how our words can tell us
the truth about God may involve us in false mysticism.
Here is the dilemma. On the one hand, you have a false
theology that talks about God as if He could be grasped
and fully contained in human concepts. On the other,
there is agnosticism that says God is completely unknowable. You can fall into anthropomorphism without necessarily picturing God with the physical characteristics of
man. All you have to do is speak of His power, wisdom,
justice, and all the rest of His perfections as if the words
applied to Him in the same way as they applied to men.
As Saint Thomas says: "The word 'wise,' said of a man,
in some degree encompasses and circumscribes the reality
it signifies." [1]

In other words, all our concepts have limits. They have

to have limits for us to understand them. In our language, wisdom is not justice. We are able to know wisdom and justice in so far as they are two different things. They are different because they are set apart by certain "definitions." To define an idea is to give it boundaries. Every reality that we are capable of grasping in a concept is hedged in by its own frontier. What is undefinable is, to us, unknowable because there is no word or idea capable of containing or delimiting its meaning. And we cannot clearly understand realities that do not present themselves to us contained in an idea.

Although it can be argued that all ideas are in some sense illusory, because there is no human concept that fully contains all the concrete reality of the thing it tries to signify, nevertheless we have to admit that conceptual knowledge gives us a sure intellectual grasp of reality. It tells us exactly what things *are*. The scientist is well aware that his idea of sulphuric acid contains and circumscribes a definite reality which is not water, not milk, not any other liquid but, quite definitely, sulphuric acid.

But there exists no word, no idea, that can contain the reality of God. We must never talk about the wisdom and justice and power and even the being of God as if these divine perfections could be fitted into the definitions of these things as they are known to us. Saint Thomas says, of every concept of the divine perfections, that "the reality [in these divine names] remains unbounded, exceeding the signification of the term." [2] All the perfections of God are unlimited and they are therefore all one identical reality. It is impossible for us to understand the notions of justice and mercy unless they are somehow divided from one another and opposed. In God, justice is mercy, mercy is justice, and both are wisdom and power and being, for all His attributes merge in one infinite Reality that elevates them beyond definition and comprehension.

Nevertheless, although all the Divine Names are objectively one identical reality in Him, they are not to be understood as synonymous by us. Like white light, broken up into different colors by the spectrum, the one Reality of God can only be attained by us under many different aspects.[3]

Catholic theology therefore safeguards two things in the concepts by which men attain to God. First, she asserts that they really do attain to Him as He is. They speak the truth about Him. But they present this truth to our minds in a mode that falls infinitely short of the Reality of God. For the justice and wisdom, mercy and power which are illimitable and inseparably identified in Him necessarily appear to us to be diverse and separate qualities. They are His infinite Being: but to us they seem to be qualities modifying His being. How can such ideas be true of Being which is above every logical category, Being which, according to the bold expression of Dionysius, is so far above being that it is "not-being"? They are only true of Him analogically. The Justice of God and His other attributes are understood by us not as modes of the illimitable Being of God but "as if they were" modes of a modifiable being. This "as if" must always be remembered, for our concepts of God are but analogies, even though they be true.

Hence every concept of God has a double aspect. In so far as it actually attains Him, it tells us what He is. For He is Wise, Just, Merciful, Omnipotent. But at the same time the same concepts tell us what He is *not*. He is *not* wise, just, merciful, omnipotent in an anthropomorphic or limited sense.

There are therefore two ways to God: a way of affirmation and a way of denial. These two ways are not offered for us to select according to our own taste. We have to take both. We must affirm and deny at the same time. One cannot go without the other. If we go on affirming, without denying, we end up by affirming that we have delimited the Being of God in our concepts. If we go on denying without affirming, we end up by denying that our concepts can tell the truth about Him in any sense whatever.

I think the way of affirmation and the way of denial can be understood if we compare them to the take-off and the flight of a plane. We start out with a concept of God, and we affirm it of Him: "God exists." This is literally and absolutely true.

I do not have to go into the proofs of the statement here, for the mere fact that there are beings means that there is Being. If God does not exist, nothing exists. If Truth does not exist, then no statement can be true, including the statement that Truth does not exist.

But now: we have a statement about God. He exists. This is an affirmation. The plane is rolling along the ground. That is to say, we are using the term "exists" as if it applied to God in the same way as it applies to you or to me, for we know that we "exist." But now we have to begin denying.

The existence of God is not the same as the existence of man. The plane (that is, our thought) is relinquishing its contact with the level on which our concept of existence is acceptable to us as positive. In proportion as we *deny*, we correct our concepts of God by stating what they cannot mean when they are applied to Him.

The plane cannot fly unless it "renounces" its contact with the ground. The theologian cannot reach God in his concepts until he renounces their limits and their "definitions." But just as Christian asceticism does not destroy the body, so apophatic theology cannot go so far in its denial as to deny everything that is positive in our knowledge of God. So, God is Being, Justice, Power, Wisdom, Mercy. We take off from this affirmation and ascend into the sky of our denials by refusing to admit that any concept of justice can delimit the divine Justice which is His own Being. And it is in this sense that Saint John of the Cross says we must renounce "clear ideas" of God: that is, we must not imagine that His Being can so be contained and circumscribed by our notion of being that our clear ideas will give us possession of Him, power over Him, union with Him.

The Fathers and the great Scholastics agree that the *via negationis* is the way to a true contact with God, a true "possession" of God "in darkness." But it must be understood that this is not merely a dialectical ascent of the unaided intellect. We shall see later that the *via negationis* of the intellect also requires a *via amoris* for the will; on this dark way both intellect and will must ultimately be possessed and transfigured by the action of divine grace in the special inspirations of the Holy Ghost.

Here is what Saint Bonaventure says, refuting the opinion of those theologians who believed in the possibility of an immediate vision of God even in this life: "The most excellent way of contemplation is to ascend by unknowing . . . as Moses was led into darkness." *Excellentissi-mus modus contemplandi est ignote ascendere.*[4]

Saint Bonaventure compares the theologian, in this way of unknowing, to a sculptor in marble. The sculptor digs his statue out of the stone by cutting away all that lies between him and the realization of his idea. Hence, says Saint Bonaventure, the contemplative theologian advances on this *via negationis* by saying: "This is not God, that is not God—*non est hoc Deus, non est hoc.* He advances by denying and by taking away—*per negationem et abla-tionem, ut sculpentes faciunt,* not by adding on.[5] (Incidentally, Saint Bonaventure belonged to an age when sculptors worked in stone and not in clay or plaster!)

And so there are two dangers to be avoided. First, we must not take our conceptual knowledge of God for what it is not. Second, we must at least take it for what it is. It must neither be underestimated nor overestimated. Both these excesses end in a practical atheism. If we attribute too much power to our "clear ideas" of God, we will end up by making ourselves a god in our own image, out of those clear ideas. If we do not grant concepts any power to tell us the truth about God, we will cut off all possible contact between our minds and Him.

I do not know which of these two is the more fatal weakness. Both are paths to false mysticism.

If you begin juggling with a system of clear ideas which, you think, delimit and circumscribe the Being of God, you will, by that very fact, begin judging God according to the measure of your ideas. In doing this, you destroy God—in so far as it is intellectually possible to do so—in order to replace Him by your system. This, says Saint Gregory of Nyssa, is clearly a form of idolatry.

What happens then? Like Job's friends, you set yourself up as a theological advocate of God. You justify His ways to men not according to what He is, but according to what your system says He ought to be. In the end, you find yourself apologizing to the world for God and demonstrating that, after all, He is not to be blamed for being what He is because it can be shown that He generally acts like a just, prudent, and benevolent man. Or rather, to help Him ascend a few degrees in the estimation of men, you present Him to them as a well-disposed and democratic millionaire. The word for this is—blasphemy. It is also atheism, because a God who depends on your ideas for His justification cannot possibly exist.[6]

But then there is the other extreme. It is a more common error, because of the appeal it makes to intellectual and moral inertia. This error says that none of our conceptual knowledge of God is objectively capable of making sense. Since our concepts do not grasp His full reality, they do not attain Him at all. It is useless to inquire whether they be true or false, for we can never know what they are. According to this error, the only justification for our concepts of God is that they are somehow symbols of our own interior states. They objectify our religious and moral ideals. They have a certain pragmatic value as slogans or rallying cries which stimulate individuals and society to moral action. Our ideas about God, we are told, have no intellectual reference to God. It does not even matter whether or not there be a God for them to refer to. But it is worth while to have these ideas. Ideas about God make people nice. Men who have no ideas about God are not nice. They behave abominably—Communists, for instance.

It is a strange paradox that this kind of thought ends up in exactly the same practical atheism as its opposite extreme. Here too we find men who embrace a shadowy god whose only justification for existence is that the thought of him moves them to live up to abstract moral standards which are not so much in him as in them. In both these heresies, such a god is the creation of man and depends, for his existence, on man's ideas of prudence, justice, morality, good and evil, right and wrong. As long as this god measures up to these ideas, he can be suffered to exist. As soon as he somehow interferes with them, the idea of him loses its pragmatic value and must therefore be either discarded or changed.

## 2

There is another form of the same error. This time, it is situated on a higher level. It demands our attention because it sometimes tries to quote Christian mystics in its favor. This is the error which holds in suspicion all religious dogmas or even philosophical doctrines, and admits only a direct, personal, and supraconceptual experience of the Absolute. The *via negationis* then becomes a frank rejection of all concepts of God. It also generally implies a studied ascetic technique by which thought and sensation are systematically suppressed and the spirit is emptied until all sensory and intellectual operations are almost completely subdued.

I am not directing these remarks against Oriental mysticism which, like Christian mysticism, rests on a basis of positive religious doctrine. I am talking of opinions which are widely scattered in the western world at the present time although they are not too well defined and admit many variations. They all have this in common: they combine agnosticism with a pragmatic respect for ascetic techniques and for "religious experience." One might sum up their content in such a statement as this: "We can only 'know' God in mystical experience. The doctrines that are connected with religious institutions, such as Churches, are an obstacle to true experiential knowledge of God. The mystic is therefore essentially a rebel against dogma."

The forms that this error actually takes are generally much more subtle than my blatant caricature. Nevertheless it sums up their substantial content.

The danger of this error does not lie in the fact that it fascinates a few intellectuals who are outside the Church and who openly remain on rather bad terms with Catholicism. The trouble really comes when the heresy technically known as "modernism" taints the Catholic atmosphere with some shade or other of this falsehood. It would be a pity if intellectuals, brought up in agnosticism and starved for religious experience, should come into the Church seeking not Truth, not God, but religious and esthetic experiences considered as somehow unrelated to the conceptual content of Catholic faith.

When a convert presents himself for Baptism, the voice of the Church's Ritual asks him what he is looking for. *Quid petis ab Ecclesia?* The answer is not: ceremonies, religious music, consolation, the prayer of quiet, mystical visions, or even interior peace. The answer is: Faith! And the Ritual, just to make it quite clear that the Church has much more to offer than the casual passing stimulations that refresh the mind and spirit of a religious man, asks another question: *Fides quid tibi praestet?* Translated into American, that question means: "What do you think you are going to get out of faith?" And the answer is: "Eternal life."

The Ritual is satisfied. The catechumen has been through his instructions, and he does not need to be told, in the words of Jesus, that "this is eternal life, that they may know Thee, the One True God, and Jesus Christ whom Thou hast sent." (John 17:3.) Nor does he need to be told that faith reaches God through concepts, since that is the meaning of Saint Paul's remark that "faith cometh by hearing—and how shall they hear if there be no preacher?" (Rom. 10:14.)

The doctrine of analogy saves the Catholic mystic from agnosticism. It keeps the two "ways" of affirmation and negation from traveling in opposite directions. It makes them parallel lanes of the same highway that leads to transcendent Truth. It explains the fact that the conceptual formulas of faith and of dogmatic theology can serve as the starting point for a mystical ascent to God. At the same time it permits dogma to serve as a sure criterion by which the enunciations of the mystic may be tested and truth may be saved from perversion by subjective illusion or by the vagaries of personal metaphor.

The "way of negation" brings us to the highest knowledge of God. It concludes, paradoxically, in a positive statement which serves as the fulfillment of the "way of affirmation."

Here are the words in which Saint Thomas describes the end of this ascent to God. "The final attainment of man's knowledge of God consists in knowing that we do not know Him, in so far as we realize that He transcends everything that we understand concerning Him." [7] "Having arrived at the term of our knowledge we *know God as unknown*." [8]

The two ways end in the same affirmation of the negative knowledge of God. It is an affirmation, because it declares that we actually *know* God. We know Him in all the positive concepts we have of Him and, besides, we know He is infinitely above all these concepts. And in this respect, our "way of negation" *adds* to our positive knowledge of God. We only deny what we know about Him in order to find out something more.

*Deum tamquam ignotum cognoscimus,* says Saint Thomas. "We know God as unknown." Far from declaring that He is unknowable, Catholic dogma knows God, and knows Him in His infinite transcendence: and Catholic mysticism knows Him by experience.

On this foundation are built Catholic philosophy and speculative theology. They are, in strict truth, sciences. In fact, they are the highest of sciences. They are not the pragmatic rationalization of vague spiritual desires. On the levels of both philosophy and theology, Catholic thought has a value that is speculative and absolute. That is to say, it arrives at conclusions about God which are endowed with a genuine scientific certitude, because they can be proved, by clear demonstration, to proceed with inexorable logic from basic principles which are self-evident, in the case of philosophy, and revealed by God in the case of theology.

Scholastic philosophy thinks on the purely rational level. But the philosopher need not do without the light of faith or the aid of grace. In speculative theology, reason elaborates the truths revealed by God and accepted by a faith which philosophy must admit to be thoroughly reasonable. Speculative theology exists and is valid as a science because of the essential conformity between the truths of faith and those of reason. Both these lights of the intellect proceed from God, and God cannot contradict Himself.

When there appears to be some discrepancy between reason and faith, it is only a sign of the essential limitation of human intelligence. True science cannot contradict revealed truth. When a scientific hypothesis *appears* to come in conflict with a dogma of the faith, the believer does not throw all science out the window in order to take refuge in an obscurantistic reaction against reason. He simply puts that particular hypothesis on the shelf and abides by the teaching of his faith, until further light is thrown on the problem.

The churchmen who rejected the hypothesis of Galileo were no more to be blamed than any of his fellow scientists who may have disagreed with him, for the time being, while waiting for further evidence. Galileo, it must be remembered, was never judged a heretic. His theory was simply considered suspicious and put on the shelf. It was accepted later on. The Church has a perfect right to demand submission of her children when she asks them to remain silent on a subject which is, perhaps, as yet incomprehensible to an unscientific hierarchy. The bishops are under no obligation to keep pace with the latest developments of physics, but they do have an obligation to preserve the deposit of revealed Truth according to whatever light God has given them.

The Catholic scientist, or philosopher, or theologian is well aware that he may have to be patient, at some time or other in his life, and withhold a favorite theory of his own merely in order to avoid upsetting an ecclesiastical superior. He knows well enough that the Church is the custodian of Truth and that, if his theory be true, it will be recognized at last. The doctrine of the Immaculate Conception was attacked by many theologians before it was finally defined as a dogma of faith.

Speculative theology concerns itself with the rational clarification of the truths of faith. In other words, it compares revealed truths with one another and with truths known to science and philosophy, and proceeds dialectically to the discovery of truths which would otherwise have remained hidden and inactive in the original articles of faith. Speculative theology seeks above all to plumb the full depths of revelation in so far as the intelligence, enlightened by faith and making use of discourse, is able to do so. But in performing this task which is essential to it, theology also throws light on all the other sciences while at the same time making a sober use of their resources.

Yet no matter how great may be the certitude of scholastic philosophy and theology, they both culminate in a knowledge of God *tamquam ignotum*. They know Him in His transcendence. They know Him "as unknown."

It is clear then that the power of scientific demonstration which is possessed by philosophy and theology, when these deal with God, is something other than the demonstrations of experimental science. The physicist deals with physical energy in such a way that it becomes subject to his control. His conclusions, if they be correct, enable him not only to make speculative judgments about material forces but also to prove his conclusions by making these forces obey him. Even if this be impossible—an astronomer cannot make the planets change their courses—still the scientist becomes, by his intelligence, the master of what he knows.

Now the first elementary truth that must be grasped by anyone who attempts to understand a scientific demonstration for the existence of God is that this demonstration, although it ends in absolute certitude, *cannot put our minds in possession of an object which they can determine, master, possess, or command.*

# CHAPTER VII

# The Crisis
# of Dark Knowledge

It is terrible to know God and not love Him. It is terrible to reach some speculative certainty concerning Him without any corresponding sense of the practical implications of that certitude.

If our conceptual knowledge of God is true and certain, then, by our very thoughts, we attain to Him, we touch Him. Yet He is untouchable and unattainable. But if that is true, how is it possible for us to think of Him without anguish?

All other certitude terminates in a clear, definite possession of the thing known. Our certitude about God lays before us a wide-open chasm of darkness. And if it is truly He that we have found, in our concepts, we realize that this darkness that exceeds our concepts gives testimony to His infinite Truth. The knowledge of all else than God makes us the masters of what we know. But our knowledge of God makes Him the Master of the soul that knows Him. If it does not, then the soul has never known Him. Only in the submission which is faith can we "know" God and find, in that knowledge, true peace.

It is dangerous to talk glibly about the infinite God. It is sometimes dangerous to talk about Him at all, unless talking of Him brings you deeper into His mystery, and finally flattens you into silence in the face of His transcendence!

Who is God? Who is He that we know only as exceeding the capacity of all our purest and most exalted concepts to contain? We speak of Him as "Pure Act," Infinite Reality, in Whom every perfection that we are capable of knowing is realized in an infinite and supereminent fulfillment. He is beyond all that we can signify by intelligence, for He is pure Intelligence. His essence is Intelligence. He is beyond all that we can signify by love or mercy. Love is His being. *Deus Caritas est.* He is beyond all that we can call power. He is all Power.

If thought, love, action, contemplation exist on earth, if they are the highest immanent perfections of man's spirit, and if all the perfections we know of are supereminently realized in God, Who is the source, exemplar, and end of them all, then how can God be anything but a personal God?

By Him we are created as we are known. When He knows us, we are. When He knows us not, we are not. His knowledge is the cause of our being. But His knowledge and His love, in Him, are One. His love is also the cause of our being. He holds us in existence by His love, as it were in the hollow of His hand.

Nevertheless, as soon as we light these small matches which are our concepts: "intelligence," "love," "power," the tremendous reality of God Who infinitely exceeds all concepts suddenly bears down upon us like a dark storm and blows out all their flames!

It is dangerous to be able to resist this whirlwind and to keep your matches lighted when the night wind blows in from His dark, infinite sea, His *pelagus substantiae*. It is perilous indeed to be satisfied with a philosophy that makes you ignore the most important consequence of God's transcendence: the necessity of faith.

Christian mysticism is born of a theological crisis. This theological crisis is precipitated by the very nature of faith. For faith, which is at the heart of contemplation, makes use of concepts and yet transcends them. It "sees" God, but only in darkness, *per speculum, in aenigmate*. To see in darkness is not to see. To understand in an enigma is not to understand but to be perplexed. The necessity of this darkness and of this enigma—this is to say, the necessity of faith—is itself the fruit of another crisis—the crisis of an apophatic philosophy. I am speaking of faith in the hierarchy of means by which we know God, not of faith as it is usually concretely found in Christians who have received it at the font and grown up with it running through their veins. They are accidentally absolved from the necessity of finding God between the horns of a philosopher's dilemma.

There is no such absolution for the contemplative. The Cross is the only way to mystical prayer.

Christian contemplation is precipitated by crisis within crisis and anguish within anguish. It is born of spiritual conflict. It is a victory that suddenly appears in the hour of defeat. It is the providential solution of problems that seem to have no solution. It is the reconciliation of enemies that seem to be irreconcilable. It is a vision in which Love, mounting into the darkness which no reasoning can penetrate, unites in one bond all the loose strands that intelligence alone cannot connect together, and with this cord draws the whole being of man into a Divine Union, the effects of which will someday overflow into the world outside him.

This spiritual crisis cannot exist where reasoning, conceptual thought, words and judgments, are believed incapable of expressing truths about God. In a universe in which there is thought to be an irreconcilable opposition between body and spirit, nature and the supernatural, concepts and contemplation, the problem of reaching union with God becomes theoretically much simpler. But this is a false solution. It makes true union with God impossible except by miracle or by accident.

According to this false view the phenomenal world, the body with its senses, language, concepts, logic, the reasoning mind, the will that is moved by love—all must be silenced and rejected. The only problem is to "deliver" spirit from matter and from discourse, for these are nothing but obstacles to union. The soul wrestles its way free from the body like a butterfly breaking out of a cocoon. Man, according to this oversimplification, is really an angel imprisoned in a body. His destiny is not a supernatural elevation of his whole being, body and soul, to divine contemplation in glory, but the reabsorption of his spirit in the kingdom of angels. Sanctity is not the supernatural fulfillment of human personality (for it takes body and soul to make a human person) but the annihilation of flesh and of individuality, to ensure the liberation of the spirit.

If there be a "crisis" in such a mysticism as this, the crisis is not intellectual but psychological: it arises from the division of man against himself in an attack on his own nature. The kind of asceticism that literally seeks to destroy what is human in man in order to reduce the spirit to an innate element that is purely divine is founded on a grave metaphysical error. The gravity of that error ought to be immediately apparent from the very fact that man's spiritual and psychological health depends on the right order and balance of his whole being—body and soul. The concept of "nature" implies the right direction of a being toward the end for which it is made. That is why animals have instincts which guide them toward the fulfillment of their proper natural ends.

Man's nature disposes him above all to seek peace in the contemplation and love of the highest Truth. It can be said that all men are born with an instinctive desire to know the Truth and an instinctive (though unrecognized) desire for the supreme happiness which is the vision of God in heaven.

Now, if man were by nature an angel, if he were a pure spirit, imprisoned, against his nature, in flesh, then the same natural instinct which drives him to seek the Truth would, at the same time, urge him to commit suicide in order to free his spirit from his flesh. The child in whom the first glimmering of thought awakens questions about the nature of things, instead of spontaneously asking his parents what things are would throw himself into a fire or out the window. He would instinctively try to destroy his body.

Although there were philosophers like the Stoics who thought suicide was a courageous act, I hardly think they can have thought it was an expression of the deepest needs of human nature! For the only reason they could argue that the act took "courage" was that it goes against our fundamental natural instinct for self-preservation. And everyone knows that no man is tempted to kill himself until he has been driven to despair by the frustration of all his natural desires for happiness—desires which tend, by their very essence, to seek their highest fulfillment in the vision and possession, by love, of the most perfect reality, indefectible Truth.

The danger of angelism is, then, quite clear. As Pascal said: *Qui veut faire l'ange, fait la bête* ("Those who play at being angels, end up as animals"). You cannot divide man's nature against itself without disastrous consequences. If perfection is sought by annihilation of the outward man and the absolute rejection of a phenomenal universe, what actually happens is that the two halves of man's metaphysical being break away from each other and start traveling roads of their own. And when the flesh becomes its own master, it ends by mastering the spirit. It is rare for an ascetic to live his whole life long as if he did not have a body. Much more common are the ones who punish themselves furiously for two or three years and then lose their morale, fall into despair, become hypochondriacs, obsessed with every fancied need of their flesh and of their spirit.[1]

There is a whole family of heresies descended from Gnosticism and Manichaeism. They are all dualistic: that is to say, they split the universe into two metaphysically irreconcilable camps, of matter and spirit, evil and good. All the evil is on the side of matter—which is the camp of the Devil. All the good is on the side of spirit, which is the side of God. Man is caught between the two: for both are at war within him. Spirit is supposed to win the day by an ascetic annihilation of flesh. But the flesh is not easily annihilated, even by a well-intentioned maniac. And so we find that in practice the Gnostics, the Cathari, the Quietists, and all those whose spirituality was so pure

that it held men to be angels by nature, were forced
in practice to ignore the flesh which so few of them were
able to conquer. Molinos had a curious theory about sins
of the flesh not being sins. No doubt we do not get a
well-rounded picture of Molinos's spirituality merely by
looking over the list of his statements that were condemned
by the Church. Nevertheless the list certainly confirms
Pascal's apothegm, for it gives us a peculiar portrait of a
soul that is half angel and half beast.

We find in the Orient something of the same strange
mixture of mysticism and lust. Millions of deeply religious
people whose view of the universe is that of pantheistic
monism are able to accept, with the most surprising indifference, the high spiritual ideals of Raja-Yoga side by side
with temple prostitution as equally credible expressions of
the same religious outlook. Different levels of spirituality,
no doubt! But, *chacun à son goût!* It is all a matter of
individual vocation. All roads lead eventually to the same
liberation, provided you are patient enough with your
burden of *karma*.

As soon as the phenomenal world ceases to be an intelligible manifestation of the Absolute, and as soon as our
thoughts and our words cease altogether to provide us
with an objectively valid means of communicating with
God, we fall into agnosticism. That is true, even though
we may have denied words and concepts their power of
mediation with God in order to do honor to the pure
spirituality of the Divine Nature. And even though this
agnosticism be adopted in order to guarantee the purity
of an interior, individual, incommunicable experience of
God, its intellectual and moral consequences will always
be regrettable.

Agnosticism leads inevitably to moral indifference. It denies us all power to esteem or to understand moral values, because it severs our spiritual contact with God Who alone is the source of all morality and Who alone can punish the violation of moral laws with a sanction worth our attention. That is why there was something peculiarly strange and funny about the feeble efforts of the bourgeois generations of the late nineteenth and early twentieth centuries to bring up their progeny with a respect for moral and social obligations but with no belief in God. The wilder lawlessness of each new growing generation was, in effect, its way of saying: "In the name of whom or what do you ask me to behave? Why should I go to the inconvenience of denying myself the satisfactions I desire in the name of some standard that exists only in your imagination? Why should I worship the fictions you have imposed on me in the name of Nothing?"

2

The crisis from which Christian contemplation springs cannot exist in a soul which believes in the total rejection of everything exterior to its own spiritual substance. But it is also quite apparent that the same crisis does not arise in a soul for whom the whole spiritual life is exteriorized in words, formulas, ceremonies, rites, laws observed for their own sake. In either case the error is generically the same, for it consists in dividing man against himself, fencing off one section of his being as a sanctuary and leaving the rest to its own devices.

The *whole man*, his body and his soul, what is within

him and what is without, has to belong to God. Saint Paul said: "Know you not that your bodies are the temples of the Holy Ghost?" (I Cor. 3:16.) He did not say the soul only was God's sanctuary. The Spirit of God dwells principally in the soul but sanctifies the whole man. *Templum Dei sanctum est, quod estis vos.* We cannot give half this temple to God and leave the forecourt to Belial. "For what agreement hath the temple of God with idols?" (2 Cor. 6:16.) And Jesus said: "He that is not with me is against me." (Matt. 12:30.) It is not enough to sanctify the soul alone, still less the body alone.

A purely interior religion, without any doctrinal structure or any liturgical expression, can from time to time produce a semblance of contemplation. A religion that is entirely outward almost never brings about anything resembling the true peace of interior and infused contemplation.

In actual fact, however, there is no religion worth the name that is entirely interior or entirely exterior. In spite of the pure spirituality of its metaphysical foundation, Raja-Yoga rests, in large part, upon ascetic techniques which exploit every resource which subtle theories of physiology can discover in the body of man.

On the other hand, the primitive cults, in which myth, symbolism, and magic strive to keep man on friendly terms with the mysterious powers that seem to govern the world in which he lives, are not merely exterior forms. They plumb the dark subconscious depths of man's being. The ceremonial dances and rites of savage tribes sometimes release hidden psychic forces in trance and ecstasy. Though these experiences are not strictly spiritual, they are at least interior: they spring from the soul, the psyche of man. And they also have a marked effect on his body. No matter what may be the spiritual level of certain primitive religions, there is no doubt that they can take possession of a man's whole being.

However, this is not usually the expression of what can properly be called a spiritual "crisis." I do not doubt that the pagan tribesman knows, from time to time, his fair share of anguish. But it is the bare, hard anguish of emotion, a physical terror intensified by superstition and allayed by drums, blood, and incantation. I would give the pagan credit for feeling much more at peace with the world at the end of one of his tribal rites than the American who comes home, tired and happy, after yelling himself hoarse over a football game. But the satisfaction of both is just about the same. It is the physical semblance of peace that comes to one who has let off steam.

The true spiritual crisis which sometimes leads to faith, the crisis within crisis that must always prepare the way for contemplation, must first of all have an intellectual element. It must be born of thought. It must spring from a respect for the validity of concepts and of reasoning. It accepts the work of intelligence. But it also sees that concepts and intelligence have their limitations. At the same time it realizes that the *spirit is not necessarily bound by these limitations*. And this is where the crisis begins.

I believe that Christ is God, that He is the Word of God Incarnate. I believe that in Christ a human nature was assumed by the Second Person of the Blessed Trinity, in such a way that it does not subsist in a proper human personality of its own but has its being from Him, subsists in Him.

I believe that the Man Christ is a Divine Person, the

Son of God. And I believe that by the grace which He
has purchased for us all by His death on the Cross and
which He has made available for us all by His Resurrection from the dead, and communicated to all who are
baptized, He has given me a share in that divine sonship.
Spiritually therefore I am living by the life of the Son of
God. My life is "hidden with Christ in God." (Col. 3:3.)
So much I believe.

These are concepts, and they are joined in intelligible
judgments. I can penetrate their meaning by an analysis
of them which compares their revealed content with the
content of other propositions revealed by God or even
with propositions known to reason. And yet they remain
mysteries to me. No amount of analysis can make them
clearly evident to my intelligence.

Nevertheless, the love of God endows man's spirit with
a kind of instinctive realization that somehow these mysteries of faith are meant to be penetrated and appreciated.
In a certain sense they are given us to be understood. Faith
seeks understanding, not only in study but above all in
prayer. *Fides quaerit intellectum.*

And Saint Paul explained to the Christian converts of
Corinth that although he spoke "the wisdom of God in
a mystery, a wisdom which is hidden," nevertheless the
Spirit of God would manifest the hidden wonders of this
wisdom. "To us God hath revealed them by His Spirit.
. . . We have received not the spirit of this world but
the Spirit that is of God: *that we may know the things
that are given us from God.*" (I Cor. 2:7, 10, 12.)

This explains the double crisis of dark knowledge. First
the philosopher, ascending to the limits of his science,
knows that God is beyond the grasp of every concept we

can have of Him. And yet our concepts about Him are true. They are most true when they are taken with this negative qualification: when they say, "God is everything that we can signify, and yet He is not what we signify because He is infinitely more."

First crisis: God is not only intelligible, but infinite and essential Intelligibility. He is essential Intellgence understanding Himself.

At the same time, since God's Truth is the supreme Good it is fitting that He should communicate Himself in the most perfect possible way to His creatures. That is as far as the philosopher can go. And that constitutes his crisis, because, as a matter of fact, as philosopher, all he knows is that God still remains infinitely beyond the scope of his philosophy. To despair of ever knowing the Truth would be to sin against the light of reason. And yet there is nothing in man that can carry him any closer to God than his own reason. It is only faith that tells us how God has, in fact, communicated His Truth perfectly to us by the hypostatic union in which a created human nature was assumed by the Word, "so that One Person was constituted by these three: the Word, a soul and a body." [2]

The second convolution of this crisis reproduces the first, but at a deeper spiritual level. The passage from philosophical understanding to faith is marked by a gift of our self to God. The moment of transition is the moment of sacrifice. The passage from faith to that spiritual understanding which is called contemplation is also a moment of immolation. It is the direct consequence of a more complete and radical gift of ourselves to God. Contemplation is an intensification of faith that transforms belief into something akin to vision. Yet it is not "vision," since contemplation, being pure faith, is even darker than faith itself.

Abraham, with his knife raised over the neck of his son Isaac, is the symbol of faith.[3] For, like the sacrifice of Abraham, the gift of ourselves in total submission to God is a sacrifice in which, far from losing anything, we gain everything and recover, in a more perfect mode of possession, even what we seem to have lost. For at the very moment when we give ourselves to God, God gives Himself to us. He cannot give Himself completely to us unless we give ourselves completely to Him: but we cannot give ourselves completely to Him unless He first gives Himself in some measure to us.

The deep secret of the mystery of faith lies in the fact that it is a "baptism" in the death and sacrifice of Christ.[4] We can only give ourselves to God when Christ, by His grace, "dies" and rises again spiritually within us.

PART TWO


REASON AND MYSTICISM
IN SAINT JOHN OF THE CROSS

# CHAPTER VIII

# The Theological Background

It is difficult to read the works of Saint John of the Cross without being impressed by the precision of his thought and by the coherence of his ideas. Even those who find themselves ill at ease with his conclusions must admit that he arrives at them by a process of strict philosophical and theological reasoning. No other Christian mystical theologian builds on such clear dogmatic foundations, or with so powerful a framework of thought. Of all those we are accustomed to regard as mystics *ex professo,* he is the closest to Saint Thomas Aquinas and to the great scholastics in the clarity of his procedure.

It would take a digression, at this point, to explain that Saint Thomas and Saint Bonaventure, as well as the great Fathers of the Church like Saint Augustine, Saint Bernard, and Saint Gregory of Nyssa, were also mystics and even "mystical theologians." In setting Saint John of the Cross apart in a peculiar species of "mystical writers" I am perhaps confusing an important issue. I am perhaps making a dangerous concession to the too-prevalent opinion that mysticism and dogma fall into watertight compartments and that "the mystics" and "the theologians" are essentially different beings with a totally different outlook on life.

Although the works of Saint John of the Cross reflect his own personal experience—since without his experience they could never have been written—nevertheless they are not mere records of what went on in his own mystical life. They are theology in a fuller sense than the writing of Saint Teresa of Ávila, of Ruysbroeck, of Tauler and the rest. I do not mean by this that the works of Teresa are not immensely rich in dogmatic truth. Saint Teresa lived the Christian faith in a way that was marvelous, and her knowledge of Christ was so personal and so immediate that she had only to put herself on paper to give a good picture of what it really means to be a Catholic; for in describing to us the life of her own soul, she left us a detailed and objective record of the whole process of transformation in Christ which is the objective of Christian belief.

Nevertheless, this "transformation" is presented to us with features peculiar to the life of a very extraordinary woman in sixteenth-century Spain. We are all called, in some way or other, to an intimate union with God in Christ. But only Saint Teresa was called to the particular degree and mode of union we read about in her books. In her writings we see Christ as He is reflected in the soul of Saint Teresa. We can easily compare this image of Christ with the visage He has revealed to the whole Church. In doing so, we see that Saint Teresa was an eminently orthodox mystic. Nevertheless, to write as a theologian one must fix one's gaze upon the Face of Christ that is revealed to the whole Church, not merely upon one's own experience of Him. The theologian who is also a mystic cannot help being guided, in his theological studies, by an intimate supernatural sense of divine values, a sort of superinstinct that reaches Divine Truth by blind flying, so to speak, on a "beam" while other theologians remain grounded in their airports or crash into each other in the mist. Nevertheless it is not expressly of his experience that the theologian writes. His mind is focused on the truths God has revealed to His Church. His chief concern is to make clear the content of revelation and to draw forth from its inexhaustible treasures new jewels with which to stun the eyes of faith.

It is true that the mystical theologian is necessarily concerned with mystical experience. But in so far as he is a theologian, he must study above all what is revealed by God concerning mystical union and the experiences that accompany it. Writers who accumulate facts of religious experience, tabulate them, and try to formulate "laws" based on common elements observed in all mysticism, treat the subject matter as psychologists rather than as theologians. These empirical studies are unquestionably very valuable. In fact, for the professional psychologist, for the historian of religion, and for other such students, they are probably more valuable than genuine mystical theology. They also serve to throw light on practical problems that arise in the life of interior prayer. The way of infused contemplation is a lonely one. Those who are drawn to it by God find inexpressible comfort in recognizing the landmarks and signposts of their journey set down in the scant accounts of others who have gone that way before them.

Some of the most beautiful and valuable pages of Saint John of the Cross are, as a matter of fact, in this category; they are observations of mystical experience, illustrated at times by Scriptural applications. Nevertheless, Saint

John of the Cross is not content with this. He realizes
that the applied sense of Scripture has no theological value,
and that the use of Scriptural texts by mystical authors is
not theology if it does not teach us some truth revealed by
God. When a mystic takes a passage from the Bible out
of its context and adapts it to his own spiritual experience,
his use of Scripture is merely literary. Employed in such
a way, a quotation from Scripture has no more theological
force than a quotation from Homer. It is not enough,
thinks Saint John of the Cross, to use Scripture as the
mirror of one's own interior life. Therefore, even though
he draws upon his experimental knowledge of mysticism,
he does not attempt to prove anything by that experience
alone. All that he says of the graces of prayer serves him
as an occasion to seek out the final theological answer, the
true Catholic doctrine on each point, in the revealed word
of God.

Saint John of the Cross does not merely *illustrate* his
doctrine by a literary use of Scripture, he *proves* it by
Scripture. More than that, he finds his doctrine in the
Bible. It is in this sense that Saint John is primarily a
theologian and not only what is loosely referred to as a
"spiritual writer." He can say, as Jesus said, that his doctrine is not merely his own but the doctrine of the Father
Who sent him.

All the deeper instincts of a true theologian warned
Saint John of the Cross that the revealed word of God
offered him greater security than did experience itself,
where there was question of a supernatural order in which
the ways were known with certitude by Him alone who
had established them. The prologue of *The Ascent* an-
nounces the plan of a true theologian:

In order to say a little about this dark night [mystical contemplation] I shall trust neither to experience nor to knowledge, since both may fail and deceive; but while not omitting to make such use as I can of these two things, I shall avail myself . . . of Divine Scripture, for if we guide ourselves by this we shall be unable to stray, since He who speaks therein is the Holy Spirit. And if in aught I stray it is not my intention to depart from the sound sense and doctrine of our Holy Mother the Catholic Church.[1]

This is not a mere form of words. *The Ascent* and *The Dark Night of the Soul*, which are simply two parts of a single book, not only follow a careful theological plan but even—and this is one of their many claims to our respect—expose to us a doctrine which seems to be continuously and coherently spread out before our eyes in the theological sense of the Old and New Testaments.

Observe how strongly Saint John insists that he is looking for the highest intellectual certitude, and that he expects to find it not in a subjective experience of God but in the objective content of a conceptual and dogmatic revelation. There is not a shadow of agnosticism in this Spanish mystic when he is properly understood. The same ideas are repeated in his prologue to *The Spiritual Canticle*. This great commentary on his own poem is much less a systematic treatise in spiritual theology than his first book, formed by *The Ascent* and *The Dark Night*. In *The Spiritual Canticle*, Saint John talks more of the positive side of mystical theology—the "lights" of mystical prayer and the stupendous joy of mystical union. The book seems to be much more personal. Much more importance is given to facts which he could only have glimpsed through the doorway of ecstasy. Nevertheless, he insists on being a theologian. The prologue tells us clearly so. He uses the same words that we have quoted from *The Ascent*.

> I think not to affirm aught that is mine, trusting to my own experience or to that of other spiritual persons whom I have known, or to that which I have heard from them (although I purpose to profit by both), unless it be confirmed and expounded by authorities from the Divine Scripture.[2]

He does not intend to rely on any purely personal revelation. His interpretation of Scripture will be guided, of course, by Catholic tradition and by the authority of the Church. He says so again here.[3] He is therefore a theologian in the Catholic sense: one who studies and clarifies the deposit of public revelation committed by God to the Church, one who studies it under the guidance of the Church, in order to find out and propound the teaching of the Church.

But there is one more accidental note which completes the Catholic idea of a "theologian" in its strictest definition. In modern times, a theologian is almost necessarily a *scholastic* theologian. He follows the methods and systematic procedure of the schoolmen. His thought is guided by the principles that were established in the Aristotelian-Christian synthesis in the thirteenth century.

It would be absurd to expect Saint John of the Cross to produce a treatise of mystical theology that would be scholastic in the academic sense of the word. A later generation of Discalced Carmelites would compile huge volumes of such material. I call to witness the heavy tomes of Joseph of the Holy Spirit which, of course, have their value. But Saint John of the Cross has a scholastic background and he makes frequent use of scholastic principles. He explains in the prologue to *The Spiritual Canticle* why he has seen fit to mix the speculative wisdom of the schools with the infused wisdom that can only be gained by prayer.[4]

## Saint John of the Cross at Salamanca and Alcalá

It is not surprising that Saint John of the Cross should write as he did, when we consider his theological background and the strict training he received. Sixteenth-century Spain had witnessed a revival of intense intellectual and spiritual activity. This was an expression of that spontaneous resurgence of Catholicism produced by the Protestant Reformation. With half Europe breaking away from the Church and rejecting her teaching authority, theologians suddenly awoke from the torpor that had descended upon them in the fourteenth and fifteenth centuries. A great renewal of theology was necessary if there was to be a corresponding revival of spiritual life. This is a fact too often ignored. The fourteenth century—in which theology was sinking to a low ebb—had nevertheless been an age of great spiritual aspirations. But these aspirations came to nothing, or went astray. Individuals like Tauler, men of sublime personal spirituality, contributed comparatively little to the growth of the Church. The dogmatic foundations of their teaching could easily have been well defined. But they were not. These mystics occupied an equivocal position in the troubled world of their time. They traversed its stage like some of the characters in Shakespeare's historical dramas, characters who are wonderful but cannot be accounted for by any rule of

art. They are simply there to satisfy the exuberant crea-
tiveness of a playwright who has made a masterpiece out
of odds and ends.

Since the sixteenth century was an age of theological
revival, it necessarily witnessed the resurrection of Catholic
spirituality, the reform of old religious orders and the foundation of new ones, the moral and ascetical reawakening
of the people and of the clergy. It also left us a mysticism
at once sublime and sane. And its mystics were at the same
time theologians, founders and heads of orders, above all,
great saints and the makers of saints. Where did all this
life and light and sanctity come from? From the teaching
and governing Church. The Church is not taught by
theologians, they are taught by her. The Church is not
sanctified by her saints; she sanctifies them, with the grace
of Christ. But the teaching and sanctifying power of the
Church are inseparable from her governing authority. In
her history, ages of light and of grace have been first of all
ages of order. This is necessary; for without order there is
no unity, and if the members of the Mystical Body are
not closely united under a common head, they cannot fully
receive the life stream of grace which is communicated
by Christ to all who are united in one will and are of
"one mind in the Lord."

The theological and spiritual revival of the sixteenth
century was due in large part to one of the greatest of the
Ecumenical Councils. I think it can be said that the mysticism of Saint John of the Cross and of Saint Teresa was a
fruit of the Council of Trent!

Salamanca was the most important university in the
Catholic world when John of the Cross registered as an
*artista* among its six thousand students in 1564.[5] A series

of great Dominican theologians had captured for Salamanca the crown that had been worn by the University of
Paris since the great days of Aquinas in the thirteenth century. Although it is significant that Salamanca was most
famous for its school of Canon Law, its faculties of arts and
theology were bursting with an intellectual life that was
unequaled anywhere. Salamanca had led the revival of
scholastic philosophy and theology by dismissing forever
from its pale the hairsplitting preoccupations of decadent
medieval thought. The celebrated *Sentences* of Peter Lom-
bard, which had been glossed and commented almost out
of existence by four centuries of intricate debate, were now
discarded forever. The *Summa* of Saint Thomas, whose
influence had shaped the chapters and definitions of the
Council of Trent, now for the first time assumed its place
as the standard text of Catholic philosophy and theology.

The *Summa* has maintained this position ever since;
and though it has never seriously been threatened by any
rival, the mere anticipation of such threat has moved the
Holy See to confirm with all its authority the unquestioned pre-eminence of the Angelic Doctor. This does not
mean that every opinion of Saint Thomas has been canonized as an object of theological faith. But the Church has
demanded that her teachers follow the basic principles of
the *Summa* because she wants their theology to be, above
all, systematic, orderly, and clear.

The intellectual atmosphere of Salamanca was pervaded
with the luminous order and rationality of Saint Thomas.
This, of course, did not prevent the social life of the student body from being as colorful a chaos as that of any
university of the Middle Ages and the Renaissance.
Compared with sixteenth-century Salamanca, or twelfth-

century Bologna, modern Oxford and Cambridge seem scarcely more riotous than Sunday schools.

The dozen Carmelites, who lived tucked away in a little corner called the College of Saint Andrew, were quite lost in this boiling sea of undergraduate excitement. They passed through its combats in a modest and unnoticed procession, walking two by two with white hoods over their lowered eyes. Not that they were not of the same flesh and bone as the rest of the university; but they knew that any signal breach of discipline would mean for them ten days in the convent jail cell on bread and water, with the prospect of a return to their house of origin if the offense were too often repeated

John of the Cross spent four scholastic years as a cleric at Salamanca. During the first three, he studied "arts," which meant Aristotelian philosophy. The works of the Stagyrite himself—his Logic, Physics, Ethics and Politics —were commented according to the spirit and the letter of Saint Thomas. This discipline left an indelible mark on the young Carmelite. His most important year was the one he spent as theologian.[6] We can tell, with great probability, what courses he followed, because the Carmelites usually sent their men to the university for the ordinary training of a priest, not for higher degrees. John of the Cross therefore probably attended the most frequented courses, which were also the most important and the most fundamental. Useless to look for him in the lectures on Nominalism, or in the course on Duns Scotus, which attracted so few students that it was always on the verge of being dropped. These were only for men who plunged deeply into the troubled waters of speculation and controversy. John of the Cross would never be one of them.

The big courses in dogma that year were those of the Dominican, Mancio, and of an Augustinian, Guevara. Another essential course was that in Scripture, taught by Grajal.

Mancio lectured after Prime each morning at Corpus Christi. His chair had previously been occupied by the great commentators of Saint Thomas—Vitoria, Melchior Cano, and Dominic Soto—who had earned for Salamanca its immense prestige. In the school year 1567-1568, Mancio was lecturing on the Third Part of the *Summa,* which deals with the Incarnation.

God's revelation of Himself to the world in His Incarnate Word forms the heart and the substance of all Christian mystical contemplation. This is just as true of Saint John of the Cross as it is of Saint Bernard of Clairvaux, of Saint Bonaventure, or any of the mystics who are esteemed for their special devotion to the Humanity of Christ. Undoubtedly the lectures on the Third Part of the *Summa* contributed much to the formation of the Carmelite mystic, if he attended them.

It seems almost indisputable that Saint John of the Cross studied that year under Guevara. Historical records show that, in these academic sessions of 1567 and 1568, Guevara lectured on the beginning of the *Prima Secundae.* Now, the *Prima Secundae* lays down the foundations of Saint Thomas's moral, ascetical, and mystical theology. Guevara must have covered his ground with great thoroughness. Although he is reported to have talked so fast that his students could not take notes, nevertheless he treated his matter very slowly. It took him a whole year to comment on the first eight questions of the *Prima Secundae.* These questions, which occupy only a few pages and would normally be dealt with satisfactorily in a couple of weeks, are immensely important. Six of them treat of man's last end, the vision of God's Essence in beatitude. From then on, the Angelic Doctor begins to discuss the faculties by which man can attain this end, the obstacles which are in his way, and the aids which have been given him by God in the natural and supernatural orders.

A mere glance at the works of Saint John of the Cross shows that he must have been familiar with more than the opening questions of the *Prima Secundae*. Nevertheless, the six brief questions in which Saint Thomas sketches, in bold strokes, his outline of that supreme contemplation which is man's last end, not only influenced Saint John of the Cross but actually provided him with the basic structure of his whole doctrine.

It will come as a surprise to many to learn that the fiercely uncompromising principles on which Saint John of the Cross builds his doctrine of complete detachment from creatures in order to arrive at union with God, are sometimes quoted word for word from Saint Thomas in these questions on beatitude. Practically the whole of *The Ascent of Mount Carmel* can be reduced to these pages of the Angelic Doctor.

The mere fact that Saint John of the Cross was able to see the tremendous implications, for the contemplative life on earth, contained in a few simple, fundamental ideas of the Angelic Doctor about man's last end, is itself evidence of Saint John's theological genius. Needless to say, it also shows that Saint John of the Cross was a true Thomist, because he could never have found what he did in Saint Thomas's treatment of man's last end if he had

THE THEOLOGICAL BACKGROUND                                    133

not been convinced, as was Saint Thomas, that "grace is the seed of glory" and that the life of faith on earth is a beginning of the life of heaven, *inchoatio vitae aeternae*.[7]

A glance at the main ideas on man's last end in the *Summa* will therefore throw much light on the theology of Saint John of the Cross. No one who has read *The Ascent of Mount Carmel* with any care can avoid being struck by the parallel development in the thoughts of these two great contemplative saints, one in the field of speculative and scientific theology, the other in the field of mysticism, or of theology as experience.

Saint John of the Cross begins all his longer treatises by pointing to the last end of man: "union with God through clear and essential vision." Saint Thomas teaches us in the *Summa* [8] that God is the last end not only of men but of all things, for all creation somehow finds fulfillment in a participation of the perfections of God. For nonrational creatures this participation is limited to being what they are meant to be. For man it is something more. We are made not only in order to exist, but in order that we may know and love Him Who is the Creator and Fulfillment of our being.

There are two levels of beatitude. One is the incomplete happiness which man can achieve on earth by his natural intelligence, contemplating and loving God after the manner of a philosopher. Perfect beatitude, which is foreshadowed in the obscure mystical contemplation of God on earth and is perfected in the light of glory, is the clear supernatural vision of the Divine Essence as it is in itself. This vision cannot be reached through any created medium, and therefore it consists in an immediate union of the glorified human spirit with the Divine Essence. This union is the only thing capable of finally satisfying man's desires for complete happiness and perfection.

Therefore (and this is the substance of the Second Question) Saint Thomas lists the satisfactions in which beatitude cannot possibly consist. His methodical elimination of all the perfections which fall short of the one supreme perfection of man in Divine Union makes us think at once of *The Ascent of Mount Carmel*. The well-known frontispiece of *The Ascent*, based on a design sketched out by Saint John himself, shows us the way of *nada*, emptiness, "naked faith" ascending straight to God by the rejection of all things that are less than God, whether they appeal to the body of man or to his spirit.

We are not surprised when Saint Thomas and Saint John of the Cross declare that man's happiness is not to be found in material possessions, honor, fame, power, pleasure, or even in the life and health of the body.[9] Much more subtle is the question in which Saint Thomas shows [10] that beatitude, objectively speaking, must necessarily be something more than the mere perfection of the soul, more even than the soul itself. We cannot achieve perfect happiness by entering into ourselves and shutting out everything else in order to relish the quiescent realization of our own spirituality. Our happiness must come, metaphysically speaking, from outside ourselves. That does not mean that perfect happiness consists in a psychological exteriorization of ourselves in created things. Far from it! But even when our happiness comes from a being other than our own spirit, beatitude cannot objectively be considered as the perfection which we receive from that Being, even though He be God. To be happy, we must be taken out of ourselves and raised above ourselves, not only to a higher level of creation but to the uncreated essence of God. God, and God alone, is our beatitude.

This statement has tremendous repercussions in Saint John of the Cross, who shows not only that our happiness is not to be sought in the enjoyment of our natural gifts and talents or in the fruition of moral goods (like virtues) for the sake of our own soul, but also that it is illusion to seek beatitude in any kind of supernatural grace or spiritual vision that falls short of the very essence of God.[11] Our happiness cannot consist in anything that happens to us, in any experience however sublime, if that experience be seen only in reference to our own perfection. God alone is our beatitude.

And now Saint Thomas brings out a second idea which echoes and reechoes on all sides from the cliffs of Mount Carmel. Union with God cannot be achieved by any operation of the senses, or even by any act of intellect that has its starting point in sense perception. This is the foundation stone of Saint John's mystical theology.[12] The reasons for this are discussed by both authors at some length. Saint Thomas devotes an article to the question whether man can arrive at perfect happiness by his own natural powers, and decides that he cannot. Only imperfect, or natural, beatitude is accessible to us without a free gift of God. Perfect beatitude, which is union with God in a clear vision of the Divine Essence, is something which exceeds the capacity of any created nature to achieve. It follows from this that God alone can give us perfect happiness by raising us to union with Himself. Our cooperation with His grace is demanded of us. There must be action on both sides. He will not give Himself to us unless we give ourselves to Him. Nevertheless, Saint Thomas can say, in a statement that must be understood in the light of the whole teaching of the Church on nature and grace, that "man becomes blessed by the action of God alone." [13] *Homo beatus fit solo Deo agente.*

Saint Thomas declares that beatitude, or union with God, is consummated in an operation of man's intelligence. In this spiritual act the mind and will of man are moved passively by God, and it is in that sense that "God alone acts." Saint John of the Cross not only follows Saint Thomas in this disputed question on the essence of beatitude but frequently uses the expression "God alone works in the soul" that is perfectly united to Him. [14]

However, although Saint Thomas considers that this act in which the soul is united to God is an operation of the speculative intellect, he is careful to point out that perfect beatitude is not found in the *speculative sciences.* [15] This important question throws light on the theme that has occupied us all through the present volume. We may be shocked by Saint John of the Cross when he says: "Any soul that makes account of all its knowledge and ability to come to union with the wisdom of God is supremely ignorant in the eyes of God, and will remain far removed from that wisdom." [16] And yet these words are only an echo of Saint Thomas, who is the supreme champion of intelligence.

The Angelic Doctor points out that the speculative sciences are all limited by sense knowledge, from which they draw their first principles. Beatitude consists in the union of man not only with what is above his own nature but with God, Who is above all created nature. Speculative sciences, on the contrary, only find God as He is reflected in visible creation, that is, in things which are below man.

These sciences can only intensify man's hunger for God and remind him of his need for the divine vision. They can never satisfy that need. It is therefore literally true to say that anyone who rests content with philosophical or theological speculation about God is "supremely ignorant in the eyes of God." [16]

There is one sentence of Saint Thomas which sums up both his own ideas and those of Saint John of the Cross on the insufficiency of any knowledge of God that reaches man on his own level through the medium of creatures: "Every knowledge which is according to the mode of a created substance falls far short of the vision of God's essence which infinitely surpasses every created substance." [17]

We read exactly the same thought in *The Ascent of Mount Carmel:* [18]

Among all creatures, the highest or the lowest, there is none that comes near to God or bears any [univocal] resemblance to His being. For although it is true that all creatures have, as theologians say, a divine impress . . . yet there is no essential resemblance or connection between them and God—on the contrary, the distance between their being and the Divine being is infinite. Wherefore it is impossible for the understanding to attain to God by means of the creatures, whether these be celestial or earthly; inasmuch as there is no proportion of resemblance between them.

*The Battle
over the Scriptures*

When Saint John of the Cross registered as a student in Gaspar Grajal's course on the Psalms, the study of Scripture was in the throes of revolution. After centuries of

peaceful allegorizing, Catholic exegetes had suddenly been
jarred by the Protestant reform and found themselves facing a battery of perilous questions. The innocent irrespon-
sibility of an earlier and perhaps more spiritual age had
led many of the saints to interpret the Scriptures with a
freedom that was consonant, no doubt, with piety, but
which often had taken them far away from the literal sense
of the revealed word of God.

The Protestant claim that each one of the faithful was
himself inspired by the same Holy Spirit Who had inspired the writers of Scripture produced a healthy reaction
in the Church, and Catholic scholars began to look back
over the Middle Ages and to wonder if perhaps the "freedom" of some of the saints had not opened the way to
pious anarchy. It was clear that if Scripture could mean
whatever any individual wanted it to mean it had millions
of different literal meanings. And that was as good as
saying it had no meaning at all. Of what use is a public
revelation made to the whole Church, if it has no one
meaning which the whole Church can agree in accepting?

The chief problems that faced Catholic Scripture scholars—and which were hotly debated at Salamanca—revolved around the interpretation of the Sacred text. The
question of a critical revaluation of the Vulgate and of the
advisability of translating the Bible into the vulgar tongue
were closely connected with this.

Saint John of the Cross relies above all on Scripture
as the source of his mystical doctrine. We cannot appreciate his theological viewpoint or correctly estimate his
attitude toward speculative thought unless we look at his
work against the contemporary intellectual background.
If the saint were a complete obscurantist, and if the de-

bates of theologians were, for him, essentially a waste of time, we might expect him to turn his back upon all these disputed questions and to treat the debaters with supreme contempt. Or at least we might suppose that he would build himself a secure nest in the forest of reaction and sing the same allegorical song as the birds that dwelt beneath its foliage, protected against the torrid rays of innovation or new doctrine.

The battle over the Scriptures had not yet reached its height at Salamanca when Saint John attended the lectures of Gaspar Grajal. But already the university was divided into two bitterly opposed factions. The "scholastic" party was conservative, the "scriptural" party was fighting for new ideas. The "scholastics" were still the more powerful group. They were the majority. They clung to the well-established method of procedure. They were suspicious of everything that savored of "criticism." They did not like investigations of the original text, still less translations into the vulgar tongue. And for them the most important task of the exegete was to discover an allegorical or "spiritual" meaning of Scripture according to the tradition of the Fathers.

The "scriptural" party believed that the whole method of scriptural interpretation should be revised. The first duty of the exegete was to discover the literal meaning of the Scriptures, and this could not be done without a scientific and critical study of ancient manuscripts in Greek and Hebrew leading to a reconstitution of the original text, which was to replace the Vulgate of Saint Jerome. These "scriptural" exegetes were in favor of translations of Scripture into the vulgar tongue. As for the spiritual sense of Scripture, they did not deny its existence or minimize its importance, but after all, the true spiritual meaning could not be reached through a faulty interpretation of the letter.

Gaspar Grajal was one of the leaders of the "scriptural" party. His appointment to the chair of Holy Scripture was a severe blow to the "scholastics" because it meant that the "scriptural" views, hitherto regarded as bold and exceedingly "modern," received a kind of official sanction. Meanwhile, another famous figure in Spanish humanism had appeared on the scene at Salamanca. This was Fray Luis de León, who was perhaps the most active and influential writer on the "scriptural" side. He had revised the text of *The Canticle of Canticles,* printed his new Latin version with a facing Spanish translation, and then added a commentary of his own which put forth some extremely radical ideas without, however, abandoning the traditional spiritual interpretation of this Song of Solomon.

Luis de León himself taught Scripture, but not when Saint John of the Cross was a student at Salamanca. In those years the friar held the chair of Nominalism and gave lectures which the young Carmelite most probably did not attend. Meanwhile, the storm was gathering. Luis de León was ready to publish a study on the authority of the Vulgate which would call for a new Latin edition of the Scriptures. In the following year, Luis de León, Grajal, and other "scripturals" were appointed as members of an inquisitorial commission for the revision of a popular commentary on the Bible by a certain Abbé Vatable.[19]

In the sessions of this commission, the "scripturals" were brought face to face with the most eminent and powerful members of the opposing party, men who believed that the authority of the Vulgate was absolutely sacred and that one could no more question its text than one could criticize the articles of the Nicene Creed. The discussions grew very heated and the whole university became inflamed. Finally, in March of 1571, Grajal, Luis de León and others were arrested and imprisoned to await trial on various charges. Luis de León was to answer for his attitude toward the Vulgate, for his Spanish translation and his "false" commentary on *The Canticle of Canticles*. On several other counts he was held as suspect of heresy. The investigations lasted four years, at the end of which Luis de León was acquitted, his ideas were pronounced to be tenable, and he returned in triumph to the faculty of Salamanca where he dominated the field of scriptural study until his death (in the same year as Saint John of the Cross) in 1591.

We can be sure that Saint John of the Cross took no part in the demonstrations that accompanied the development of the scriptural question at Salamanca. Even if his temperament and attraction to solitude had not prohibited him from doing so, the rule of his order would have made it impossible, without serious disciplinary consequences. Nevertheless, both his work and his life bear witness to the fact that he took an extremely intelligent interest in what was going on. Because he was a saint, he was able to accept the doctrine proposed by a party without at any time suffering himself to be confined by the narrowness of party spirit. His sympathies are sober and untechnical —and they all lie with the progressive, the "scriptural" side.

Later on, when Saint John of the Cross's commentary on his own *Spiritual Canticle* (which is also a commentary on *The Song of Songs*) came, in manuscript, under the eyes of Luis de León, it aroused the admiration of this

friar, who was a friend and supporter of Saint Teresa.
Both Saint John of the Cross and Saint Teresa prefer to
handle Scripture in the vulgar tongue—they generally
quote it in Spanish, although that was considered "bold."
On the other hand, Saint John of the Cross feels that he
can be quite content with the Vulgate. Why? Because
he is not a technical specialist and because he knows that
for his own purposes the Vulgate is sufficient. The Council
of Trent has declared that the text of Saint Jerome is always safe to follow and indeed that it should be followed
by preachers. We may suppose that Saint John of the
Cross felt the need for a new critical edition of the Scriptures. Nevertheless, since no such edition was produced
in his time or even for centuries after his time, he took
the only practical course that was open to him, in following the Vulgate. Only in the twentieth century has
serious progress been made in the edition of a new Latin
translation of the Bible for the use of Catholics. If he re-
lied on the Vulgate, Saint John of the Cross was not afraid
to make use of other versions of Scripture known in his
time, and it can be said of him, generally, that his work
is impregnated with the principles of scriptural interpretation that were taught by the progressive school of Luis
de León.

The most important effect of this was that Saint John
of the Cross took great pains to respect the literal meaning of Scripture. He was not a scientific student of ancient
texts, and his interpretations of the literal sense are sometimes incorrect. Nevertheless his arguments from Scripture are generally much more solid and more convincing
than those, say, of Saint Bernard of Clairvaux, precisely
because Saint John of the Cross was more cautious, more

objective in his use of Scripture and did not show the same outspoken disdain for "the letter" as did Bernard. It is true that Saint John of the Cross claims to be almost exclusively interested in the "spiritual" sense of Scripture. But this term "spiritual sense" is not used in a strictly technical way. Sometimes Saint John of the Cross follows an allegorical tradition sanctioned by the practice of the Fathers. Sometimes he interprets scriptural figures according to the more rigorous laws of typology admitted by the most scientific modern commentators. And sometimes his "spiritual" sense is simply the literal sense of a passage, seen in its implications for the interior life.

It would be useless to deny that Saint John of the Cross sometimes interprets Scripture incorrectly and that some of his arguments from Scripture collapse because they have been constructed on Vulgate texts which do not accurately convey the meaning of the original Hebrew. It is true that he sometimes makes use of the accommodated or applied sense of the Scriptures. But it is very significant that he never uses this sense in order to prove anything. He usually warns the reader that this "accommodated" sense is nothing but a manner of speaking and is not to be taken as the strict sense intended by the inspired author.

On the whole, however, the scriptural doctrine which forms the foundation of Saint John's theology of the mystical life rests on an objectively valid interpretation of the Bible. The mystical theology he claims to find in the Bible is really there.[20] And this is a great deal more than can be said for some of his predecessors.

# CHAPTER IX

# Faith and Reason

Saint John of the Cross did not sever his contact with the intellectual world of his time when he ended his course of theology at Salamanca. Soon after the beginning of the Carmelite reform, the Discalced Carmelites opened a college for their young clerics at the University of Alcalá.

It is very significant that the third monastery founded in an order dedicated to penance and contemplative prayer and to preaching the interior life should have been a college. Saint Teresa had suffered too much from half-educated directors. She wanted the priests of the reform to be well grounded in their theology; she even declared that, for her part, she would have been willing to soften some of the rigors of the Rule if this would help to bring learned men into the Order.[1]

Saint John of the Cross was sent as Rector to the new college. He had to supervise the clerics in their studies and preside over weekly disputations in theology and philosophy. He was in constant contact with the university faculty.

Under the masterly direction of this saint, the Carmelite students at Alcalá were living the lives of intellectuals and of mystics at the same time—and finding no contradiction between the two. It is said that in Saint John's time practically all the students at the college were "great contemplatives." Each could apply to himself the rhyme:

> *Religioso y estudiante,*
> *Religioso por delante.*[2]

A story told of Saint John at Alcalá throws another sidelight on his attitude toward the intellectual life. He had been asked by someone to write a book on the two patron saints of the town. He refused, on the grounds that he was only capable of producing a biography that would be a "work of piety" rather than of objective history. It is a great pity that more biographers of saints have not had as good sense as Saint John of the Cross.

Later on, in 1579, Saint John was chosen as Rector of another house of studies, this time in the small university town of Baeza, in Andalusia. He organized the program of studies and presided over the disputations, in which he took part, arguing, distinguishing, and resolving problems with all the finesse of a true scholastic theologian.[3]

It is clear, then, that if Saint John of the Cross was severe in criticizing incompetent teachers and directors it was precisely because he realized the importance of sound teaching and spiritual direction. It is true that God Himself, and God alone, forms contemplatives and makes men saints. It is true that the mystic is guided in a sacred, personal, and intimate way by the inspirations of the Holy Ghost. Nevertheless, God does not normally teach us the ways of interior prayer without making use of other men.

No matter how solitary a man may be, if he is a contemplative his contemplation has something of a social character. He receives it through the Church. All true and supernatural contemplation is a share in God's revelation of Himself to the world in Christ. The Church is the Mystical Body of Christ, prolonging His Incarnation, manifesting Him still in the world. She is in full possession of His revelation. She alone dispenses the treasures of His grace. It is possible that there are saints and contemplatives who have never made any confession of Catholic faith and have never formally associated themselves with the visible Church. Nevertheless they cannot be saints unless they belong, at least invisibly, to the Church. They cannot belong even invisibly to the Church unless they accept in some rudimentary form the fundamental truths of revelation which she propounds to men.

The teaching of the Church is therefore not an evil which the contemplative must bear patiently, as a test of his humility. It is the solid nourishment of his whole interior life. Even though contemplation grows best in silence and solitude, nevertheless the contemplative loses nothing by human contact with a spiritual director or a teacher of theology. The silence that favors contemplation is not something absolute, excluding all recourse to speech. On the contrary, spiritual conferences, conversations, study, and direction are occasions of light and grace for the soul that has dedicated itself to a life of solitude and prayer. The contemplative life is a life of charity. And charity is always twofold. It has one object: God. But it reaches Him both directly, in Himself, and through other men. Our interior life dies out unless there be a constant vital contact with God through both these avenues. If we do not let ourselves be directed by other men, who speak in His name, we cannot pretend that we are directed by Him. For Christ said to His Apostles: "He that heareth you heareth me, and he that despiseth you de-

spiseth me. And he that despiseth me despiseth Him
that sent me." [4]

Saint John of the Cross remarks, in one of his maxims:
"The soul that is alone and without a master and has
virtue is like the burning coal that is alone. It will grow
colder rather than hotter." [5]

Some people believe that the Catholic Church is the
only one that exacts submission to teaching authority and
that outside the sphere of her influence all spiritual men
are free as the wind—they can believe anything they like
and practice any form of asceticism they please and never
have to render an account of themselves to anybody.
Actually, wherever the contemplative life is taken seriously, the first thing required of the novice is the willingness to submit to a master, to obey, to renounce his own
judgment, to practice humility and to learn a doctrine of
the interior life from a spiritual master. Let us consider
a few statements on the relation of the *sadhak* (Hindu
aspirant to the contemplative life) to his spiritual director,
the *Guru*. Ramakrishna, who exercised a tremendous religious influence in nineteenth-century India, once said:
"He who thinks his *Guru* is a mere man will never progress in the spiritual life."

A novice in a Cistercian monastery is taught to listen
to the instructions of his abbot and of his novice master
with the same reverence he would pay to the voice of
Christ, because faith shows him that these men speak to
him in the name of Christ. But the Hindu *sadhak* is asked
to believe far more than this. He must not only consider
his *Guru* to be a representative of God, he must see the
Divinity itself living and acting in him. To pursue the
thought of Ramakrishna: "Before the disciple attains to a

realization of the Divinity, he must first see the *Guru* invested with the light of the Divinity. It is the *Guru*, whose form has mysteriously been assumed by God, who will later show him God. And then the disciple will realize that the Guru and God are one and the same." [6.]

Saint John of the Cross makes a much more moderate statement: "Never consider thy superior to be less than God, be the superior who he may, for he stands to thee in the place of God." [7] Saint John explains how the humility and prudence of the saints will not permit them to base their lives on subjective inspirations and feelings of grace, or even on manifest visions and revelations, without recourse to authority and to the teaching of faith. What is more, he even adds that it must first of all be judged at the bar of reason!

### 2

The ascetic doctrine of Saint John of the Cross would have been much better understood in the past if all his readers had taken the trouble to observe that the saint has much less respect for visions than he has for common sense. He is quite definite in teaching that you can make much more progress to sanctity by following the light of reason than by indulging in an unregulated taste for extraordinary penances and for suspicious spiritual "experiences."

Before we examine some of these passages, let us consider one that has reference to the relations of the contemplative with his director or his teacher of theology. These statements are taken from one of the most important chapters in *The Ascent of Mount Carmel.*[8] We shall be returning to it again. It is the chapter in which Saint

John explains why it is no longer fitting for Christians to ask God for supernatural signs and private revelations, although this was often done by the saints of the Old Testament. Saint John tells us that even Moses and Gedeon sought human confirmation of the supernatural signs that had been given them. He is discussing the passage of Exodus (4:4-15) in which God tells Moses after various miraculous signs to seek the advice of his brother Aaron. "Speak thou with him," says the Lord to Moses, "and tell him all my words and I will be in thy mouth and in his mouth so that each of you shall believe that which is in the mouth of the other." Here is the commentary of the Spanish Carmelite:

Having heard these words, Moses at once took courage . . . for this is a characteristic of a humble soul which dares not to treat with God alone, neither can be completely satisfied without human counsel and guidance. And this is the will of God, for *He draws near to those who come together to treat concerning truth in order to expound and confirm it in them upon a foundation of natural reason.*[9]

Words like these show us something of the true character of Saint John of the Cross. His teaching is deep, but it is also simple. Above all, it is sane. It displays a wisdom born of natural equilibrium and of supernatural experience. The last thing many men would look for in a mystic would be a positive need for the advice and guidance of other men. Yet this is precisely one of the characteristics of a truly interior soul. The mystic is led by a sure spiritual instinct to seek God wherever He may be found. And the Spirit of God, Whose function it is to unite men with God by love, also unites them to one another in Him. Humble and limited as our poor speech may be, the Spirit of God uses it as an instrument for His action upon our souls. Anyone who has seriously devoted himself to the interior life will recognize that there is almost as much peace and spiritual profit to be derived from conversation with an enlightened director as from an hour of contemplative prayer.

This is the doctrine of Jesus Himself. Saint John of the Cross remembers the words of Christ: "Where two or three are gathered together in my Name, there am I in the midst of them," and he paraphrases them. He says:

Where two or three are met together in order to consider that which is for the greater honor and glory of my Name, there will I be in the midst of them. That is to say, *I will make clear and confirm in their hearts the truths of God*. And it is to be observed that He said not where there is one alone there will I be; but, where there are at least two. In this way He showed that God desires not that any man by himself alone should believe his experiences to be of God, or should act in conformity with them or trust them, but rather should believe the Church and her ministers for God will not make clear and confirm the truth in the heart of one alone, and thus such a one will be weak and cold.[10]

Let us resume what has so far been proved by these quotations. They have shown us first of all that mystical contemplation rests on a doctrinal basis. They have demonstrated that even for a Saint John of the Cross, who has sometimes been considered the enemy of scholastic thought, the study of scholastic theology not only is no obstacle to the contemplative life, but is its necessary foundation. More than that, where spiritual doctrine is shared by master and disciple, there are more than human powers at work. The Holy Ghost is acting in them. Christ is "in the midst of them." Above all, it is *preferable* for the contemplative to be guided by the Holy Ghost through the Church and her ministers than for him to follow the light of extraordinary and completely private experiences. To be more exact: his willingness to submit to the guidance of a qualified spiritual master will give evidence that his personal and interior inspirations (without which, of course, there is no mystical life) really come from God.

One more point: Saint John of the Cross has just told us that when spiritual men converse together on interior doctrine, God works in them in order to "expound and confirm" the truth in them *upon a foundation of natural reason*. It is time to speak at some length of the place of reason in the teaching of Saint John of the Cross.

# CHAPTER X

# Reason in the Life of Contemplation

It is true that Saint John of the Cross begins *The Ascent of Mount Carmel* with the statement that the soul cannot arrive at union with God unless it enters into "darkness" with respect to everything that can be known and desired not only by its sense faculties but also by the will and the intelligence. In other words, there is a certain sense in which faith and contemplation "darken" and "blind" man's reason. I think we have said enough of the limitations of man's conceptual knowledge of God for this statement to be properly understood. It merely means that we cannot rely on any clear and intelligible concept of God to delimit and to circumscribe His being as He really is in Himself. Faith takes man beyond the limits of his own finite intelligence. It is therefore "dark" to him, because he has no longer any faculty with which to see the infinite Truth of God, which is nevertheless intimately present to his spirit in the obscurity of theological belief. Saint John of the Cross admits, of course, that faith is never contrary to reason.[1]

Unfortunately, many readers of the great mystics—of whose teaching Saint John of the Cross is an outstanding and characteristic example—proceed from this statement to the false conclusion that reason has no place in the mystical life. But, as a matter of fact, it is spiritual suicide to base your life on an ascetic doctrine that is essentially antirational. It is true that reason alone cannot make us saints, and that Christian virtue must necessarily function on a higher level than the naturally acquired virtues of a pagan philosopher. Otherwise we will never arrive at the perfection that is demanded of us by our vocation to the perfect sonship of God in Christ. The saint is one who is born not of blood, not of the will of the flesh, not of the will of man, but of God. (John 1:13.) Nevertheless Christ, the Light of the World, Who enlightens every man coming into the world, gives us a natural participation in the Divine Light of God; and this is our human reason. He has not given us our reason for nothing. Consequently, not only has reason something to do in the supernatural life, but God has ordained that we cannot normally arrive at sanctity without making use of reason. And this is the teaching of Saint John of the Cross.

The Spanish Carmelite lays down as a fundamental law of the spiritual life that God wishes us to sanctify ourselves, with the help of His grace, by the use of our natural faculties in His service. In other words, grace does not destroy nature, but elevates it and consecrates it to God. Men do not become saints by ceasing to be men. We do not reach mystical union by separating the soul from the body and trying to live like angels. However, Saint John of the Cross certainly never misused the theological axiom "grace builds on nature" in order to defend an easy-going and materialistic spirituality. Reason must serve us in our struggle for perfection. But it does not fight under its own standard. Reason alone is not our captain. It is enlisted in the service of faith. We must think out the moral implications of our supernatural faith. We must use our minds in order to know and keep the commandments and counsels of God.

Saint John of the Cross emphasizes the importance of reason in the mystical life in those chapters of *The Ascent of Mount Carmel* [2] where he contrasts two kinds of mysticism. On one hand there is the straight way to Transforming Union, the way of "Night," *nada,* pure faith. This is true Christian mysticism, a direct development of the life of sanctifying grace, the theological virtues, and the gifts of the Holy Ghost.[3] On the other hand there is a mysticism which is not exactly false—since it abounds in experiences which may be genuinely supernatural—but which is a deviation from the direct path to sanctity and divine union. This kind of mysticism thrives on visions, revelations, extraordinary manifestations and signs. Saint John of the Cross does not deny that God often communicates in this way with some of His saints. But he insists that these unusual experiences are not to be sought after or desired, because they have no essential connection with sanctity and are not capable of manifesting God to us as He really is. On the contrary, there is always great danger that the appetite for visions may turn us aside from the only true road to God which is the way of perfect faith.

It is here that reason comes in. Its most important function in the mystical life, according to Saint John of the Cross, is to keep the contemplative from getting off the straight road to divine union, which is the way of faith. One of the chief characteristics of Sanjuanist asceticism is that it demands constant critical sifting of spiritual experiences and the rejection of spiritual inspirations which fall outside the realm of pure faith. The instrument of this interior asceticism is nothing else but our inborn light of reason. Reason, acting in the service of faith, must question and evaluate and pass judgment on all our most intimate and spiritual aspirations. It must examine, with merciless objectivity, everything that presents itself to us as a supernatural impulse. It must question every interior voice. It must plunge our purest "lights" into the dark sea of faith. The great paradox of Saint John of the Cross is that his asceticism of "night" cannot possibly be practiced without the *light of reason*. It is by the light of reason that we keep on traveling through the night of faith.

One might compare the journey of the soul to mystical union, by the way of pure faith, to the journey of a car on a dark highway. The only way the driver can keep to the road is by using his headlights. So in the mystical life, reason has its function. The way of faith is necessarily obscure. We drive by night. Nevertheless our reason penetrates the darkness enough to show us a little of the road ahead. It is by the light of reason that we interpret the signposts and make out the landmarks along our way.

Those who misunderstand Saint John of the Cross imagine that the way of *nada* is like driving by night without any headlights whatever. That is a dangerous misunderstanding of the saint's doctrine.

Saint John of the Cross severely criticizes those who keep asking God for signs, visions, and extraordinary experiences. And he explains why:

Although God may answer them, this method is not good, neither is it pleasing to God, but rather it is displeasing to Him.

. . . The reason for this is that *it is lawful for no creature to pass beyond the limits which God has ordained for his governance in the order of nature. In His governance of man He has laid down rational and natural limits* wherefore the desire to pass beyond them is not lawful.[4]

Again he says the same thing more clearly:

With respect to divine visions and revelations and locutions God is not wont to reveal them, for *He is ever desirous that men should make such use of their own reason as is possible.*[5]

In other words, the obstacles we meet on the way to contemplation and sanctity must be removed not by miracles but by common sense guided by the light of faith and animated by the power of divine grace.

### 2

Saint John of the Cross aims at nothing more or less, in his asceticism, than the right ordering of man's whole being, in which man's senses become subject to his reason and his reason in turn consecrates itself, and all else that is man's, to God by supernatural faith. The perfection of this order is achieved when man is able to love God "with his whole heart, his whole mind, and all his strength." This is the fulfillment of the first Commandment. It also corresponds to a description of sanctity which we find in Saint Thomas, who says that man reaches relative perfection on this earth when there remain no obstacles to prevent him from loving God with all his being: *ut ab affectu hominis excludatur omne illud quod impedit ne affectus mentis totaliter in Deum dirigatur.*[6] According to the Angelic Doctor, man must seek above all else to love God with all his power (*ex toto posse suo*) to arrive at a state in which everything in him is ordered to the love of God. Saint John of the Cross says the same thing: "The soul that is perfect is wholly love . . . all its actions are love, and it employs all its faculties and possessions in loving." [7]

The Carmelite mystic declares that this is the summary of all he has to teach: "Herein is contained all that the spiritual man ought to do and all that I have to teach him, so that he may attain to God through union of the will. (He is speaking of the first Commandment, to love God with our whole heart.) Herein man is commanded to employ all the faculties and desires and affections of his soul in God." [8] It is quite clear that Saint John of the Cross conceives that this perfection is only attained in mystical union, for which the soul is prepared by the "dark night" of passive purification.

No mere ascetic training can give the soul such complete control over all its faculties as to be able to recollect them at will and consecrate them entirely to the love of God, so that there remain no instinctive first movements of love for anything else but Him. God Himself must take the soul to Himself in a state of "passive recollection" before it is able to "love with great strength and with all its desires and powers of spirit and of sense which could not be if they were dispersed in the enjoyment of aught else. . . . [Therefore] God keeps in recollection all the energies, faculties and desires of the soul both of spirit and of sense, so that all this harmony may employ its energies and virtues in this love and may thus attain to a true fulfillment of the first Commandment." [9]

However, a word of warning is necessary here.

To isolate this statement from the rest of Saint John's teaching would lead us into serious errors. It is true that the final perfection of the soul, the complete union of love with God, is produced passively in the soul of God. This work is accomplished by the mystical "dark night" of the spirit, not by the active night of asceticism. Nevertheless, asceticism is the ordinary and normal preparation for the graces of mystical prayer and for passive purifications.

Let me clarify all this. First of all, what do I mean by asceticism? I mean the active self-purification by which the soul, inspired and fortified by grace, takes itself in hand and makes itself undergo a rigorous spiritual training in self-denial and in the practice of virtue. My stress is on the word active. The initiative is left to us. God merely suggests and inspires the things that are to be done. We either accept or refuse His suggestions.

"Mystical" or passive purification takes place without our initiative. Our consent has nothing essential to do with it. However, trials imposed on us by exterior agents do not come under this heading. Sickness, for instance, is not a mystical purification! It may well accompany such purification, however. Passive purification is a work done on the soul by God, from within the soul itself, just as the graces of passive prayer are infused into the soul from its own depths.

Our definitions are now established. Sometimes writers describe the interior life as if it were made up of two successive, clearly distinct stages. The first is "ascetical," in which we are active; the second "mystical," in which we are passive. They leave one with the impression that the man who leads an interior life first exercises himself for years in many busy practices of virtue. Then suddenly one day he goes limp. For the rest of his life he just floats, and receives mysterious illuminations. There are other authors who maintain that there are two distinct ways to perfection, one purely ascetical, the other mystical. But I am not talking about this opinion here, except to say that I do not hold it.

In practice, the interior life never enters a stage in which man is continually passive in everything. Nor is there any stage in the real interior life in which there is not already some degree of passivity. The borderline of the mystical life is crossed, however, when the soul is habitually guided in a passive manner by God both in prayer and in the practice of virtue. This passivity may not always be clearly marked. Generally speaking, there remains a constant need for active cooperation with grace. Hence the imperative need for asceticism. Without asceticism, the mystical life is practically out of the question. But asceticism does not need to find expression in strenuous exercises of mortification, still less in spectacular and extraordinary macerations. On the contrary, the true path of asceticism is a path of simplicity and obscurity, and there is no true Christian self-denial that does not begin first of all with a whole-hearted acceptance and fulfillment of the ordinary duties of one's state in life. Everyone guided by grace will spontaneously desire to add something on his own account to the sacrifices demanded by Providence and by his state of life. But the best of these mortifications will always be the ones that are seen by God alone and do not attract the attention of other men or flatter our own self-complacency. It is very bad in practice to allow ascetics to indulge in penitential rivalries with one another, for this generally fixes their attention upon themselves and gives them a narrow outlook, depriving them of the interior liberty which is absolutely necessary for progress in the ways of prayer.

One conclusion necessarily flows from all this. Asceticism, properly understood and practiced, is absolutely necessary for Christian perfection and for the contemplative life. In fact, it can be said that the mystical life, although essentially independent of our efforts, is made by God to depend on our generosity in accepting sacrifice.[10]

There are two cogent reasons for this. First of all, God will not grant the soul the special inspirations of passive prayer and purification unless it has first proved itself faithful in cooperating with the ordinary inspirations of grace. Secondly—this is very important—when passive purifications begin they demand even greater courage and self-denial on the part of the soul than were exacted from it by active mortification. At the beginning of passive purification the soul is still largely active. God does not submerge it all at once in His divine action. Much active virtue is required to bear the suffering which is produced passively by God in the depths of the soul. But He aids us in this trial by special grace.

# 3

The whole work of asceticism is summed up by Saint John of the Cross in the formula "directing all the strength of the soul to God."

What is the strength of the soul? Its faculties, passions, and desires. When these are all directed by the will to God, we have reached that relative and limited perfection which can be attained by ascetic effort and which disposes us for mystical prayer. But the will itself is blind. By itself alone it cannot direct the strength of the soul to God. The will itself must be brought into line with *reason* in all its movements of desire. Hence, as Saint John of the Cross declares: "When these passions are controlled by *reason* with respect to God, so that the soul rejoices only in that which is purely for the honor and glory of God . . . it is clear that the strength and ability of the soul are directed to God and are being kept for Him." [11]

Speaking of the passions, he says again: "From these affections, when they are unbridled, arise in the soul all the vices and imperfections which it possesses, and likewise, when they are ordered and composed, all its virtues. And it must be known that if one of [these passions] *should become ordered and controlled by reason,* the rest will be so likewise. . . ." "Wheresoever one of these passions is, *thither will go likewise the whole soul and the will and all the other faculties.* . . ." [12] If reason, by the perfect control of one passion, can direct all the other passions and the will and all the faculties of the soul toward man's proper end, the soul will be at peace. And Saint John makes it quite clear that this peace and interior silence, the result of ascetic self-control, create the only atmosphere in which graces of mystical prayer can flourish. "Tranquillity and peace (in which the passions do not reign) *are necessary for the wisdom which by natural or supernatural means the soul is capable of receiving.*" [13]

The conclusion is inescapable. Mystical prayer is a gift of God to a soul purified by ascetic discipline. This is only achieved when all the passions and faculties are controlled by reason. Mystical prayer depends, *per accidens,* on the right ordering of the soul by reason. In this sense, therefore, *reason is the key to the mystical life!* The psycho-

logical explanation for this is found in the words of Christ
which the Church has appointed to be read as the Gospel of
the proper Mass of Saint John of the Cross in the Carmelite Missal: "The light of thy body is thine eye. If thine
eye be single [that is to say, if it sees clearly, without
blurring or double vision] thy whole body will be full
of light; but if it be evil thy whole body will be full of
darkness. *Take heed therefore that the light which is in
thee be not darkness.*" [14]

The light which is in us is reason, or intelligence. This
not only is the eye which helps us to see and understand
created things as they really are; but above all it is the
"eye" which receives the infused light of faith and of
contemplation. True contemplation is a "loving knowledge of God" which actually requires the coordinated
action of supernatural knowledge and love. Nevertheless
it is formally situated in the intelligence, as Saint John of
the Cross and Saint Thomas would agree. We have seen
what it means to keep the "eye" of the intelligence clear.
Our spirit is darkened by its attachments. Spiritual blindness is the fruit of emotion, passion, inordinate desire.
One more quotation from Saint John of the Cross will
remind us of the fact:

However little a man may drink of this wine [of rejoicing in
created things for their own sakes] it at once takes hold upon
his heart and stupefies it and works the evil of darkening the
reason . . . so that if some antidote be not at once taken against
this poison whereby it may be quickly expelled, the life of the
soul is endangered.[15]

The antidote which Saint John prescribes is the "crisis,"
the discriminative separation of true and false values which

we discussed at the beginning of this book. This discrimination is of course arrived at precisely by the work of reason.

4

It would, however, be a fatal error to suppose that because Saint John of the Cross assigns so important a part to reason in the ascetic purification of the soul, that this purification is operated entirely on the level of natural virtue. When he says that all the powers of the soul must be set in order by reason, Saint John of the Cross definitely does not mean that they are *merely to conform to a rational and natural ideal*. The good order of the soul with which we are concerned here is not simply an ethical or moral perfection. Saint John of the Cross is not considering merely the level of perfection on which men refrain from cheating each other in business, go to Mass on Sundays, give alms now and then to the poor, and lend their lawn-mower to the people next door without even cursing under their breath.

When he says the "powers of the soul must be ordered and controlled by reason," Saint John of the Cross is speaking of a supernatural perfection, achieved under the guidance of grace according to principles revealed by faith. A natural, or ethical, perfection is one in which reason directs all the powers of the soul to God considered as the Author of nature and as the last end of man's natural aspirations. But every Catholic theologian knows that all men are living under a supernatural order in which they are directed by God to a supernatural end—and if they fail to reach that end, they cannot make up for it by a substitute on the natural level. There is, in fact, no natural beatitude. A life of virtue must somehow, at least implicitly, be directed to a supernatural end and controlled by grace, or it will end in loss.

Reason must direct the soul of man to God according to the supernatural plan He has revealed to us, and which we can only know by faith. But is this enough? Saint John of the Cross is much more precise. I will let him display his precision in a concrete case. Remember the end he has in view: all the strength of the soul must be entirely consecrated to the love of God. A situation arises in which the soul finds itself taking sensible pleasure in created things, and this pleasure is connected with the love of God through these things. Is this pleasure profitable to the soul? Does it help us to love God or not? How can we know? We must ascertain what it is we love: God, or the pleasure. The end, or the means. The answer is to be found in the intention of our will. In what does the will actually rest? In what does it seek its ultimate satisfaction? If in God, then the pleasure it finds in created things is only a means. That pleasure is well ordered. It helps us to praise God. It sanctifies the soul. Here are the words of Saint John of the Cross:

When as soon as the will finds pleasure in that which it hears, sees and does, it soars upward to rejoice in God—to which end its pleasure furnishes a motive and provides strength—this is very good. In such a case not only need the said motions [of pleasure] not be shunned when they cause devotion and prayer, but the soul may profit by them and indeed should so profit. . . . For there are souls who are greatly moved by objects of sense to seek God.[16]

However, it is easy for us to deceive ourselves in judging the purity of our intentions when we taste great pleasure in created things. A devout man can form a habit of attachment to some created pleasure by frequently using it, in good faith, as a motive of prayer. In actual fact, his desire for the pleasure soon becomes greater than his desire to pray. Without his realizing it, he has made prayer the motive for indulging in his pet pleasure. This can very easily happen, for example, in the case of a sentimental friendship.

In determining whether or not the intention of the will is directed to God through the use of some created pleasure, many theologians are content to prescribe an "act of purity of intention." To make such an "act" means to express a desire that the pleasure may give honor and glory to God. Indeed, this act need not even be formal and explicit. It may be virtual. Saint John of the Cross, in common with all Catholic theologians, recognizes the supernatural value of a pure intention. However, he also warns us that because of the blindness of our soul it is quite possible for us to be at the same time sincere and deluded in our good intentions. Our sincerity will ensure that our will is indeed directed to God in the order of intention, but because we have deceived ourselves, our will actually takes its rest not in God but in a creature. We *say* that we want to please God, and perhaps we mean it; but because we have allowed ourselves to be beguiled by the love of pleasure for its own sake, we are unconsciously seeking to please ourselves. Our formal dedication of the act to God may not strictly speaking be hypocritical, but it is nevertheless a cloak in which our unrecognized self-love comes forth disguised. Such an act can never be formally sinful, since it proceeds from a good intention. But the absence of any theological fault does not mean that the act cannot produce harmful spiritual effects. Saint John of the Cross asserts that psychologically such acts weaken the soul and confirm it in a bad habit. This should be plainly evident to all who are willing to consider that the laws of human psychology are not suspended by formalistic acts of pure intention. The saint says:

Great caution must be observed herein [in the pleasure we take in created things, under the pretext of glorifying God by them] and the resulting effects must be considered; for oftentimes many spiritual persons indulge in recreations of sense under the pretext of offering prayer and devotion to God; and they do this in a way which must be called recreation rather than prayer, and which gives more pleasure to themselves than to God. And although the intention that they have is toward God, the effect which they produce is that of recreation of sense, wherein they find weakness and imperfection rather than revival of the will and surrender of themselves to God.[17]

Saint John of the Cross asserts that a spiritual person can tell, by experience, when he is using created pleasures with a pure intention and when not. The sure sign is a certain inward liberty of spirit, in which one is aware that he is not held captive by pleasure. The pleasure itself remains indifferent, neutral. One loses sight of it in God. God alone matters. He alone is in the soul's focus. Everything else is blurred out of vision.[18]

When we experience this interior liberty, we can fully trust our pure intentions in the use of created pleasures. But the Carmelite mystic declares—and this is the most important point of all—that when this liberty is not experienced *we cannot trust reason alone to guide us* in our selection of means. And now we see that reason has its limitations, even when it is directed by principles of faith. Saint John says about this:

One who feels not this liberty of spirit in things and pleasures of sense, but whose will rests in these pleasures and feeds on them is greatly harmed by them and should withdraw his will from the use of them. For although his reason may desire to employ them on the journey toward God, yet inasmuch as his desire finds pleasure in them which is according to sense [i.e., according to the context, *inordinate*] . . . he is certain to find hindrance rather than help in them, and harm rather than profit.[19]

And yet, not one word of this changes the essence of the problem. Reason remains the key to the ascesis of Saint John of the Cross, in the sense that reason is the one all-important instrument by which we cooperate with divine grace and put into practice the teachings of our faith. We are sanctified by self-denial, by the Cross of Christ, by loving God with all our strength. This is the teaching of our faith. How do we carry it out? I return to the beginning of Saint John's *The Ascent of Mount Carmel*. We must have a "habitual desire to imitate Christ" in all that we do. In order to conform our lives to the life of Christ, we must meditate upon His life "so that we may know how to imitate it." And in order to do this well, we must renounce "every pleasure that is not for the honor and glory of God." Our motive in all this is the "love of Jesus Christ." [20]

Faith gives us our principles. It shows us our supernatural end and the means to achieve it. It gives us a supernatural motive. But the success or failure of our practical application of these principles *depends on our ability to decide which of our acts are really for the honor and glory of God and which are not*. God is always at

liberty to enlighten us by an infused light which will
help us to make this decision in a manner that transcends
our ordinary human mode of practical judgment. Such a
light is a gift we cannot strictly merit. Therefore, as far
as our own active cooperation with God is concerned, our
practical decisions *depend on the clarity and efficiency of
our reason and will, guided by ordinary grace and illumined by the infused theological virtues.* However, this
clarity and efficiency, in their turn, depend on our generosity in self-denial, and this generosity is proportionate to
our love. Faith tells us that we must seek God before all
created pleasure. But in the way of active asceticism it is
our reason that should pass judgment on the purity of our
intentions and tell us what our will is really doing—
whether it is really tending to God or resting in created
things.

The simplest and most uncompromising solution to the
problem is found in the severe counsels which the saint
put down at the beginning of the *Ascent.*

If there present itself to a man the pleasure of listening to things
that tend not to the service and honor of God, let him not desire
that pleasure, neither let him desire to hear them.

In other words, the reason must subject all our movements
of desire to a keen supernatural scrutiny and refuse the
will all liberty to love what is not for the glory of God.
All that is required of the will is to obey the dictates of
reason guided by faith and grace. However, we must preserve our sense of proportion. We are still human beings!
Our passions may still be strongly attracted to the pleasure they naturally desire. They may even taste something
of that pleasure, in spite of the resistance of the will. In
that case, says the saint:

*It suffices that although these things may be present to his senses, he desire not to have this pleasure.* And in this wise he will be able to mortify and void his senses of this pleasure and leave them, as it were, in darkness.[21]

Note carefully the difference between the two instances cited by Saint John: one in which *the will* rests in sensible pleasure, the other in which *the senses* rest in this pleasure but against the dictates of the will. In the first case, reason becomes helpless. It is blinded by the attachment of the will to an inordinate pleasure. Its most specious decisions are consequently apt to lead the whole soul into extreme peril.

In the other case, pleasure is *felt* but not *desired*. The will is free. Consequently the reason remains clear. Its decisions are reliable and true. We can advance with confidence, albeit with extreme care. Our intentions are perhaps as pure as we think they are. Thanks to the loyalty with which reason is serving God's grace, our acts are supernatural in their object, their end, and their circumstances.

The practical conclusion of all this is important. Saint John of the Cross holds that, in the practice of that active asceticism upon which, *de facto,* our spiritual progress normally depends, we must never formally allow our *will* to seek any created pleasure for pleasure's sake. It is not enough that this pleasure be moderate and licit according to the standards of natural reason. If the pleasure be formally sought for its own sake alone, and if the will does not pass beyond that pleasure to rest in God rather than in the pleasure itself, then according to Saint John of the Cross, the act, while not necessarily being formally sinful, will have harmful consequences for the soul because it will cause it to rest in created pleasure and will thus blind it to the supernatural light that should lead us, by the way of the Cross, to union with God.

However, if the will does not rest in created pleasure but goes beyond it to God by a truly pure supernatural intention—even though that intention may be only virtual —then the pleasure not only does no harm to the soul but may even make a considerable accidental contribution to its spiritual good. These are abstract principles which must be applied with good sense and moderation in actual practice. Many souls would be greatly harmed by a false understanding of these principles. Narrow-minded scrupulosity would have exactly the opposite effect to that desired by Saint John of the Cross: it would rob the soul of true spiritual liberty and make it unable to devote itself entirely to the love of God.

# CHAPTER XI

# "Your Reasonable Service"

Saint Paul wrote to the Christians of Rome beseeching them, as he besought all the churches, to practice asceticism. It was necessary that they do so if they were to fulfill their vocation as Christians. Self-denial is the characteristic of those who follow Christ, because the sign of the Christian is the sign of the Cross. We are incorporated by Baptism into the Mystical Body of Christ, but we must grow in Him, proving ourselves by good works to be the Sons of God. The principle of this growth and of these works is the Spirit of God, the Spirit of our adoption as sons of God. "Whosoever are led by the Spirit of God," says Saint Paul, "they are the sons of God. If you live according to the flesh, you shall die. But if by the Spirit you mortify the deeds of the flesh, you shall live." [1] And so, the Apostle adds: [2] "I beseech you, therefore, brethren, that you present your bodies a living sacrifice, holy, pleasing to God: your reasonable service."

What does it mean for us to sacrifice our bodies to God? Christians do not throw themselves into volcanoes, like Aztecs. What is this sacrifice? Saint Thomas Aquinas makes clear the theology of Saint Paul. We can sacrifice our bodies to God by accepting martyrdom—that is to say, by suffering a violent death that is inflicted on us for our faith or for any of the other Christian virtues. We can also sacrifice our bodies to God by fasting and abstinence and other works of asceticism. But we are not permitted, for the sake of self-denial, wantonly to destroy the health of the body. This would incapacitate us for the third way in which we must sacrifice our bodies to God: that is, in good works and worship. Saint Thomas briefly discusses the qualities of this self-sacrifice. He emphasizes the fact that it must be guided by faith and by a pure intention and above all that it must be a "reasonable service."

Reason brings with it decency and order. Saint Thomas quotes another principle of Saint Paul's: "Let all things be done among you with decency and in order." [3] Our asceticism is reasonable, orderly, and decent when our exterior actions are ordered to interior virtues and when, among these virtues, all are directed to the growth of the supernatural life of faith, hope, and charity in our souls. Our exterior acts of mortification or prayer are means to a spiritual end, not ends in themselves. Now, the rational use of means to an end demands that the means be proportioned to their end. As Saint Thomas observes, with Aristotelian balance and good sense: "A doctor tries to give his patient as much health as he can, but not as much medicine as he can: for he only prescribes as much medicine as the patient seems to need for his health." [4] A man who takes medicine not because he is ill but because he has a sort of compulsion complex about medicine is a hypochondriac. There are also spiritual hypochondriacs who take many medicines they do not need while at the same time avoiding the penances that would really do them good—the ones that exact discipline from their will and their reason. The true measure of asceticism, says Saint Thomas, is charity. Self-denial is the mark of the Christian only because it is the negative predisposition for that charity by which alone it can truly be known whether or not we belong to Christ. We have to deny ourselves because, in practice, love that is centered in ourselves is stolen from God and from other men. Love can only live by giving. When it steals and is stolen, it dies, because it is no longer free.

Saint John of the Cross repeats the teaching of Saint Thomas and Saint Paul in a passage that will surprise many of those who have never given the Carmelite the benefit of a careful reading. This is another illuminating chapter of *The Dark Night of the Soul*—one in which Saint John describes a certain self-willed gluttony for exterior penance which he calls an imperfection of "beginners." He goes on to say that this kind of asceticism is "no better than the penance of beasts." [5]

This seemingly contemptuous term has a precise meaning for Saint John of the Cross. He would not have used it otherwise. Why beasts? Remember Saint Paul's distinction between the "animal man" (*animalis homo*) who does not understand the things of God and the "spiritual man who judgeth all things." [6] Here is Saint John's exegesis of the text: "By the animal man is here meant one that uses sense alone; by the spiritual man, one that is not bound or guided by sense." [7] It is the traditional interpretation of these expressions. In fact, the Douay version of the Bible translates *animalis homo* as "the sensual man."

Avidity for exterior mortifications is a kind of sensuality in reverse. It drives the penitent to punish his flesh because of the pleasure he takes in these exercises. However, it would betray ignorance of religious psychology to label all such manifestations of religious enthusiasm as "masochism." A careful distinction must be made between the excesses of a psychologically healthy soul and the aberrations of a neurotic. Saint John of the Cross is not here talking about a sick mind but about spiritual imperfection. Therefore, it must be said at once that no healthy mind takes pleasure in pain as such. A morbid love of suffering for its own sake would be an indication of neurosis. Saint John of the Cross is talking not about neurotics but about athletes. The pleasure such men derive from their fasts and penances springs not from the pain which they inflict upon their bodies but from the sense that they are doing things which are objectively painful without suffering as much as one might expect. In other words, they taste a delightful sense of having somehow risen above pain by courage and moral stamina. Far from being neurotic, this is a very healthy natural instinct. It is good for man to rejoice in the exercise of fortitude. If most men did not feel satisfaction in overcoming obstacles, they would be so weighed down by depression at the labor of negotiating them that they would probably never face them at all. And yet, the highest fortitude is that in which we overcome obstacles without any appreciable feeling of satisfaction. The bravest man is not the one who never feels fear, but the one who overcomes the greatest fear and goes through danger cool in the presence of terror.

But if the instinct to rejoice in one's moral strength is basically healthy, the abuse of it is a moral imperfection. The purpose of mortification is to liberate the spirit and make it plastic in the hands of God. The man who allows himself to become absorbed in an inordinate attention to penitential exercises for their own sake ends, in fact, by being constantly preoccupied with what he is doing to himself and how he is taking it. Instead of getting away from himself, he has imprisoned his spirit in a labyrinth of self-will and self-deception. The exercises that ought, by rights, to bring him to a state of liberty and detachment have ended, rather, by making him more attached than ever to his own will and his own judgment.

Now, the secret of detachment, as we have seen, consists in acting not according to the impulses of our own fancy and good pleasure but in following the guidance of reason enlightened by faith, whether the path it points out to us should suit our tastes or not. For members of religious orders the path of faith and reason is also the path of obedience. Here is how Saint John of the Cross describes the imperfection which he calls "spiritual gluttony." First: What is the essence of this disorder? It consists in following the attraction "of the sweetness and pleasure which they find in [penitential] exercises, and *striving more after spiritual sweetness than after spiritual purity and discretion which is that which God regards and accepts throughout the spiritual journey.*" [8]

The reader should by now be attuned to implications of the word "discretion" in Christian asceticism. It might better be translated here as "discrimination," and it conveys the idea of a purified spiritual sensitivity by which the ascetic distinguishes what is fine, in the interior life, from what is gross. Discretion in its highest sense is a kind of spiritual instinct by which we immediately recognize the difference between impulsions of pride (even under the most spiritual of disguises) and the inspirations of divine grace.

Saint John of the Cross goes on:

Besides the imperfections into which the seeking for sweetness of this kind makes them fall, the gluttony which they have makes them continually go too far, so that they pass beyond the limits of moderation within which the virtues are acquired and in which they consist. For some of these persons, attracted by the pleasure which they find therein, kill themselves with penances and others weaken themselves with fasts, by performing more than their frailty can bear, without the advice of any, but rather endeavoring to avoid those whom they should obey in these matters; some indeed dare to do these things even though the contrary has been commanded them.[9]

The situation is one which anyone who has lived in a fervent contemplative monastery will easily recognize. And it must be said that it is perhaps better, after all, when monks are eager to do too much penance than when they seek to do as little as they can. For the passion that drives men to undertake hard and seemingly heroic things provides good raw material for sanctity. With wise direction, you can make something of such men. But what can be done with people who have decided beforehand that every obstacle is insuperable and that all hardships are unbearable and that every mortification is extreme? They turn whole monasteries into hospitals, and their spiritual directors must rest content if they can get them to keep the fasts of the Church and say their prayers of obligation. Returning to Saint John of the Cross and his spiritual athletes, we find the Carmelite mystic once again demonstrating, without any ambiguity or compromise, that reason is the cornerstone of his asceticism. He says:

These persons are most imperfect and devoid of reason; for they set bodily penance before subjection and obedience, which is a penance of the reason and discretion, and therefore a sacrifice more pleasing to God than any beside. [Their attachment to bodily penance] is no more than the penance of beasts, to which they are attracted, exactly like beasts, by the pleasure and desire which they find therein. Inasmuch as all extremes are sinful, and as in behaving thus such persons are working their own will, they grow in vice rather than in virtue.[10]

It is significant that some of the strongest language used by Saint John of the Cross is poured out on the heads of men who defied reason with an inordinate love of bodily penance. But the most important thing about this paragraph of *The Dark Night* is that it lays down the fundamental principle to which we have already alluded, and which is the test of true discretion.

The success or failure of a man's spiritual life depends on the clarity with which he is able to see and judge the motives of his moral acts. To use a term canonized by ascetic tradition, the first step to sanctity is self-knowledge. It is the function of reason to judge these motives, to try the purity of our intentions, and to evaluate the objects of our desire and all the circumstances that surround our moral activity. But this work of reason is obstructed and fouled by a habit of acting on impulse every time we are prompted by the instinctive motions of passion and desire.

Now, the impulsions of desire which present the greatest problem in the ascetic life are not those which reach out for an object that is manifestly evil. On the contrary, the biggest task of reason, in the spiritual life, is to unmask disordered impulsions that seem at first to be spiritual and aimed at the highest good. The reason why so many pious men fail to become saints is that they do evil for the glory of God.

The apparent ruthlessness of Saint John of the Cross

consists in the fact that he turns the merciless light of an
intellect purified by the fire of God upon scores of objects
and desires which seem, to the misguided, to belong to the
very essence of sanctity and Christian perfection: and he
condemns them all. Not that they are all evil: but the mere
fact that they are not good enough means that they are
not worthy of our desire. We must turn aside from them
and look elsewhere. Not only the good things of the
world are to be renounced by the ascetic but even some of
the highest gifts and favors of God. Not that we should
formally refuse a gift of God: but we must always be
careful to receive His extraordinary favors in such a way
that our desire is centered on the Giver, not on the gift
itself.

But the pleasures of the interior life are so great and so
pure; they so far transcend the crude joys of sense and of
this world, that they exercise a terrible attraction upon the
soul that meets them along its road to God. The thought
of these pleasures, the memory of them and the hope of
their recapture move a man to the very depths of his spirit
and almost turn him inside out with the vehemence of
great desire. He will do the wildest things if he believes
that it will bring back two minutes of the joy he has once
tasted in what seemed to be a vision of God. He will go
to the ends of the earth to hear some unutterable word
that once left him suspended between time and eternity.
He will kill himself to hear some echo of that sweet voice.
But Saint John of the Cross tells him that every one of
these impulsions must be slaughtered with the blade of
reason and that the way to God is a way of emptiness,
without refreshment and without pleasure, in which we
seek no light but faith and hear no voice but that of faith

—so that, in the end, we must always walk in darkness. We must travel in silence. We must fly by night.

That is why some of the saint's maxims chill the enthusiasm of immature contemplatives with incomprehension and surprise. Is it really the author of *The Living Flame of Love* telling us these things?

Enter into account with thy reason to do that which it counsels thee on the road to God, and it will be of greater worth to thee with respect to God than all the works which thou doest without this counsel and all the spiritual delights which thou seekest.

Blessed is he who puts aside his pleasure and inclination and regards things according to reason and justice in order to perform them.

He that acts according to reason is like one that eats of substantial food, and he that is moved by the desire of his will is like one that eats insipid fruit.[11]

Another maxim—this time rather curious—brings us to a new aspect of our subject. It reminds us of the doctrine which readers more readily associate with Saint John of the Cross—that of passive prayer and of the infused light and love of the Holy Spirit. It recalls that sometimes the soul is, indeed, passively moved by spiritual impulsions that proceed from another.

Consider that thy guardian angel does not always move thy desire to act, though he ever illumines the reason. Wherefore stay thou not for desire before thou perform a virtuous deed since reason and understanding suffice thee.[12]

Perhaps Saint John was thinking of the Quietists, who believed that those who followed the interior way of spiritual prayer could never permit themselves to perform any act of virtue without feeling themselves positively and sensibly urged to do so by an interior impulsion from God.

This is one of the few places where Saint John of the Cross refers to the mediation of angels in our mystical life —a subject which is emphasized by Pseudo-Dionysius. In any case, here he is definitely talking about mysticism. The reason does not play an active part in mystical experience as such. Contemplation is, strictly speaking, mystical in proportion as our faculties are moved passively by special inspirations from God. There is a level of prayer in which the faculties are not totally absorbed in God. But when the will and reason can still act on their own initiative, even though they do so in conjunction with some passive movement received from God, our contemplation is less pure.

Nevertheless, there is an essential continuity between these two levels of spiritual activity. The doctrine of Saint John of the Cross on this point is, once again, based on the teaching of Saint Thomas. Here is the Thomistic principle which is reflected in the maxim we have just quoted from Saint John of the Cross. The spiritual life of the Christian is an ordered ascent to perfection. From the beginning of this ascent to the end, man is moved, enlightened, strengthened, led, and elevated by the action of God. At first, God acts on man through the instrumentality of man's own reason, enlightened by grace and directed by the virtues. Later on, God moves the spirit of man in a more direct and intimate fashion, through the special inspirations which we are disposed to receive by the seven Gifts of the Holy Ghost. But whether man be led by his reason or moved directly by God, the end is the same and the work done is essentially the same, for in either case God is bringing the spirit of man into divine union by the perfection of faith, hope, and love.

# CHAPTER XII

# Between Instinct and Inspiration

The precise relation of reason to the mystical life has begun to be clear. Reason has such an important function in the life of man that his supernatural happiness is made to depend, in some sense, upon it. Reason holds the key to the mystical life. That key has been placed in its hands by God. What does this mean? Not that we can find our own way into mystical contemplation by thought or study. Not that the life of virtue which perfects our reason can, strictly speaking, merit graces of infused prayer or divine union. Not that contemplation elevates reason to a high degree of efficiency in its own order by lucid discourse and brilliant intuitions of the truth.

Saint Gregory Nazianzen calls the soul of the spiritual man—the mystic—an instrument played by the Holy Spirit: *organum pulsatum a Spiritu Sancto*. The Holy Ghost draws from this instrument harmonies and a melody of which reason and the will of man alone could never even dream. It is this music vibrating on the well-tuned strings of a perfect human personality that makes a man a saint. It is when special harmonies are wrung from a human instrument that the Holy Ghost makes a man a contemplative. What part has reason in this silent song

that God sings for Himself and for His elect in the soul of
a mystic? It is the function of reason not to play the instrument but only to tune the strings. The Master Himself does not waste time tuning the instrument. He shows
His servant, reason, how to do it and leaves him to do the
work. If He then comes and finds the piano still out of
tune, He does not bother to play anything on it. He
strikes a chord, and goes away. The trouble generally is
that the tuner has been banging on the keys himself all
day, without bothering to do the work assigned to him:
which is to keep the thing in tune.

It takes much discretion and delicacy of soul to keep
this instrument in tune. The strings must not be pulled
too tight, or left too slack. Reason must judge the right
measure of self-denial that will keep all the faculties of
the soul responsive to the keys when they are struck by
God. This work belongs already to the supernatural order.
Reason could not perform it without grace, without the
infused virtues. How is it done?

I think the task of reason in keeping the soul attuned,
by virtue, to the inspirations of grace can be summed up
as a process of elimination in which the movements of disordered passion and ill-regulated instinct are judged and
rejected. The soul of a man who is mature in Christian
asceticism is like the well-trained ear of a musician, sensitive to the slightest modulations of pitch in a voice or instrument. The mediocre ascetic is one who, morally speaking, never knows when he is flat. Eccentric mortifications
are attempts to sing truer than the pitch that has been
given by God: they have the effect of a loud voice singing
sharp in a flat choir, where only the organ is true.

All this is just another way of saying what has been

said before: that reason disposes the soul for passive union with God by the active work of "discretion," discrimination. There is another term for it: "the discernment of spirits."

The task of reason, illuminated by grace and perfected by all the acquired and infused virtues, is to make sure that we clearly distinguish between temptation and the light of grace, between the urges of emotion and the instinct of supernatural love, between the guesses and fancies of a lively imagination and the lights of the Holy Ghost. The movements of supernatural light and love which come to us on a human level, by the inspirations of ordinary grace, help reason in its own connatural function of perfecting the soul in virtue, that is, of keeping it in tune. But above that level there is another set of faculties, belonging to the same unified organism of grace. These are habits which perfect the action of the soul on a level higher than that of its own natural mode. They are called the Gifts of the Holy Ghost. It is when the soul is dominated and led by special inspirations of God, through these Gifts, that it is said to be leading the mystical life.

All the virtues, whether acquired or infused, natural or supernatural, dispose the soul to act according to the standards of perfection laid down for a rational being ordered to a supernatural end. Nevertheless, on the level of the virtues, where the soul moves itself in a human mode, according to the guidance of reason, by the light of grace, its activity is weakened and obstructed by many involuntary imperfections. Why is this? With infused charity, sanctifying grace, and a host of virtues, reason should run smoothly. To some extent, it does. But let us return to our instrument and its tuner. The difference between the per-

fection of a soul that operates only on the level of the virtues, *humano modo,* and of one that is moved on the
higher level of the Gifts, by special inspirations of God,
is something like the difference between a symphony
played by a piano tuner and one played by a genius. Reason can manage to get along in the supernatural life, with
grace and the virtues. It is like a skater who can go forth
onto the ice with a well-founded hope that he will not be
carried off on a stretcher. He can truthfully say: "I know
how to skate." But that does not make him a champion
hockey player, and if he feels the urge to go in for figure
skating his attempts had better be modest, or he will
break a leg.

If there were such a thing (and perhaps there is!) as a
kind of natural inspiration which would suddenly make a
piano tuner play like a genius, and send a wooden-legged
skater unexpectedly spiraling down the pond with the
grace of a sparrow hawk, it would give a good idea of the
working of the Gifts of the Holy Ghost. To these can
strictly be applied the formula of theologians concerning
that grace which works in us, but without our own initiative: *in nobis sed sine nobis.* The Gifts attune us to special
inspirations which enable us to arrive at supernatural judgments and decisions with an ease and efficacy that would
be entirely impossible if we were moved by our own
faculties, even under the guidance of ordinary grace. These
inspirations are more than suggestions of grace. They
more than point out an action for intelligence or love to
perform. Instead of letting our faculties move themselves,
the Holy Ghost directly acts in them, while they remain
passive. Thus they have the impression of suddenly arriv-
ing at a new level of supernatural knowledge or a more

intense degree of love without having the faintest idea how
they got there.

At the same time, it is very important to realize that
the inspirations of the Holy Ghost, by means of the Seven
Gifts, are generally not at all spectacular or dramatic
either in their object or in their mode of activity. After
reading the lives of the saints and the experiences of the
mystics, some people become convinced that the mystical
life must be something like a Wagnerian opera. Tremendous things keep happening all the time. Every new motion of the spirit is heralded by thunder and lightning.
The heavens crack open and the soul sails upward out of
the body into a burst of unearthly and splendid light.
There it comes face to face with God, in the midst of a
huge *Turnverein* of flying, singing, trumpet-playing
saints and angels. There is an eloquent exchange of views
between the soul and God in an operatic duet that lasts at
least seven hours, for seven is a mystical number. All this
is punctuated by earthquakes, solar and lunar eclipses, and
the explosion of supersubstantial bombs. Eventually, after
a brief musical preview of the end of the world and the
Last Judgment, the soul pirouettes gracefully back into
the body and the mystic comes to himself to discover that
he is surrounded by a hushed, admiring circle of fellow
religious, including one or two who are surreptitiously
taking down notes of the event in view of some future
process of canonization.

It is generally safe to say that noise and turmoil in the
interior life are signs of inspirations that proceed from our
own emotion or from some spirit that is anything but
holy. The inspirations of the Holy Ghost are quiet, for
God speaks in the silent depths of the spirit. His voice

brings peace. It does not arouse excitement, but allays it because excitement belongs to uncertainty. The voice of God is certitude. If He moves us to action, we go forward with peaceful strength. More often than not His inspirations teach us to sit still. They show us the emptiness and confusion of projects we thought we had undertaken for His glory. He saves us from the impulses that would throw us into wild competition with other men. He delivers us from ambition. The Holy Spirit is most easily recognized where He inspires obedience and humility. No one really knows Him who has not tasted the tranquillity that comes with the renunciation of our own will, our own pleasure, our own interests, without glory, without notice, without approval, for the interests of some other person. The inspirations of the Spirit of God are not grandiose. They are simple. They move us to seek God in works that are difficult without being spectacular. They lead us in paths that are happy because they are obscure. That is why they always bring with them a sense of liberation. "He is the Spirit of Truth" (John 14:17) and "the Truth shall make you free." His inspirations make us clean. They deliver us from coarseness and from limitation.

And in the light of the Holy Ghost we can be at the same time happy and sorry: happy because of God's truth, sorry because of what, by His truth, we see that we have been. Happy, again, because of what we know we can become, in Him. We find strength and humility, confidence and caution together in this light which teaches us the way of knowledge in darkness by filling us with a miraculous love. One last thing: the light of the Holy Ghost does not leave us pleased with ourselves but pleased with God only. If it permits us not to be displeased with ourselves, it is because it has brought us into a deeper union with Him: He is all we love, and other men: not our own selves.

The light of the Holy Ghost has no part in the sanctimonious self-admiration of the Pharisee who loves the vision of himself rejoicing in a vision.

2

Sanctity consists in a perfect union of mind and will with God. It means the total consecration and submission of all our faculties to God's Truth and to His Love. Therefore, the whole work of our sanctification, which is performed on one level by reason and the virtues and on another by the Holy Ghost acting directly through His Gifts, can be summed up as *the perfect obedience of our whole being to the will of God*.

That is why the whole spiritual life can be reduced in practice to one simple formula: doing the will of God. The formula must not be oversimplified. It must not be applied mechanically and without understanding. It can never become a matter of mere routine, for the sanctity God asks of us is found not in the obedience of mules but in the "reasonable service" proper to beings endowed with freedom and with intelligence.

Saint John of the Cross, together with Saint Thomas Aquinas, holds that reason and virtue can only bring us to a relative and limited perfection in our obedience to God. On this first level, only a certain degree of divine union can be achieved. The work of active asceticism needs to be completed passively by the supremely delicate intervention of God the Sanctifier. On the first level, the soul can at least arrive at a state in which the will rejects every desire which reason, enlightened by grace, recognizes to be contrary to the will of God. But, as Saint John of the Cross says, "unintentionally and unknowingly, or without having the power to do otherwise [the soul] may well fall into imperfections and venial sins and natural desires."[1]

These habits are like living roots from which, in spite of our best intentions, we constantly suffer a regrowth of bitter, tenacious offshoots of imperfection. The highest sanctity demands that even the roots of bad habit be dug away and cleared from the garden of the soul. This work cannot be performed by reason alone. It requires the direct intervention of God in passive or mystical purifications of the soul.[2] Nor is the so-called Night of Sense sufficient for this. Perfect sanctity is not in fact to be achieved without the radical cleansing of the spirit in fires of infused love equivalent, in all their spiritual effects, to the flames of purgatory itself. This is the real Dark Night—the Night of the Soul.

Saint John of the Cross declares without hesitation or ambiguity that the active, or ascetic, purification of the soul can never suffice for perfect sanctity. He writes:

I can only say, in order to prove how necessary is the night of the spirit, which is purgation, for him who would go farther, that none of these proficients, however greatly he may have exerted himself is free at best from many of those natural affections and imperfect habits *the purification whereof is necessary if the soul is to pass to divine union.*[3]

However, this passive purification and the sanctity which follows from it are both gifts of God. It is good for us to desire them. We can and should pray for them. We cannot resolve to attain them. Perfection in the active work of asceticism, and the total generosity of our conscious fulfillment of the will of God will dispose us to receive them. And there is one thing more. God will not undertake the passive purification of our spirit unless we first give Him our generous and intelligent cooperation in the preliminary purification of the interior senses.

## 3

The Night of Sense is a period of trial in which the faculties of the soul begin to be moved passively by God without losing their own power to move themselves. It is called a Night, not because the reason and will are themselves "darkened," or deprived of their own natural light and strength, but because they are hampered in their ordinary mode of activity. The intelligence cannot naturally know anything without acting upon the material it receives from the senses. The will also needs this material in order to act on the natural plane. In the Night of Sense, the infused action of God upon the mind causes it to become weary of reasoning. The same hidden action makes the will grow tired of desire. Instead of reasoning, the intellect is drawn to rest in a simple intuition of the truths of faith. Instead of pouring itself out in the quest of particular ends, the will withdraws itself into the unified and simple love of God, the One End of all our striving.

But since the infused action of God on the soul is still very tenuous, and since the experience it produces is vague and obscure, the faculties find themselves in a state which seems to them equivocal. And because they cannot clearly apprehend what is happening to them, they fluctuate between anguish and consolation. They can never quite ascertain why they are in anguish or why they are consoled. Their own activity is not yet seriously obstructed (as it may be later on), but it gives them no satisfaction and seems to be more or less fruitless. And yet they do not at this stage realize how they should comport themselves in order to remain simply and fruitfully passive under the mysterious action of God. Furthermore—and this is important—God does not always act in them in this special way. When He is not acting in them, they must not remain passive but do something for themselves: otherwise, neither God nor the faculties will be acting and the soul will be idle. It is very difficult to tell, in the beginning, when God is infusing these delicate and passive inspirations into the soul.

Finally, it is a law of the mystical life that the faculties of the soul remain passive in the strict sense of the word only when they are absorbed by God in rapture and lose all power to move themselves.[4] Otherwise, their passivity is only relative. It is therefore very important to understand in what sense and to what precise degree the mind and will of man remain passive in the Night of Sense and in the Prayer of Quiet. This is important for two special reasons. First, because the faculties, which remain capable of acting on their own account, can frustrate the delicate work of God by ill-advised activities of their own, especially at the time of prayer. Second, because if they remain completely inert they will fail to do the simple work of cooperation which God still demands of them.

In short, the principle I wish to emphasize is this: that

although formal discursive meditation is practically impossible in the Night of Sense, and although, at this time, the beginnings of infused and passive motivation by God demand that the activity of the mind and will be *purified, simplified, and reduced to unity,* there nevertheless remains work to be done both by the mind and by the will. This is especially true at the beginning of our daily mental prayer. For, during the Night of Sense, the divine action does not usually take hold of us without our first disposing ourselves in some way to receive it. Only later on, as we become more habitually immersed in the Prayer of Quiet, does the passive light of God come upon us and envelop our faculties in the translucent semidarkness of "unknowing" at the most unexpected moments of the day.

In the Night of Sense the infused inspirations of contemplative prayer work principally on the will. It is the will that is first subjected to the passive movements of the Holy Spirit. It is the will that first of all begins to be absorbed and held captive under the spell of God's mysterious presence. For God makes Himself immediately present to the contemplative soul not by knowledge but by love. Thus, from the very first, love plays a pre-eminently important role in contemplation, even though contemplation remains formally an act of the intellect.

But if the will is absorbed and enfolded by the power of secret grace, in the beginnings of infused prayer, it can still move itself. It can still get free. And if it be misled by the intelligence, it may strive to get free and to act of its own accord, instead of resting in the serene darkness of divine love. The success of our cooperation with the inspirations of God in this state therefore *still depends largely on the supernatural discretion of our reason.*

It is quite true that when the will begins to be absorbed in the mysterious and delightful love which God produces passively in it, through the Gift of Wisdom, this faculty becomes momentarily independent of reason, at least in the sense that it now begins to be guided directly by God in the intimacy of an experience of values that are not made known to it through the intelligence. The will, suddenly touched by the flame of love in the wise darkness of its own secret passivity, in some sense "learns" and "knows" the things of God in a way that reason cannot fathom. Nevertheless, the will alone cannot formally elicit the estimative judgment that subjectively decides the real value of this experience. That is why the Gift of Wisdom shares its inspirations between the will and the intelligence. It has to do so. For the will, though passively moved by God, is only delicately moved and remains subject to the direction of the intelligence. If reason does not see something of the value of what the will is tasting, it will be likely to call the will away and deprive the whole soul of supernatural nourishment and joy.

Therefore, although it is important to realize that too much reasoning is an obstacle to the infused action of God upon the will, in this Night of Sense and in the Prayer of Quiet, it is equally important to remember that a certain discreet, intuitive action of our intelligence is required of us by God in this state. In fact, the successful cooperation of our soul with His infused graces depends on a passivity that is supremely humble *because it is intelligent*. After all, since humility is truth, it presupposes a supernaturally enlightened intelligence. Consequently, we are bound to conclude that reason has a very important, though secondary, part to play in the Night of Senses. Here again, reason is lodged in its usual crucial position on the borderline between nature and the supernatural. It is the sentry placed by faith to stand guard over the inner fortress of the soul, which is the will, and to examine every stranger who presents himself at the door. Here in the penumbra of faith which descends upon the soul in the Night of Sense, reason must be a particularly vigilant and courageous sentry, and refuse admittance to all those instincts of human nature which present themselves as noisy friends of prayer, and who seek admittance to the fortress in order to carry on their own peculiar kind of celebration. Above all, reason must be firm in excluding many of his own good friends. Talkative intellectuals would not be welcome in the silence and simplicity of the inner solitude where the will rises to an ineffable meeting with the true God beyond the level of concepts. Only those who have acquired some familiarity with the practice of interior prayer can realize what a delicate and courageous task is here assigned to the intelligence—which remains responsible, in large part, for the purity of the will, without which contemplation is impossible. This task is all the more delicate because it requires that reason sacrifice first of all its own natural propensity to settle problems by much discourse and analysis. It must supervise what goes on in the house of the soul not with much intricate self-examination and elaborately dictated plans of action, but with a wise economy of prudent decisions, born of silent reflection in which reason is a submissive listener and God's grace suggests what is to be done.

# 4

There is another difficulty. It explains why the intelligence has to renounce something of its own primacy here, and wait upon the will. The reason is not admitted to the depths in which the will is held enthralled by an obscure experience of immediate union with God. The intelligence, itself enlightened less directly by God, knows something of what is going on: but does not know it all. It is now playing a role secondary to that of the will. If one might be permitted the expression, it is as if the will had become a source of information for the intelligence. This explains, perhaps, why the theologians of the Augustinian tradition thought that the will was the highest faculty in the soul: they were basing their decision on the experience of this prayer in which the will (as any Thomist would readily agree) is in fact acting on a higher plane than the intelligence because it is in more immediate contact with God.[5] If the will really held primacy over all the other faculties in the soul, this situation would not be hazardous at all. The reason would have nothing to do but acquiesce in whatever information might come to it through the experience of the will. Furthermore, the soul would now be perfectly ordered: the will would have possession of God, the reason would obey the will directed by God, and all the other faculties would follow. In that case, one might conclude that the highest beatitude was nothing more than the Prayer of Quiet or the prayer of full union in which God is possessed without being known.

There are great dangers latent in a state of soul in which the will is in immediate experiential contact with God but the intelligence is not enlightened in a way that measures up to this union of love. If God kept the will permanently in union with Himself, these dangers would be relatively insignificant. He does not in fact do so. As the contemplative emerges from the Night of Sense and enters deeply into the habitual practice of the Prayer of Quiet, with occasional touches of the prayer of full mystical union in which all the faculties are absorbed, the will comes into contact with many objects of pleasure which are spiritual but not, for all that, divine. Hence the need of great discretion.

The action of God in passive prayer has deepened and enlarged the natural power of the will to taste spiritual pleasure. There is nothing miraculous about the new spiritual capacities which the soul discovers in itself. They are part of its nature, but their exercise had been frustrated and stultified by attachment to the pleasures of sense. Now they have been set free and have begun to recover some of their inborn freshness and vigor.

What are some of these capacities? I will mention only one, by way of example. It is the metaphysical sense of being and of all the transcendentals. Many people cannot even grasp the abstract notions of being, truth, beauty, unity, as they are proposed by philosophers. They have no capacity to appreciate these realities, which remain, to them, mere words. In order to excite the interest of those who live on the level of sense experience, and who are unfamiliar with thought and philosophical intuition, you have to present them with concrete, particular, existing samples of being, truth, and the rest. The intellectual level of our modern civilization is fairly indicated by what those who live in "the world" see all around them from

morning to night on billboards and hear from night to
morning on the radio and over television. "Being,"
"Truth," "Beauty" are appreciated only in their most
fragmentary and particular manifestations. A hundred
million big beefy citizens are on the verge of drinking cans
of ice-cold beer. A hundred million young women made
out of pneumatic caramel are using soap, stockings, ciga-
rettes, automobiles, and a million other things, in such a
way that the beholder is invited to dwell upon the fact
that they are women. This is all that rates as "Being" in a
world that has finally decided to blow itself up.

When, by the practice of prayer and interior discipline,
a man has freed himself from useless preoccupation with
whatever is fragmentary and particular, and can make
temperate use of material things without being too much
distracted by them, and when God has enlarged his capacity for spiritual joy by infused graces of prayer, he begins
to taste some of the pleasures that ought to belong, by
natural right, to every human soul, but which most men
have forfeited or forgotten.

Metaphysically speaking, the values that can be proved
and enjoyed in sense experience of particular things can
all be enjoyed in a concentrated and much higher form in a
spiritual intuition of the transcendental properties of being. Let me explain in a way that ought to be acceptable
even to those who secretly lament the fact that they do not
have infinite stomachs, in order to devour all the fried
chicken in the universe. You cannot gain possession of
all the being and all the goodness contained in all the food
in the world by grimly sitting down to the task of eating
everything in sight. Despite the ambitions of Gargantua,
our bodies are not equipped for this feat, and even if they

were, we would fail. But all the reality and all the goodness of everything that exists and is good can be spiritually
tasted and enjoyed in a single metaphysical intuition of
being and of goodness as such. The clean, intellectual delight of such an experience makes all the inebriation procured by wine look like a hangover. I am not now talking
of anything mystical: merely of the natural intuition of
pure being, pure goodness. Here the being and goodness
which are shared by all particular things are grasped in a
single luminous intuition which floods our whole spirit
with light and exhilaration. It is a kind of natural ecstasy
in which our own being recognizes in itself a transcendental
kinship with every other being that exists and, as it were,
flows out of itself to possess all being and returns to itself
to find all being in itself. In a moment of rich metaphysical illumination we rise above accidents and specific differences to discover all things in one undifferentiated
transcendental reality, which is being itself.

The foundation of this experience is, no doubt, a sudden intuitive penetration of the value of our own spiritual
being. It is a profound metaphysical awareness of our own
reality—not of the trivial, psychological surface-self that
is engaged in the pursuit of many temporal desires and in
the flight from many fears, but the deep substantial reality
of our own personal being. In this moment of light, the
soul may taste something of the inborn liberty that is due
to it as a thing of spirit. It may even pass from this to an
intuition of the Absolute Being Who infinitely transcends
our highest concept of being and of spirit. In this metaphysical intuition of being of which I speak, the intelligence does not enter into an immediate vision of the Infinite Being. If God is realized, He is still realized by

inference from created being. He is known as reflected in
the vital depths of our own spirit, of which He is the
Creator and which is the mirror that receives His image.

And yet, the metaphysical intuition of being and of
its transcendental properties is a very great thing. It cannot be arrived at without some moral purity, and its natural effect is to strengthen the soul and help it to get free
from dangerous attachments. Beyond this intuition is
another—the intuitive appreciation of the Absolute Being
of God, an intuition which is not only speculative but
qualitative, tinged with affectivity, by virtue of the analogical light shed on the idea of the Creator by the intense
vitality and joy which the spirit realizes in itself as His
creature. So great a thing is this intuition that the pagan
philosophers thought it was the highest beatitude: and
indeed it is the highest beatitude that man could ever
arrive at by his natural powers alone.

This pleasure, this intellectual fulfillment which is a
partial answer to the deepest need of man's spiritual being
—his need for contemplation—is accessible to nature. But
it is quickly and more perfectly attained under the guidance of grace. However, those who experience the spiritual
fulfillment that comes with the first beginnings of infused
prayer are almost never aware of the distinction between
what is essential to true contemplation and what is merely
an accidental natural accompaniment of contemplation.
They seem to think, as a matter of course, that everything
that happens to them in connection with what they feel to
be the movement of divine grace is simply to be labeled
as "a grace" and left at that. They apparently suppose
that, as soon as you reach the prayer of quiet, the distinction between nature and grace vanishes into thin air: you

are a mystic, therefore you no longer have anything to do with "nature."

As a matter of fact, in all the levels of the mystical life until the soul has finally passed through the "Night of the Spirit," the movements of grace and the inspirations of the Holy Ghost are at work in a spiritual organism that not only exercises natural functions but, as we have seen, begins to rediscover in itself capacities that nature never knew it had. The lights of prayer that make us imagine we are beginning to be angels are sometimes only signs that we are finally beginning to be men. We do not have a high enough opinion of our own nature. We think we are at the gates of heaven and we are only just beginning to come into our own realm as free and intelligent beings.

Spiritual vanity enters into this and affects our attitude toward the graces of prayer. We want everything to be "extraordinary" and supernatural. Everything that moves within us has to be the finger of God. And if God is acting we have to be passive. We are eager to persuade ourselves that the delights we feel are mystical and that we cannot resist them. We want to be drunk with joy, and therefore we believe that every spiritual inebriation is necessarily "sacred." And because it is sacred, it must not be examined by reason. But this is precisely where reason needs to do its most important work in the spiritual life.

It would be extremely dangerous to leave the will to itself and the whole soul under the command of the will, when the will remains, as ever, a blind faculty, and is blinder than ever in a night full of inebriating delights, some of which find their source in God and some of which are merely the self-discovery of hidden spiritual potentialities in our own nature. To deny the intelligence any power to discriminate between the impulsions that move the will and sometimes carry the whole soul out of itself in an access of strange rapture would be as prudent as uncaging a hungry lion for the greater glory of God. By no one is more harm done in the world than by men who were at the point of becoming mystics but whose mysticism degenerated into an irrational surrender to every passion that knew how to dress up as an angel of light. This irrationality has never been the teaching of the Catholic Church or of Christian mystics. Nor has it been admitted by the truly wise men of any land or any religion. We have seen that it is certainly not the doctrine of Saint John of the Cross.

# CHAPTER XIII

# Reason and Reasoning

The interior asceticism demanded of our reason by Saint John of the Cross cannot be practiced without the highest supernatural heroism. It demands of reason an unswerving fidelity to faith, which will reject the dramatic appeal of every supernatural stimulation that tends more to self-glorification and to interior excitement than to pure submission to God. It is a sacrifice of our intelligence which is, at the same time, one of the highest and most honorable ways of exercising our intelligence for, in the end, it protects our soul against a thousand illusions in the ways of mystical experience.

Saint John of the Cross is severe in his criticism of contemplatives who are too ready to accept all their interior locutions, that is, all the words and sentences which seem to be formed passively as though clearly spoken within their souls by God or by one of His angels. Saint John does not care whether or not these locutions may be connected with some really supernatural grace. He is convinced that the habit of accepting them, taking complacency in them, and recalling them to mind with satisfaction is a dangerous obstacle to progress in interior prayer. This will no doubt surprise those whose spiritual reading consists mostly of revelations and locutions supposedly uttered by Our Lord and His saints to pious women. Saint

John of the Cross would declare that even though these mystics were in good faith, many of the messages they thought they were receiving from heaven were, in fact, received from themselves. "The desire which people have for locutions," he says, "and the pleasure which comes to their spirits from them lead them to make answer to themselves and then to think that it is God who is answering them and speaking to them. They therefore commit great blunders if they put not great restraint upon themselves. . . . I knew a person who had these successive locutions and who among them formed some that were very true . . . but others were sheer heresy." [1]

The saint then goes on to explain why these locutions, even though they may be true, should be rejected. They create an unnecessary atmosphere of activity in the soul, which should be quiet and recollected in faith in order to receive the inspirations which really lead to divine union and which are not sensed after the fashion of words, for the mind and will are moved by them directly and without the medium of concepts. This passage gives a good idea of the condition in which the soul must be kept by reason, in cooperation with grace.

The Holy Spirit illumines the understanding which is recollected and illumines it according to the manner of its recollection, and the understanding cannot find any other or greater recollection than in faith; and thus the Holy Spirit will illumine it naught more than in faith. For the purer and more refined in faith is the soul, the more it has of the infused charity of God; and the more charity it has, the more is it illumined and the more the gifts of the Holy Spirit are communicated to it, for charity is the means and the cause whereby they are communicated to it. [2]

This luminous passage could serve as a summary of the mysticism of Saint John of the Cross. It certainly shows

us with the greatest clarity just what reason has to do in
the mystical life. Reason must keep the soul pure and
recollected. How? In faith. That is, by keeping the eye
of the intelligence exposed to the light of the Truth God
has revealed to His Church, instead of letting it be distracted by emotional experiences of a more spectacular
and personal character. Why? Because the light of faith
opens the way for infused charity. Sanctity consists in
charity, and the more we grow in charity the more
scope the Holy Ghost has to work on us with His inspirations which lead us to divine union. This divine union,
however, is nothing else but the perfection of charity.
Saint John concludes by distinguishing between the action
of the Holy Ghost in locutions, and His action through
the theological virtues and the gifts. He says:

In the one manner [through locutions] is communicated to the
soul wisdom concerning one or two truths, but in the other is
communicated to it *all the wisdom of God in general, which is
the Son of God, who communicates Himself to the soul in faith.*[3]

I will leave this tremendous statement without comment
for the moment. Discussion of it would interrupt the work
that still needs to be done on our present topic. We shall
later on see more of this communication of the Word by
faith.

For the present, I have a humbler task in hand. Yet it
is important. As I proceed with it, I would call the attention of the reader to the difference between "reason" and
"reasoning." Reason is a light, reasoning a process. Reason
is a faculty, reasoning an exercise of that faculty. Reasoning
proceeds from one truth to another by means of argu-
mentation. This generally involves the whole mind in
labor and complexity. But reason does not exist merely

in order to engage in reasoning. The process is a means to an end. The true fulfillment of reason as a faculty is found when it can embrace the truth simply and without labor in the light of a single intuition.

The intelligence of man is, by nature and by predisposition, intuitive. It is made to see the truth in one glance. However, since man is not an angel, his intelligence is bound up with his senses. And because it depends on sense knowledge it cannot at once contemplate all truth in a few primary intuitions. It starts from some intuitions of its own—which are rather poor in content—and proceeds laboriously from the knowledge of one sensible reality to another until it acquires enough material to behold something of the profound truth contained in the intuition with which this process began. I spoke a moment ago of the metaphysical intuition of being. This is simply a deeply spiritual penetration of a truth that is intuitively realized in a crude form by every man who lives: that a being cannot at the same time and in the same sense be and not be what it is. This principle is not usually a source of openmouthed wonder to those who hear it. Yet it becomes a matter of enthralling spiritual experience when it is seen in the light of the affective connotations thrown on all being by a sudden metaphysical appreciation of our own reality—of the fact that we ourselves *are*, and of all that this means! On this level, the intuition of the simplest and most obvious of all truths becomes too sublime for explanation—and we return to the inarticulate helplessness that confronted us at the beginning of all, when we were forced to throw up our hands and stammer: "whatever is, *is*." And indeed it might seem strange, to some, that there have been men whose whole lives have been thrown into a revolution by the sudden experience of the fact that they existed, and that the world was real!

Now, all contemplation is, by its very essence, an intuition. Saint Thomas gives the broadest possible definition of contemplation when he calls it a simple intuition of the truth—*simplex intuitus veritatis*.[4] This covers the contemplation of the speculative philosopher who beholds the whole range of his science in the intuitive appreciation of a few fundamental principles. It also covers the contemplation of the mystic who receives the Word of God into his spirit in the simple light of faith intensified by wisdom and understanding. It is because contemplation is essentially intuitive that our minds must remain peaceful and receptive and not indulge in too much useless reasoning when they are exposed to the infused light of the Holy Ghost.

The fact that mystical contemplation is essentially an experiential penetration of Divine Truth by love and passive illumination from God has important consequences. It means that in the order actually established by God, the Holy Spirit can raise to contemplation persons whose knowedge of God is confined to a few primary articles of faith. For, as Saint Thomas points out,[5] all the articles of faith are contained in a few fundamental revealed truths. In fact, he reduces the whole teaching of faith to the two propositions which, according to Saint Paul, must be believed *ex necessitate medii* by all who would attain their supernatural end. "He that cometh to God must believe that God exists and that He is a rewarder of them that seek Him." [6] The deepest truths about God and the whole economy of our Redemption through the Incarnation and death of Jesus Christ are implicit, says Saint Thomas, in these two articles. It would seem that every religious man possesses an intuitive grasp of the existence and providence of God and therefore even those who are incapable of elaborating their knowledge of God by study can nevertheless be perfected in faith by the illumination of God's grace and by other means which His providence is free to dispose of in their regard.[7]

All Catholics who have received the proper instruction and have come to live their faith possess at least a minimum knowledge of God that is simple and elementary, but nevertheless complete. Many of them have never had a chance to elaborate this knowledge by study, and they may not be capable of reasoning about it at length. And yet we know that there are and always have been many Christians of "simple faith" whose knowledge of God has reached profound depths, without their ever having had any ability to express to others what they knew. Their knowledge has remained intuitive. It has never resolved itself into analytic thought. There is nothing to prevent God from leading these souls from their primary intuitions of the truths of faith into a deep, though inexpressible, experience of the reality of those truths. The reason for this is that contemplation itself is essentially intuitive, and discursive reasoning does not therefore have any part in contemplation as such.

However, it is here precisely that many spiritual writers fall into an error which is quite contrary to the teaching of Catholic theology. The mere fact that *some* souls of "simple faith" have risen, without instruction or analysis, to mystical contemplation does not permit us to infer that therefore discursive knowledge, intelligent study, logical meditation, and other mental disciplines are either useless or positive obstacles to our growth in the life of prayer. On the contrary, the exercise of our intelligence in meditation and in the prayerful study of revealed truth is the ordinary way by which we must dispose ourselves for contemplative prayer. This is very easy to prove. It follows from what we have said about the nature of the human mind and about the conditions under which it labors. We have seen that in the natural order our knowledge proceeds from the intuitive grasp of a few self-evident first principles, through a process of discursive reasoning on the evidence of sense experience, to conclusions in which the mind rests, once again, in intuition. It is the same in the order of faith. When we begin, the first principles of our belief are apt to be vague and cold to us, because we cannot see below their surface. They do not fully engage our interest because we do not even suspect what they contain. We have to study the implications of these truths, exercise our mind on their consequences, proceed step by step to examine what they really mean. As we thus study and meditate on what God has revealed to us of Himself, the growth of truth and faith in our souls brings with it a corresponding growth of love for God, and this love in its turn excites us to greater interest and to a more careful and thorough study of our faith.

Now, as Aristotle somewhere says, when a man is learning to play a harp he has to think of every movement he makes. He is conscious of the distinct effort to find each proper note and to strike the right string. But when he is a proficient player, he no longer is aware of what he is doing with his fingers. His mind is not concerned with each separate movement to be made. His hands move easily over the strings as though by instinct, and the mind of the musician is no longer concentrated on technical details but loses itself in the enjoyment of the music he is drawing from the instrument. In the same way, when we have learned how to meditate, the truths of God present themselves spontaneously to our minds. We do not always have to work them out by discourse: we need only to enjoy them in the deep and satisfying gaze of intuition. And yet this intuition will be a sterile thing if it remains purely speculative. In practice, the soul that has been seeking God by love and finds Him by meditation, feeds its love by gazing on Him. Those who seek Him truly will find that the gaze of the intellect that has reached the perfection of meditation is, itself, singularly unsatisfying. It cries out for more than it has. It is not satisfied with the fruit of study. It seeks the Face of God Himself —but does not know where to turn to find Him.

The fact remains that by acquiring proficiency in meditation we reach a stage in which the truths of God present themselves to our minds without labor and without search. We can see them at a glance. When the mind is capable of these mature intuitions, it is more or less disposed to receive the gift of contemplation, through special inspirations of the Holy Ghost.

2

And now we come to another extremely important point. The man of prayer who has so familiarized himself with the truths of faith in study and meditation that he can call them to mind in a simple intuition *does not automatically become a contemplative by this mere fact alone.*

This should be obvious from experience. Contemplative prayer does not, strictly speaking, consist in a dry glance which comes and goes in a few seconds. It absorbs the mind and will in a prolonged, fruitful, and loving gaze in which the intuition of divine truth does not quickly come to an end but remains with us and gradually floods and pervades our whole being with unsuspected depths of meaning. This intuition holds us by some obscure but inexplicable charm. It captivates us. It keeps us prisoners. It will not allow us to escape from the hidden power that works on the depths of our spirit, even though we may hardly be able to tell what is going on.

If, on the other hand, the mind has reached the term of meditation and can grasp the truth in a simple intuition on the natural level: what happens? There may be a flash of clarity that penetrates the mind for a moment. But *it does not last*. Usually, its effect is not to inspire rest and loving absorption but to *stimulate more reasoning*. It shows the mind new avenues down which it travels, not without a certain excitement. If, however, no further thought is stimulated, the mind simply sees the truth as a whole, in an intuition that is without much life and which exercises no power over it. It sees it in the dry, cold light of familiarity. It can gaze upon it without inspiration for a moment or two. It can even force itself to rest in the cold view of its intuition, in the hope that contemplation "may come." But in actual fact it must be admitted that this is not contemplation at all. Since the soul is *not* in a passive contemplative state it will either become distracted or go to sleep. If it cannot go on reasoning, it should exercise itself simply and without strain in acts of love, or use the words of short, ejaculatory prayers.

John of Saint Thomas, a seventeenth-century Dominican and commentator on the Angelic Doctor, points out
that without a special inspiration from the Holy Ghost,
through one of the contemplative Gifts, contemplative
prayer is impossible. He says:

Bare faith alone leaves the mind in obscurity and consequently
those whose contemplation proceeds solely from an act of faith
fall quickly into boredom and cannot continue for long. And so
for contemplatives who seek to penetrate the mysteries of faith
the Gift of Understanding is necessary, and they must use it.
But those who say they can get along in contemplation with
reason and bare faith have practically no idea of what contemplation really is. They either daydream or fall asleep in their contemplation, because faith alone does not contemplate, it *assents,*
in darkness.[8]

This passage may create a confusion in the minds of some
readers familiar with the language of Saint John of the
Cross, for whom contemplation is always accomplished
in "naked faith." But actually what Saint John of the
Cross means by "pure faith" is faith illuminated by the
Gifts of understanding and wisdom, and not the mere
virtue of faith acting *humano modo.* For, according to
the Thomistic doctrine on the Gifts and virtues, Christian sanctity, which consists essentially in the perfection
of charity supported by the other theological, moral, and
intellectual virtues, cannot in fact be reached unless the
virtues are perfected by the action of the Holy Ghost
through His Gifts.

The virtues themselves can be defective for two reasons
—either because of the subject in which they function, or
because of an intrinsic limitation in the virtue itself. To
say that the virtues fall short of perfection "because of
the subject in which they function" is just a technical

way of saying that a man may fail to become a saint by not practicing enough virtue. This defect is remedied by a more generous cooperation with ordinary grace and more wholehearted practice of the virtues. When the "subject" pulls himself together and goes into action with the proper degree of fervor, this defect disappears. But, according to Saint Thomas, the second insufficiency, inherent in the very character of the virtues as such, can only be remedied by other habits, new "fixtures" so to speak, with a special function in our interior life.

Faith, then, on its own level as a virtue, is a simple assent to authority proposing a truth to be believed. It does not contemplate the truth, it does not plumb the depths of that truth with wonder and understanding: it just says "yes." This act of assent, however heroic it may be under certain conditions, only takes a moment. True, the assent may revolutionize a man's entire life. But bare faith alone remains a cold-blooded assent to authority. Such an assent cannot, of itself, produce the loving absorption and intimate understanding of the truth which is contemplation.

Naturally, one may say that the submission to divine authority which brings adult converts to the faith is, in practice, very often accompanied by a deep religious experience of peace, a sense of the discovery of totally new horizons and the awareness of a profound psychic transformation. One literally becomes a "new man" under the touch of grace—and this transformation may well be the object of an experience bordering on true mysticism or at least analogous to infused contemplation. But the very reason for this is that in such conversions faith is intensified in its action by strong affective elements, espe-

cially of charity, and even by inspirations of the Gifts of
the Holy Ghost which are all present in the soul from
the moment of its justification. But the very fact that
all conversions do not have this experiential element and
that, indeed, many conversions are hardheaded and "cold,"
lends weight to the Thomist argument which distinguishes bare faith from faith illumined by the Gifts.
And I may add, parenthetically, that the convert whose
faith is emotionally "cold" and is not inflamed with an
element of quasi-mystical experience is not therefore less
virtuous or less pleasing in the sight of God. It may, in
fact, require great charity to allow oneself to be led, in
spite of temperamental or hereditary disinclination, by
force of rational demonstration alone, to an unemotional
acceptance of the faith.

### 3

We have been introduced, in these last pages, to the
Gift of Understanding. This is one of the three Gifts of
the Holy Ghost which are ordered primarily to perfecting
the spirit of man in contemplation and bringing him to
mystical union with God. We have also seen that the
function of reason in the degrees of prayer in which
the intelligence is still free and bound to contribute its
own share of co-operation with the action of the Holy
Ghost, is to keep the whole soul attuned to the special
inspirations by which the Divine Spirit prepares the soul
for mystical prayer and union.

Therefore, one of the most important tasks of the intelligence, as it waits on the frontier of mysical prayer, will
be to recognize the messengers that come to it from God,

and especially those in the service of the Gifts of Knowledge, Understanding, and Wisdom. If reason is to communicate with these secret agents sent by God, it must speak their language. It must be prepared to establish contact with them. It must be in possession of a password.

This contact is established by the ascetic preparation of the soul. Detached from the desire of created things, the spirit is ready for the inspirations of the Gift of Knowledge, which shows us created things as they truly are, in relation to God. Exercised in meditation on the truths of faith, the intelligence is ready for the pure intuitions of the Gift of Understanding which penetrates the mysteries of faith without hesitation, doubt, or error. Finally, on fire with the love for God's Truth, the will and intelligence together are ready for that experience of God which brings the soul to know Him in His infinite goodness through the experience of union in the Gift of Wisdom.

It is especially important to consider the role assigned in the contemplative life to the Gift of Understanding. John of Saint Thomas has some interesting pages on the subject, and they intimately concern us here, since the inspirations of the Gift of Understanding enlighten the intelligence of man, perfecting it in faith by giving it a superhuman insight into the realities which faith accepts in blind submission to authority.

The function of the Gift of Understanding is to purify the soul of all formal error in matters of faith and to dispose the mind to make clean-cut and accurate judgment as to what is and is not of faith. John of Saint Thomas spends much time in defining with the utmost theological accuracy the sense in which the inspirations of the Gift of Understanding lead us to a judgment in matters of faith.

One conclusion of his is particularly important for us here. He distinguishes the modes of judgment proper to the three contemplative gifts. The judgments made by knowledge and wisdom are analytical: they are based on the knowledge of causes and effects. But the judgments made by the Gift of Understanding are simple and discriminative. By an interior instinct and impulsion of the Holy Spirit, the mind, enlightened through the Gift of Understanding, plunges to the invisible spiritual realities which are conveyed to it under sensible images and concepts which fall short of the immense perfection of the Godhead. Therefore, as John of Saint Thomas explains:

It follows that the Gift of Understanding is particularly useful for contemplation because by it the Holy Spirit sharpens the intelligence and makes it more subtle and enables it to press forward in light, not in darkness, even though it advances in the divine Night, that is to say when its course leads it through the obscurity of negation. Transformed from power to power by the Spirit of the Lord, this Gift penetrates, by contemplation, into His glory. The most striking evidence of this is had when the light of the Holy Ghost rises upon the soul and makes it realize that God is exalted above every created thing. . . . It is proper to the Gift of Understanding to raise up the heart of man and lead it to a high sense and knowledge of the things of God penetrating and understanding that the things of God exceed every comparison. And by this lifting up of the heart, the heart itself is not exalted—as happens in the case of acquired knowledge, for knowledge puffeth up and the proud heart goes before a fall—but by the Gift of Understanding the heart is lifted up to exalt and praise God, and not its own self.[9]

Clearly, then, it is the Gift of Understanding that man's intelligence must turn to in order to become perfect in that interior discrimination which is its chief office in the contemplative life. The special inspirations of the Divine Spirit can never, strictly speaking, be merited by us or acquired. Reason can and must dispose itself for the reception of these inspirations, as we have seen. And even though we may have the best of intentions, the wrong use of our faculties, especially at the time of prayer, can completely spoil the delicate work of these inspirations on which both our progress and our perfection depend.

We have seen that the Night of Sense and the Prayer of Quiet are a stage of crucial importance in the mystical ascent. Many arrive at this degree of prayer, which is the borderland of mystical contemplation, but do not advance any further. The reason is that they do not know how to co-operate with the subtle movements of the Divine Spirit and they frustrate His work in their souls in several different ways.

A few souls let the gifts of God fall out of their hands by complete inertia and inactivity. Many more trample the delicate new growth of prayer underfoot with a great deal of useless activity. Most souls, even if they happen to keep their activity within bounds, nevertheless waste their time and efforts doing the wrong thing.

Perhaps the most common fault is that too many contemplatives remain tangled up in externals. They are so busy concentrating on means to arrive at contemplation that they have no time for contemplation itself. Or else they are so occupied with particular ways of mortifying themselves that they never get free from preoccupation with themselves. Yet this freedom is the purpose of all mortification. In short, the secret of progress in the interior life is to escape from ourselves as quickly and as completely as possible and give ourselves entirely to God. This can generally be done quite simply, and without a multitude of techniques and observances, if we will only attune ourselves to the voice of His Spirit and take care to give God not what He desires of somebody else, in some other situation, but precisely what He asks of *us*. In doing this, we will give Him our whole selves. He asks nothing more of us, for as soon as we give ourselves completely to Him, He gives Himself completely to us.

# CHAPTER XIV

# Intelligence
# in the Prayer of Quiet

Saint John of the Cross and Saint Teresa of Ávila have both left us detailed studies of the ways of contemplative prayer, and better than any other mystics they have described the practical details of our co-operation with the Spirit of God in the degree of prayer which most interests us here. They both agree that in the Night of Sense, and more still in the Prayer of Quiet, the faculties of the soul are in some measure passive. But they also agree that these faculties are still free to act of their own accord and that consequently they are capable of either helping or hindering the work of God. And they both agree that in order to help the action of grace our faculties must engage in some very simplified activity which, at the actual moment of passive prayer, consists in nothing more than the effort to keep themselves passive. Outside the time of prayer they must do more. But in any event, it takes mortification to maintain the soul in a state of alert receptivity during the first stages of passive prayer when grace acts almost unnoticeably on the soul and when the imagination is drawn away by many distractions.

Here is a summary of one important chapter in Saint Teresa's life. It tells us what our soul can do and may do as well as what it must do and must not do in the Prayer of Quiet.[1]

The saint first reminds us of the nature of the Prayer of Quiet. This "beginning of all blessings" and the "pledge of great things to come" is the first definite taste of mystical prayer. For, while it is possible that infused contemplation may begin during that arid part of the Night of Sense in which God's presence is not felt, nevertheless the Prayer of Quiet very evidently absorbs the soul in a state of passive recollection and floods our whole being with an indescribable interior peace flowing from a profoundly intimate and actual sense of the Presence of God. The dark water of the soul has suddenly been touched with sunlight from heaven. Suffused with the clarity of God, it awakens to a new life, discovers itself to be a different being, rests in an unknown joy. And yet this sense of God is not sharply defined, for the soul is still dazzled by His light. The spirit rests in deep tranquillity, rocking gently like a ship anchored on a quiet harbor while the sun rises upon a new world through noiseless and translucent mist.

So much for the Prayer of Quiet. The business about the ship is mine, not Saint Teresa's. Perhaps it has obscured the issue. The expressions she uses at the beginning of the particular chapter I am considering suffice to convey her meaning. They are: "quiet," "recollection," "satisfaction," "peace," "very great joy," "repose of the faculties," "sweet delight." William Blake knew of the Prayer of Quiet and thought of it as a moonlit night.

Very well. In this prayer, the faculties are passive. Yet they can act.

They are passive. That is to say, they can do nothing

either to acquire this blessing or to keep it. It is a pure gift of God. It is not produced by any deliberate technique. Our efforts can only dispose us to receive it as a gift. Hence the Prayer of Quiet must be sedulously distinguished from natural analogues of mystical experience which can be acquired by man's efforts. The soul can become *recollected* by its own efforts. It can become "centered" in a deeply satisfying and fruitful experience of rest. Even human love can sometimes produce this effect, although human love is far more apt to produce restlessness than rest. The soul that has acquired a high degree of ascetic emptiness and recollection can, in this state, produce a willed intellectual reflection on the metaphysical being of God present within itself. This may sometimes be heightened by a natural inspiration of the kind we have referred to—a metaphysical intuition of being.

In the Prayer of Quiet, the experience is something more. The whole soul feels itself to be enlightened, vitalized, lifted up to a new plane of being, delivered to some extent from material limitations. It has an extraordinary sense of lightness and freedom, like a boy who has just been liberated from a classroom or a bird that has got out of its cage. But beyond and above all this is the Divine Reality in which this experience takes place. The soul has not arrived at God by thought or reflection. It does not perceive Him in any image or concept. Yet it is "in Him." It is swimming in His light. He envelops it like a cloud of gold. And the most essential factor of this experience is the soul's discovery of God in His immanence and His transcendence. Everything that the soul experiences flows from this central mystery that God is in all things and in the soul, and that He is nevertheless infinitely above the soul and above all things.

And now: more of Saint Teresa. She makes fun of people who have tasted this pleasure and try to recapture it by their own efforts. But she makes fun of them very tenderly because, after all, she has been through it all herself. Beginners in prayer get this wonderful interior feeling. They no longer dare to move. They stay transfixed, with closed eyes, scarcely daring to breathe, for fear it might go away. Or else, as soon as the spark of love is kindled in their souls, they start piling on wood— by useless reasoning and lofty considerations. This immediately smothers the fire. Saint Teresa sums up her opinion of the uselessness of our own efforts to acquire this degree of prayer:

What a strange kind of belief it is that when God has willed that a toad should fly, He should wait for it to do so by its own efforts. . . . Our souls are weighed down by the earth and by a thousand impediments and the fact that they want to fly is of no help to them; for, though flying comes more naturally to them than to a toad, they are so completely sunk in the mire that they have lost the ability.[2]

## 2

And now: what do the faculties do in the Prayer of Quiet? We must make a distinction. When the soul is actually engaged in the Prayer of Quiet, the faculties have one kind of function; outside the time of prayer they have another. Furthermore, the grace of quietude has a different effect on different faculties.

First, let us look at the faculties of the soul when it is in the Prayer of Quiet. The exterior senses are recollected.

This is generally the fruit of active recollection, but is intensified by the action of the Holy Spirit upon the depths of the soul. The interior senses—especially the imagination and memory—may be recollected or they may be quite distracted. When the soul is deeply absorbed in passive recollection, the imagination and memory are almost entirely inactive. Or if they act at all, their movement is no longer noticed in the depths of the soul.

Sometimes, however, these faculties may be distressingly busy. The same applies to the intelligence. Sometimes it rests in a reverent appreciation of the fact that the will is receiving news of God that is more direct than the understanding itself can yet attain to. But at other times reason and imagination can make a lot of noise. Our exterior soul preaches sermons, reforms monasteries, reproves heretics, passes in review the faults of other contemplatives, evolves complex theories of the interior life, undertakes the spiritual direction of whole convents of nuns, urges bishops to lead a more prayerful life, and finally itself becomes Pope to govern the whole Church with universal acclaim. While all this is going on, the will, hiding in a bomb-proof shelter in the center of the soul, clings with extreme distress and desperation to the hope that God will not evade her entirely and leave her alone with the arguments of the fatuous monster outside the door. Under such conditions, it will be understood that there is very little of the Prayer of Quiet in the true sense, which implies sensible peace and rest in the presence of God. If we allow that the will is praying at all, and that it is passive, then it is suffering that arid quietude which belongs to the Night of Sense properly so called. As quietude grows on us and takes fuller possession of the will, this faculty gains a fuller command over the others. But here is the interesting thing: it controls them *passively*. That is to say, in its direction of the rest of the soul the will itself is *passively moved by God*. This point is very important. It offers the only possible justification for the fact that the will, in this as well as in other degrees of mystical prayer, holds sway over the reason. Naturally speaking, the intelligence of man is the noblest faculty in his soul because it is normally deputed to guide the will by the light of God.

Let us look more closely at the will in the state of quietude. The will is the faculty which is most completely passive in this state of prayer. It is by the will that God's love lays hold on the soul here, and draws it to Himself, without any of the other faculties quite realizing how all this is taking place. This explains two things: first, the fact that the soul can be at the same time united with God in passive recollection and still suffer distractions, and second, the fact that the soul cannot form for itself any clear or adequate idea of how this union takes place. Why? Because God has passively united the soul to Himself, not through the intelligence but through a blind faculty: the will.

Here is what Saint Teresa has to say on the subject:

The soul has such satisfaction in God that although the other two faculties may be distracted, yet, since *the will is in union with God* for as long as the recollection lasts, its quiet and repose are not lost, but the will gradually brings the understanding and memory back to a state of recollection again. For although the will is not yet completely absorbed it is so well occupied, without knowing how, that, whatever the efforts made by the understanding and memory, they cannot deprive it of its contentment and rejoicing: indeed, *without any labor on its part,* it helps to prevent this little spark of love from being quenched.[8]

Here is a paradox! The will which, being passive, is "doing nothing" is, in fact, doing everything in the Prayer of Quiet. The other faculties, which are still active, are in fact doing nothing and less than nothing because their activity is a nuisance and tends to impede the work of God. But, as the saint points out, thanks to the passive action of the will moved directly by the inspirations of God, the undesirable activity of these other faculties is kept under control and does not have too bad an effect. The solution of this apparent problem comes from the fact that the will, when passively moved by God, is in fact acting in a much higher and more perfect sense than when it is moved only by itself. Also, since God is infinitely beyond every limitation, when the will becomes the prisoner of His love and is, so to speak, withheld from doing anything but His will, it then at last becomes perfectly free with the freedom of God Himself! *Ubi Spiritus Domini, ibi libertas!*

Nevertheless, we have seen that in the Prayer of Quiet the will is not in fact completely captivated by God. It does not become completely powerless to act for itself. It retains its natural tendency to follow the guidance of the intelligence. If the reason and imagination, by force of persuasion, can convince the will that their own natural lights are somehow preferable to the obscure and tenuous consolations it is receiving in secret, they may win it over to their own side. Saint John of the Cross asserts without hesitation that, as soon as this happens, supernatural and passive prayer comes to an end, even though a strong sense of consolation and a specious feeling of passivity may persist in the will. We shall discuss some texts of Saint John of the Cross on this point, in a moment.

This brings us once more to the truth upon which I have been insisting for the last three chapters: that even in passive prayer, the progress of the soul and its co-operation with God depend to a great extent upon the supernatural discretion exercised by our intelligence. Here are proofs of that thesis from Saint Teresa.

# 3

When a contemplative has reached the Prayer of Quiet, what must he do with his understanding?

First: in general, that is to say, *outside the time of actual absorption* in passive prayer, the intelligence has the following important things to do. It must recognize, says Saint Teresa, the great gift God has bestowed upon the soul. It must realize the importance of living up to the favor it has been granted. It must continue to exercise itself, very simply, in self-knowledge, that is to say, in humility, yet at the same time it must produce motives of confidence and stimulate the will to desire progress in this way of prayer. It will recognize, says the saint, that this grace is the "pledge of great things to come." It must also humbly understand, as she says, that many other souls are now depending on it, for God does not give these graces to us for ourselves alone. He pours out His joy upon the whole world through the chosen, though perhaps obscure, vessels He has seen fit to fill to overflowing with the wine of interior prayer. Above all, the intelligence must show the will the importance of persevering in prayer and self-denial and of not returning, as Saint Teresa says, in a time-honored ascetical cliché, to "the fleshpots."

Much more important is the discretion and good behavior of our reason *at the actual time of passive prayer.* I quote Saint Teresa herself:

What the soul has to do at these seasons of quiet is merely to go softly and make no noise. By noise I mean going about with the understanding in search of many words and reflections with which to give thanks for this benefit and piling up its sins and imperfections so as to make oneself realize one does not deserve it. . . .

The soul will lose a great deal if it is not careful about this, especially if it has a lively understanding, with the result that when it begins to hold discourse with itself and think out reflections it will soon begin to fancy that it is doing something worth while if its discourses and reflections are at all clever.

Pursuing the comparison of the "little spark" which she uses all through this chapter, Saint Teresa warns the reason against piling on too much wood. However, it can do something on its own part to help build up the fire:

A few little straws laid down with humility (and they will be less than straws if it is we who lay them down) are more to the point here and of more use in kindling the fire than any amount of wood—that is, of the most learned reasoning—which will put it out in a moment.

There is one consideration above all that the reason must use at the time of prayer: it must realize that this is a gift of God and recognize its own incapacity to add anything substantial to the work that is being done. This sentence of Saint Teresa is classic:

All that the reason has to do in this state is to understand that there is no reason, save His goodness alone, why God should grant us so great a favor, and to realize that we are very near to Him. . . .[4]

Nevertheless, prayer of petition is not excluded even from the moments of passive absorption in God. These petitions remain wordless and simple, but they reach out to embrace the needs of souls in the world and of all who depend upon us for the grace of God. Finally, meditation is never abandoned entirely by the soul that has reached this state. He may sometimes have to return to formal discursive meditation, but only outside the time of passive prayer. Saint John of the Cross agrees. In any case, one will always have before his eyes the simple idea of Christ's Cross and remember that the only way to divine union is the narrow road that Jesus traveled before us.

A wrong idea of the function of reason in the beginnings of the mystical life would lead inevitably to spiritual stagnation. Under the pretext of remaining in a state of passive receptivity without directing any formal acts of love or understanding toward God, the contemplative would let himself be carried along by habit and routine. If he were to some extent a virtuous man, he would be able to go on for some time acting virtuously out of sheer force of habit. But soon these virtuous actions would become hollow. They would be merely external, without any interior fervor of will. The condition of our nature in its present state makes it obnoxious for any man formally to renounce the active pursuit of perfection at any time. Passive graces from God only modify the character of man's activity, elevating it to a higher plane and giving more and more of the initiative to God Himself. But God will not ordinarily grant these passive inspirations to souls that are not consumed with a constant and generous desire to co-operate actively with His ordinary grace.

It is true that spiritual inertia can bring, to certain

souls, an illusory sense of peace. But this peace is just as unhealthy as the quiescence of a stagnant pond. The real rest to which man is called by God and to which the highest faculties of his nature urge him to aspire, is paradoxically found in the highest activity of those faculties. Man is said to "rest" in perfect union with the knowledge and love of God because here there no longer remains any obstacle to impede the action of his spirit in God, and there is no more weariness because labor is no more.

The Flemish mystic Blessed John Ruysbroeck had some powerful things to say about the Beghards and other precursors of the Quietist heresy. His statement, though in an entirely different context, makes one think of what John of Saint Thomas said about the impracticality of a contemplation that was not inspired by the Holy Ghost, but procured by what one might call "stalling" on an act of faith. Ruysbroeck says:

It is true that as soon as a man empties himself and abstracts from all images in the sensible part of his soul, and becomes idle, remaining inactive in his superior faculties, he enters into a natural state of repose. . . . But the man who really loves God cannot rest here, for charity and the inward action of the grace of God do not remain idle. . . . The interior man cannot bear to stay for a long time closed up in himself in a state of merely natural repose. . . . This kind of repose is not permitted. . . . It brings man into a condition of complete blindness and to the ignorance of all knowledge . . . he collapses into himself and loses the power to act . . . it is a sterile idleness . . . in which he forgets not only himself but God and everything else besides, especially when he is called upon to do a little work!

Ruysbroeck goes on to show in the clearest language that this inertia quickly leads to the opposite pole of the spiritual life from contemplation and divine union because it

makes a man incapable of receiving the light of truth by
confirming him in stubborn self-will. Where the intelligence and will are completely stultified, the spiritual life
ceases to be possible at all.

Without any inward and loving attention to God, this man will
be capable of the worst errors, for he turns away from God in
order to concentrate on himself with natural love. All he is looking
for is consolation, sweetness and satisfaction. . . . Everything
he does is done for his own personal interests, not for the honor
of God. . . . His life is guided by natural self-love and therefore
he is entrenched in his own will and incapable of self-forgetful-
ness.[5]

The only way a contemplative can avoid this disastrous
mistake is to use the intelligence God has given him in
the service of faith and love. He must possess the discretion and supernatural insight which come from humble
and constant attention to the inspirations of divine grace
in his soul. It is not always an easy task to distinguish the
inspirations of grace from false natural inclinations that
bear a man away from God. Since the Holy Spirit leads
the contemplative soul into passivity, it does seem, in fact,
that our faculties are sometimes tending to inactivity and
inertia. Only a soul that has achieved maturity in contemplative prayer can quickly and easily tell the difference
between stagnant inactivity of the faculties and the fruitful, passive motivation of the mind and will by the inspirations of the Holy Ghost.

A child who rides for the first time on a train by night
sees nothing going by outside the windows and therefore
complains that the train has stopped. Sometimes a train
traveling through darkness, or in a tunnel, gives one the
feeling of traveling backwards. The same thing happens

to a soul that is visited by darkness and interior trial. So, too, when two trains are together in a station and one begins to move, the people in the other feel as if they were the ones who were moving. This applies to the spiritual life also. A contemplative who has come to a standstill in the midst of a fervent community can imagine that *he* is moving and that the others are standing still. The basis of his error is the progress that is being made by his companions.

The function of discretion in the beginnings of mystical prayer is to discover the true way that lies between extremes. Reason guided by faith must be on the alert and give the will sufficient light to reject either impulses to overactivity or tendencies to sloth.

Now, in making such judgments as these, it is often fatal to apply broad general rules indiscriminately to all souls. Such rules are necessary: but in actual practice, the direction of contemplatives, while dominated before all else by the principles of sane and Catholic theology, is also an "art" even more than a science. This means that the director must possess a special flair for solving particular problems in the light of their own peculiar circumstances. He cannot do this unless he himself possesses some experience of contemplative prayer. Activity which would be useless and even harmful for one soul would be quite insufficient for another. And the same soul will need to work more with its faculties at one time than at another. In a word, what would be good in one set of circumstances would be evil in another, and each case must be judged, with great humility and circumspection, on its own proper merits. That is why it is so dangerous to let contemplative souls fall into the hands of directors who have pet theories about the spiritual life, who are passionately devoted to one side or another in some disputed speculative question, and who chop or stretch their penitents in order to make them fit, by violence, into the Procrustean bed of their own cherished opinion.

# 4

One of the most delicate questions to be decided in the contemplative life is, as a matter of fact, whether or not a soul may be considered as receiving graces of passive or infused contemplation. Many matters concerning the conduct of this soul will depend on the answer to this question. There is a general agreement among the best theological and ascetic authorities in this field, that when a soul reaches contemplation, its discursive activity, meditations, particular formal affective acts of will, and so on must all be greatly simplified and reduced. As a matter of cold fact, they also admit that when contemplation is clearly passive, or infused, the activity of the faculties is at least to some extent impeded by the action of God.

Unfortunately, this problem of the borderline between active and passive states of prayer, between what is "acquired" and "infused" is the subject of very hot theoretical debate. Those who are impatient with the opinion that says "infused" contemplation begins very soon and that therefore meditation ought to be dropped quite early in the spiritual life are apt to vent their wrath on their poor penitents and force some of them to go on meditating and producing much more activity than is good for them when they are fairly well advanced. Those, on the other hand, who hold that almost any kind of aridity at prayer is a sign

of the infused action of God will risk letting some beginners waste their time in daydreaming and idleness and so
jeopardize their chances of progress.

However, I would like to point out that even profound
differences in doctrinal opinion do not necessarily imply
an equally great divergence in the practical paths to be
followed in forming souls. I am merely quoting the
thoughts of an eminent Jesuit theologian of our time,
Father J. de Guibert,[6] and of one of his disciples. Father
Lebreton says that, no matter what may be the views of
the various schools regarding the proximate call to infused
contemplation, they all recognize in practice that infused
contemplation is a gift of God and the best way for a
man to dispose himself for this gift is renunciation and
humility. All equally agree that as long as the soul finds
profit and peace in the ways of meditation and affective
prayer, these should not be dropped. Therefore, in practice,
no matter what theoretical views a director may hold, he
will not encourage an interest in mysticism which produces a proud contempt for the "ordinary ways" of the
spiritual life and weakens the soul in its mortification and
devotion to prayer. But he will place no obstacle in the
way of a soul who possesses deep humility and a fervent
desire to reach union with God, and who is also strongly
attracted to silence and solitude and to simple wordless
forms of prayer.

In actual practice, the opinion of Saint John of the
Cross, who is recognized as the greatest of the Catholic
mystical theologians, is the most authoritative guide in
deciding when a soul is ready to drop discursive meditation, for the time being at least, and hold itself in a
state of receptivity in which it is largely passive under

the secret guidance of divine grace. Saint John's three signs of the soul called to contemplative prayer are well known.[7] We need only run through them quite briefly here.

Two of these signs are negative, one is positive.

First sign: the inability to meditate. Saint John is precise. He is not simply speaking of a soul that cannot meditate, but of one which was once able to make fruitful discursive meditations and now can no longer do so. The use of the mind and imagination at prayer used to be easy and pleasant. Now it has become intolerably hard and wearisome. This sign by itself alone means nothing.

Second sign: lack of interest in *particular* objects of thought. The emphasis is on the word particular. The soul is very keenly interested in something, or rather "Some One," Who remains, nevertheless, undefined. The soul fails to satisfy this positive interest by directing its thoughts to particular things. The mind and will find no rest and no satisfaction in anything on earth or even in heaven. By this last remark, I mean that the soul is no longer satisfied with any idea of God or of heaven that can be represented to it in the imagination. In other words, the soul has come face to face with the distinction between God in Himself and God as He is contained in our concepts of Him. This can be the source of great anxiety and distress, because we naturally tend to identify God with our ideas of Him, and the fact that we are no longer able to feel any sensible affection for a mental image or idea of God persuades us that we have ceased to love God Himself. People who do not understand this distinction often break down completely under the strain of forcing themselves to feel sensible devotion for some particular representation of God in their minds, or for some statue or holy picture that used to fill them with spiritual consolation.

The third sign is the most important of all. For without it we cannot decide that a soul is called to passive prayer merely on the basis of the other two, which could arise, for instance, from tepidity or bad health.

The third sign is a positive attraction for solitary contemplative prayer. I will let Saint John of the Cross himself describe the attraction:

The third and surest sign is that the soul takes pleasure in being alone, and waits with loving attentiveness upon God, without making any particular meditation, in inward peace and quietness and rest, and without acts and exercises of the faculties—memory and understanding and will—at least without discursive acts, that is without passing from one thing to another; the soul is alone with an attentiveness and knowledge, general and loving as we said, but without any particular understanding, and adverting not to what it is contemplating.[8]

This is almost the same condition that was described above by Saint Teresa. However, Saint John of the Cross observes the soul in an earlier and more arid stage of the same prayer in which there is almost no consciousness of pleasure and sweetness in this passive attention to God in the "cloud of unknowing." Saint John of the Cross here only excludes a certain mode of activity: discursive acts. The soul is still engaged in something quite definite. Attention is a precise activity of the mind. It implies also activity of the will. Knowledge is an act of the intelligence. The difference is not between activity and inactivity but between two kinds of action—between reasoning and intuition. The soul gazes with the desire of love into the darkness where God is hidden and gradually loses sight of every other object.

Everything that Saint John of the Cross has written about this state of prayer forces us to conclude that reason has an important function in it: that which we have described as the discernment of spirits. It would be useless for the Saint to tell contemplatives how to conduct themselves in this kind of prayer if they could not understand his instructions and use their minds and wills to put them into effect. And, as we have seen, the first thing the reason must do is resist an impulse to analyze its condition discursively and make long speeches about it. When this kind of prayer gets a stronger grip on the soul it becomes sweet, consoling, and even at times inebriating. Here too reason must be careful. For, as Saint John points out:

When such persons begin to be recollected the devil is accustomed to offer them ample material for distractions, forming conceptions and words by suggestion in their understanding, and then corrupting and deceiving it most subtly with things that have a great appearance of truth.[9]

In another extremely interesting passage, the Saint goes on to say:

In this way with hardly any trouble the devil works the most serious injuries, causing the soul to lose great riches and dragging it forth with the tiniest bait like a fish from the depths of the pure waters of the spirit where it had no support or foothold and was engulfed and immersed in God.[10]

The Spirit of God acts quite differently in the soul He has called to contemplative prayer, inclining it to solitude, simplicity, and peace. Here are some of the passages in which Saint John of the Cross describes the inspirations of the Divine Spirit.

The Spirit of God has this characteristic in the soul in which He dwells, that He forthwith inclines it toward ignorance [i.e. of "particular things"] and unwillingness to know the business of other people, especially things that are not to its profit. For the Spirit of God is recollected within the soul itself and turns to it rather that He may draw it forth from extraneous things than in order to lead it among them. And thus the soul remains in complete unknowing with respect to the things that it knew formerly.[11]

The saint is simply repeating what he has already told us in the "second sign" of the beginning of contemplation. The movement of divine inspiration inclines the mind away from particular and definite knowledge of God in concepts which seem to delimit His perfections. It creates a distaste for representations of Him which are powerless to do justice to His infinite reality. But, still more than this, it makes the soul mortally weary of the thousand trifling curiosities and passing events which engage the minds of men. One might collect a large number of texts from the Carmelite mystics and string them together to form a sort of anthology on the first stages of contemplative prayer. But I will not do so, for beautiful as they are, they are all very much the same. Rather than quote them all word for word, I need only recall that the "three signs" of Saint John of the Cross contain all the essentials of this state of prayer. They are sufficient to indicate how the Holy Ghost "anoints" the soul with the unction of its special graces, "sending after it the fragrance of His ointments wherewith He draws the soul and causes it to run after Him." Saint John of the Cross goes on to remind us that mystical contemplation has no other end than to make us perfect in the theological virtues: especially in charity.

These ointments are His divine inspirations and touches which
. . . are ordered and ruled with respect to the perfection of the
law of God and of faith, in which perfection the soul must ever
draw nearer and nearer to God . . . until it comes to such a
delicate and pure preparation that it merits union with God and
substantial transformation in all its faculties.[12]

He repeats what he has told us, in substance, in the "three
signs": "God here secretly and quietly infuses into the
soul loving knowledge and wisdom without any intervention of specific acts." [13] In a beautiful sentence, the
saint describes how the soul responds to the delicate inspirations "of the Spirit of Divine Wisdom, the loving,
tranquil, lonely, peaceful, sweet ravisher of the spirit."

At times the soul will feel itself to be tenderly and serenely ravished and wounded, knowing not by whom, nor whence, nor
how, since the Spirit communicates Himself without any act on
the part of the soul.[14]

This contemplation is a paradise of peace, interior liberty,
spiritual growth. The soul is at last clean not only in its
substance, which is suffused with the light of sanctifying
grace, but also in its faculties, which are now delivered
from base absorption in all that is accidental and transient.
It rediscovers its own essential dignity, and rises above its
former slavery to desire. But what is much more than
this, the soul is beginning to move in a new world, a
"new creation," something that transcends the level of
its own nature, the hanging gardens of contemplation,
suspended halfway between earth and heaven.

But notice: Saint John has said: "the Spirit communicates itself without any act on the part of the soul." True.
The touches of mystical grace which now begin to be
experiences by the soul have no dependence on any activity

of our faculties. Yet this, as we have clearly seen, does not mean that all work of the intelligence and will has suddenly come to an end. Saint John of the Cross is even more definite than Saint Teresa in stating exactly what must be done by our faculties in this "Prayer of Quiet." Incidentally, he seems to demand much less of us than Saint Teresa, but remember that she was considering the whole life of the contemplative, in prayer or out. Saint John is chiefly talking about what is to be done at the time of prayer. The activity he requires of the soul must be elicited by the understanding and will together. It is very simple. It has three stages or "moments."

First: a remote general disposition to receive the inspirations of passive or mystical prayer. The "chief care of the soul will be to see that it places no obstacle in the way of the guide, who is the Holy Ghost." [15] It must choose a good spiritual director. That is very important in the eyes of Saint John of the Cross. For the rest, this task of "removing obstacles" from the path of divine grace resolves itself into the "discretion" or "discernment of spirits" to which we have so often alluded. The soul will be careful not to mistake the impulses of self-love or the suggestions of the Devil for inspirations of the Holy Ghost.

Second step: as soon as the mind is recollected in prayer and the will is centered upon God and able to rest in Him, there remains but one very simple activity to be performed. The soul keeps itself in an attitude of "simple knowledge or awareness," so as to receive the infused knowledge and love which come to it from God. This is an activity, indeed. But it is so simple, and already so much dominated by the absorbing action of the Divine Spirit, that Saint John of the Cross does not hesitate to contrast it with the "natural activity" of the soul, which he forbids at this time. "Natural" activity is simply that discursive series of acts which are proper to our reasoning minds. The proper attitude of the soul is described by the saint in these terms:

In order to receive [these graces] the soul must be quite dis-encumbered and at ease, peaceful and serene, according to the manner of God; like the air which receives greater illumination and heat from the sun when it is pure and cleansed and at rest.[16]

Finally, the third moment. As soon as there is a positive indication (which the soul must recognize by experience) that it is being passively drawn by God into deep interior silence and solitude and absorption, the faculties abandon all activity whatever. They no longer need to keep themselves in a state of simple awareness. They relinquish even this plainest of all acts and let themselves be drawn away in the sweet and powerful gravitation by which God quietly submerges them in the darkness of His love.

At that moment, the consciousness of our false, everyday self falls away from us like a soiled garment, heavy with moisture and with mire. The "deep self," which lies too deep for reflection and analysis, falls free and plummets into the abyss of God's freedom and of His peace. Now there is no more advertence to what goes on within us, still less to what happens around us. We are too far below the surfaces where reflection was once possible. Sunken in God, the soul knows Him alone, and only knows Him obscurely. No longer realizing what it knows, or what it loves, or even what it is, the spirit is carried away into eternity like a dead leaf in the November wind.

When this comes to pass, and the soul is conscious of being led into silence, and hearkens, it must forget even that loving awareness of which I have spoken, so that it may remain free for that which is desired of it; for it must exercise that awareness only when it is not conscious of being brought into solitude or rest or forgetfulness or attentiveness of the spirit which is always accompanied by a certain interior absorption.[17]

I do not pause to comment on this extremely interesting passage, which enumerates several different ways in which the faculties are carried off into passive prayer. There is a great difference between "forgetfulness" and "attentiveness of the spirit"; also this passive "attentiveness" is something more intense and more pure than the "simple knowledge and awareness" which was actively elicited by the soul itself under the attraction of grace. In any case, the activity of reason has here ceased. The faculties have been taken over by God, though not completely absorbed by Him. Mind and will have nothing to do but rest in forgetfulness of themselves and of all things.

# PART THREE

# DOCTRINE AND EXPERIENCE

# CHAPTER XV

# The Mirror
# of Silvered Waters

We cannot completely understand Saint John of the Cross or Saint Gregory of Nyssa unless we remember that their mysticism is centered upon Christ. Even though their mystical theology be apophatic, their supraconceptual experience of God cannot in fact be achieved without Christ. What is more, it cannot even be arrived at without a concept of Christ as the Incarnate Word of God. This is essential to Christian mysticism. "No man comes to the Father but by Christ." (John 14:6.)

Some writers outside the Church pay the great Christian mystics the homage of a certain respect. The saints themselves would not have thought themselves flattered by it. Saint John of the Cross is treated by some as if he lived as a pantheist behind a Christian façade. This accords with the theory that the great mystics of every religion live together at the summit of their own Olympus, far above the mists of religious doctrine, priesthood, liturgy, sacrifice, church discipline, and all the other tiresome things which separate the common run of men into religious groups. The Christian mystics of "Night" are supposed, in practice, to have left Christ outside the gates of their own contemplative Eden. Ideas of an Incarnate Word

are all very well for simple people. Devotion to the Cruci-
fied Jesus, meditation on His Sacred Humanity are thus
supposed to bear the same relation to apophatic Christian
mysticism as does *Bakhti yoga* to the purer *Raja Yoga* of
India. *Bakhti yoga* is a respectable though admittedly
inferior mysticism in which the adept arrives at union with
the Absolute conceived under a personal form.

This amusing theory can easily be arrived at if one
neglects to read the most important chapters in Saint John
of the Cross and passes over his most fundamental doctrines as if they did not exist.

In actual fact, the mysticism of the Spanish Carmelites
is not centered upon Christ considered as a Divine Person
with an assumed Human Nature that no longer needs to
be mentioned in the best mystical circles, but upon Jesus
Christ, true God and true man, *Deum verum de Deo vero,*
consubstantial with the Father and born in time of the
Virgin Mary, Who died on the Cross to redeem mankind from sin and Who, in His risen glory, ascended into
heaven, taking our human nature with Him so that
we are all at least potentially enthroned in heaven with
Him. *Consedere fecit in caelestibus in Christo Jesu.*[1]

This much at least is required to make a mystical doctrine Christian. But the teaching of the Spanish Carmelites, of the French Cistercians, of the Italian Franciscans,
of the Greek Fathers, of the mystics of the Egyptian
Desert, is not only Christian but Catholic. That is to say
that not only is it centered on the historical Christ, but
that its contemplation is nourished by and lives in that
extension of the Incarnation which is the Mystical Body
of Christ: His visible Church.

All that we have said about the place of reason in the

mysticism of Saint John of the Cross still needs to be completed by his conception of the relation of reason to revealed truth and to ecclesiastical authority. For Saint John of the Cross, concerned as he is exclusively with practical problems of the spiritual life, "reason" and "intelligence" are never considered in the abstract, as though man might be living in a hypothetical state of "pure nature." Reason interests Saint John of the Cross precisely because it has an important place in the supernatural order in which the whole human race now actually finds itself. For all men have a supernatural end—the vision of God. They are to achieve this end by the use of their natural faculties, especially of their intelligence and will, aided by the grace of God. Grace will never fail anyone who does what is in his power to seek God. Hence, as Saint John of the Cross realizes, in common with all Catholic theologians, the loss of souls is due not to their arbitrary exclusion from God's favor but to the fundamental irrationality of minds that do not accept the faith which is proposed to them as fully reasonable and as the only means of satisfying the highest aspirations of man's intelligence and will.

Now, in the last few chapters I have described at some length the activity of man's intelligence in the interior purification of his soul by "discretion" and the "discernment of spirits." The diagram which serves as the frontispiece of *The Ascent of Mount Carmel* proposes to the contemplative three roads by which he may travel. Two of them are wrong roads. One of these leads nowhere, the other only brings us to our supernatural end after a weary and roundabout journey. Those who travel by these two wrong roads are guided by a purely subjective standard of values: they obey the impulsions of passion and of desire. Desire is blind. It judges things only in relation to ourselves. Hence, these two roads are illumined by the light of illusion. The third road, the true one, is the way of *nada*, "nothingness," the rejection of all subjectivism, in order to take things objectively. Now, for a theologian, the objective reality of things is what they are in relation to God, considered both in Himself and as our last end. To travel the way of *nada*, man must strive to become perfect in the theological virtues. He can only do this by the constant exercise of his intelligence and will, either actively or on the passive and mystical level. The function of the intelligence is to guarantee the purity of faith, hope, and charity, not by much reasoning and subtlety but by the constant ascetical discernment between the illusions of subjectivism and the true light which comes from God.

So far, so good. But now a serious problem arises. Is this relentless exercise of purifying intuition something that we learn by direct personal inspirations from God? If this is so, then we are in peril of being confined to the subjectivism from which we are trying to escape. Are we to distinguish the inspirations of God from the impulsions of wishful thinking by a merely interior standard? Then that standard will always run the risk of being arbitrary and therefore irrational. Hence, the intelligence is only defeating itself in this "discernment of spirits." It is reasoning in favor of unreason. It has become the instrument of another subjective impulse. It is the servant of mood and desire. For, even though God might give us a sure interior "sense" by which we could "feel" the difference between right and wrong—and He has in fact given us such a sense—nevertheless He does not leave us to make our moral judgments solely by the standards of a delicate interior "sensation." For it is much easier to pervert an inward "sense," which is something undefined, than to tamper with the light of reason. Judgment by an interior "taste" or "feeling" is apt to be something quite individual. Artists can agree on the value of a good painting because they somehow feel that they react to it in the same way. Yet their reactions remain quite personal.

But truth reveals itself to the light of reason in a way that can be shared in the same way by all who use that light. One who understands a truth can convey his understanding to another by evidence and demonstration. The truth that is thus transmitted from one mind to another produces the same objective certainty in both, even though it may at the same time have quite different subjective repercussions in different spirits.

Therefore, when Saint John of the Cross lays down reason as one of the foundation stones of the mystical life, it is because, for him, reason completely fulfills its office only when it subjects a man to the guidance of faith. And the faith which reason serves is not a purely subjective, personal, and incommunicable thing. This faith is objectively centered in God Himself, as He is revealed to the whole Body of the faithful. Hence, we come to a very important conclusion: reason is the key to the mystical life *in so far as it helps a man to shape his whole life by the teaching and authority of Christ living and acting in His visible Church*. This Church, moreover, is a perfect organic unity, with one clearly defined creed, one body of laws, one worship, one visible head. The mysticism of Saint John of the Cross is not merely reconcilable with an authoritative Church and a dogmatic system—it is actually impossible without them.

I am not basing this assertion on the saint's declarations that he submits all his statements to the teaching authority of the Church. Such protestations might be made merely as a matter of form, without constituting any substantial part of the doctrine thus presented. However, we have seen that for Saint John of the Cross the mystical life is in concrete fact impossible without an uncompromising ascesis of the will guided by the intelligence. But this interior ascesis is summed up in the concept of "pure faith." And objective faith, as it is conceived by Saint John of the Cross, is the faith proposed to men by Christ through an authoritative Church. Furthermore, the very subjection of our intelligence to the doctrinal and moral authority of this Church is one of the most essential characteristics of Saint John's ascesis of "reason."

Having said this, which is already very much, I will proceed to say much more. There is hardly a page in *The Ascent of Mount Carmel* in which Saint John of the Cross does not impose upon reason the task and the strict obligation of judging and banishing from the soul not only every spiritual aspiration which is out of harmony with the mind of the Church, but even every mystical inspiration and impulsion which, even though it may be supernatural, *even though it may come from God,* is nevertheless a potential temptation to break away from public revelation and doctrinal authority. Saint John of the Cross would be the last man in the world to dispense the mystic from subjection to the *Magisterium.* Even though it would be possible for a contemplative to receive into his soul all the mysteries of the faith direct from God, Saint John of the Cross is only writing for mystics who are formed, by God, according to His ordinary way, by mediate revelation. The Carmelite theologian has a very special reason for insisting on this. His ascesis of "pure faith" demands the most absolute humility, obedience, and interior self-denial on the part of the soul. This self-denial is impossible without the fundamental gift of one's whole self in the submission of one's highest faculties to God. And this submission is nowhere more complete than when we receive God's word through a human representative. It is more perfect to believe God's truth when it is preached to us by the successors of the Apostles than it would be to receive it directly, in visions and private revelations. As Christ said to Saint Thomas: "Blessed are they who have not seen, and have believed." [2]

Here is what Saint John of the Cross has to say on this vitally important subject:

We must be guided in all things by the law of Christ the Man-God and by that of His Church and of His ministers in a human and visible manner, and by this means we must remedy our spiritual weaknesses and our ignorances, since in these means we shall find abundant medicine for them all. If we leave this path we are guilty not only of curiosity but of great audacity: nothing is to be believed in a supernatural way save only that which is the teaching of Christ the Man-God and of His ministers who are men. [3]

This passage is taken from one of the two most important chapters of *The Ascent of Mount Carmel*. It is absolutely essential for the true understanding of Saint John's mystical theology, for here alone do we see the real purpose behind his relentless attack on every kind of private revelation and his rule that under every circumstance we must turn away even from genuine visions, revelations, raptures, locutions, and so on in order to rest in "pure faith," which is the only proximate means of union with God.

The doctrine of this particular chapter brings out two aspects of his interior asceticism. We have just seen one of them. Submission to authority is all-important because it requires perfect humility, obedience, and interior detachment, without which spiritual liberty can never be attained. This is what makes obedience to the Church and her ministers eminently reasonable. And it is in this sense that Saint John is always contrasting "reason" with the movements of irrational subjective inspiration and ill-defined mystical "attractions." This is the negative side of his interior asceticism—and the least important. We shall pass on in a moment to the positive work of faith itself, in which, according to the terminology of Saint John of the Cross, union is actually achieved. Meanwhile, let us tie up the few loose ends that still remain in our discussion of reason.

First: a clear statement of the saint on private revelations. The saint's doctrine is extraordinarily strict. In fact, it is much more rigid than that of most Catholic theologians, although in practice the Church's caution in accepting "private revelations" may encourage one to adopt the standards laid down by the Spanish Carmelite. When he speaks of revelations, the saint is referring to the direct intuition of hidden truths, and particularly of truths which could not possibly be known in any natural way. He has already discarded lower forms of extraordinary mystical experience—visions of saints, interior locutions, and what not. The saint wastes very little paper on prophecies of the end of the world. He now says that no private revelation concerning the mysteries of God is to be accepted by the soul even—mark this well!—even though it be in confirmity with what God has already publicly revealed to the Church. Here are his words:

Since, then, there are no more articles to be revealed concerning the substance of our faith than those which have already been revealed to the Church, not only must anything new which may be revealed to the soul be rejected, but the soul must be cautious and take no notice of various other things involved therein, and for the sake of the purity of the soul it behoves it to keep the faith even though the truths already revealed to faith be revealed to it privately; and to believe them not because they are now revealed anew but because they have already been sufficiently revealed to the Church; *rather it must close its understanding to them holding simply to the doctrine of the Church and to its faith, which, as Saint Paul says, cometh through hearing.*[4]

On the other hand, we must well understand the saint's contempt for everything that falls outside the domain of pure faith. He is not trying to deprive contemplatives of lights and experiences and visions on the ground that it is pride to aspire to anything but the level of faith on which the ordinary faithful actually live. Far from it. The explicit purpose of Saint John of the Cross is to teach souls the way to the highest possible union with God. Why then does he set aside everything that is popularly regarded as the very essence of "mysticism"? Because it is not good enough, it is not the real thing. However sublime these extraordinary graces may be, they are in actual fact less perfect than the true mystical graces which fall in the direct and "ordinary" path to sanctity. And why? Because these visions and prophecies are essentially less supernatural.[5] And for this very reason they cannot bring the soul to divine union. They have no power of themselves to transform the soul in God.

2

The highest possible contemplation of God is the vision which the saints enjoy in the glory of heaven. According to Catholic tradition, three great saints are thought to have enjoyed an immediate vision of the Divine Essence even while they were on earth. It is in this sense that many Catholic theologians interpret passages of Scripture relating the visions of God granted to Moses, Elias, and Saint Paul. This immediate vision of God is, by its nature, in the *ordinary* line of Christian mysticism, for it is essentially the same as the Beatific Vision, the normal end and fulfillment of the Christian life. Of course, it is a most extraordinary grace if we consider it to have been granted to three men still in this life. That, however, has nothing to do with the essence of the vision which, in the case of Moses, Elias, and Saint Paul was only extraordinary in the circumstances under which it was granted. Saint John of the Cross treats these visions in their proper turn, as he passes through every possible category of spiritual experience in *The Ascent of Mount Carmel*. He does not treat them like the revelations of which we spoke a moment ago. He does not consider the immediate vision of God granted to Saint Paul an extraordinary grace in the same sense as would be a private revelation of divine mysteries. He does not consider the vision of Saint Paul under the aspect of a "temptation." No doubt that grace is so rare that the ordinary everyday mystic Saint John is

writing for would never have a chance to form an attachment to it! But I did not introduce the subject of this
immediate vision of the Divine Essence in order to indulge
in futile speculations. The only point that concerns us
here is contained in one significant remark which Saint
John of the Cross makes about this fleeting glimpse of the
Godhead that was granted to Moses, Elias, and Saint Paul.
Of this rare grace, which opened to them for a moment
the doors of heaven while they were still on earth, he says
the following words: "God performs such a thing *in those
that are most strong in the spirit of the Church* and in the
law of God as were the three I have mentioned above." [6]

This is a singular confirmation of the thesis that our
growth in mystical contemplation and our progress toward
divine union is proportionate to our union with the "spirit
of the Church." Yet nothing could be more obvious to
anyone with the most superficial knowledge of Catholic
theology. Mystics are made by the same Holy Ghost
Who is the Divine Teacher of the Church, and the life of
contemplation is simply the full flowering in the individual soul of the grace which is poured out through the
whole Church. It is the same Holy Ghost Who guides
the Church in the definition of a Catholic dogma and
who secretly infuses the light of faith into each Christian soul that assents to the dogma. When a Catholic
makes an act of faith in an article proposed to his belief
by the Church, he is actually sharing, though in a dark
and inchoate manner, in the contemplation by which
God knows and loves His own Divine Essence. The
activity of faith, hope, and charity perfected by the
Gifts of the Holy Ghost depends entirely on the presence of the Father and on the missions of the Word and

Holy Spirit in the intimate depths of the soul itself. It is only possible for me to make an act of faith in God because God has deigned to draw my soul and its faculties into the mysterious circuit of personal relations which constitute His own infinite Truth and His eternal Contemplation.

With this consideration, we have finally come to the end of our long analysis of reason in the mystical doctrine of Saint John of the Cross. The human mode of intelligent activity which is necessary to keep our souls in perfect submission to the guidance of grace is only a predisposition for the really important activity in which the soul and God work together as one in the soul's own faculties. This is the activity of the theological virtues, particularly in the superhuman mode they achieve when they are perfected and elevated by special inspirations through the Gifts of the Holy Ghost.

## 3

Since the act of faith is the first step toward contemplation and toward the beatific vision, it is extremely important to have an exact notion of what faith really is. Faith is a supernatural virtue, the function of which is to enable the intelligence of man to make a firm and complete assent to divinely revealed truth, not on account of the clear intrinsic evidence of statements about God, but on the authority of God Himself revealing to us what we do not actually see.

This intellectual assent is made by a free act of the will illuminated and guided by grace and preceded by a rational judgment of credibility which is not, however, an internal motive of faith. The Catholic Church has consistently defended the intellectual character of the act of faith. It would be a serious error of doctrine to hold that faith was a "blind movement of the will." Yet the Church also defends the essentially obscure character of faith. It is not and cannot be an assent to intrinsic evidence. It is essentially the "argument of things which appear not." We believe what we do not see, and therefore the act of faith is not purely intellectual: it is elicited under the impulsion of the will.

Then, again, the Church defends the essentially supernatural character of faith. It is a gift of God. It is produced under the inspiration of grace. This inspiration acts directly upon the faculties of the soul which are moved, so to speak, by the "finger of God." In every act of faith, the Holy Spirit takes our will, which has been deflected away from God by sin, and "corrects" its aim and at the same time illuminates the understanding, so that we believe.[7]

Finally, what is the object of faith? God Himself. Faith terminates in God in the sense that every article of revealed truth ends in God or refers to God, and also in the sense that everything we believe is accepted by our mind in submission to the authority of God.

With this brief outline of the essentials of faith, we can understand the theological weight of the categorical affirmation made by Saint John of the Cross that "faith alone is the proximate and proportionate means by which the soul is united to God."[8] And again: "this dark and loving knowledge, which is faith, serves as a means to divine union in this life even as, in the next, the light of glory serves as an intermediary to the clear vision of God."[9]

Saint John is simply echoing the famous expression in which Saint Thomas called faith a beginning of eternal life—*quaedam inchoatio vitae aeternae*. The same doctrine is taught by the Church herself in the Catechism of the Council of Trent,[10] where we read:

Faith so sharpens the power of the human intelligence that it can penetrate heaven without effort and, flooded with the light of God, it becomes able to reach first of all the Fount of light, thence proceeds to all things below God . . . in such a way that we experience with great exultation the truth that we are called out of darkness into His admirable light, and rejoice with exceeding gladness.

Returning to Saint John of the Cross, let us consider a stronger statement than any we have yet quoted, on the power of faith to unite the soul of man to God. It is simply a repetition of the doctrine of the Church we just cited. Saint John of the Cross says:

Such is the likeness between faith and God that there is no other difference save that which exists between seeing God and believing in Him. . . . And thus, by this means, God manifests Himself to the world in a divine light which passes all understanding. *And therefore the greater is the faith of the soul, the more completely is it united to God.*[11]

Clearly then, both the Catholic Church and Saint John of the Cross, the greatest mystical Doctor of the Church, teach that faith gives us the same possession of divine truth in obscurity as the blessed, and indeed God Himself, enjoy in clear vision.

We have now returned to the central paradox of apophatic mysticism. Faith is a vision of God which is essentially obscure. The soul knows Him, not because it beholds Him face to face, but because it is touched by Him in darkness. Now, as Saint John of the Cross has just said, the purer our faith, the more perfect is our union with God. But since faith is essentially obscure, the purity of faith is proportionate to its darkness. Therefore, as Saint John points out at the very beginning of *The Ascent,* pure faith is "as dark as night to the understanding." It is, in fact, the darkest of the "three nights," and in this night takes place "the communication of God in the spirit, which is ordinarily wrought in great darkness of the soul." [12]

Conclusion: in the deepest spiritual darkness, in the most profound night of unknowing, in the purity of naked faith, God unites the soul to Himself in mystical union.

# 4

Ascending by a spiral course we are once again confronted with the same intellectual landscape that engaged our eyes toward the beginning of the present study. But now we see it from a higher altitude. It is time to give final and definite shape to our conclusions on the role of concepts in contemplation. This will finally place dogmatic theology in its proper relation to the mystical life.

In an earlier chapter, we took up the philosophical validity of concepts of God. It is now our task to determine, once for all, how the conceptual knowledge on which an act of theological faith depends can contribute to the mystical union of the soul with God. The problem at issue has been presented in the last statements we quoted from Saint John of the Cross.

The saint said that we are united to God in pure darkness. Hence pure faith, which is the proper atmosphere for divine union, goes beyond all clear conceptual and scientific knowledge of God. Saint John of the Cross says that faith "blinds and dazzles the understanding." Precisely, then, it must rob the mind of its clear conceptual knowledge of the things of God. Furthermore, we have seen that, in practice, the soul that enters the state of infused contemplation does in fact lose its inclination to dwell on precise and particular objects of knowledge. It seeks God in a darkness that is above concepts. It finds Him, we cannot doubt his terms, beyond all knowledge.

This, of course, is true. Once we have clearly established that Saint John of the Cross does not reject conceptual knowledge and scientific theology as such, we must admit that he holds, in common with Saint Thomas and all the greatest theologians, that infused wisdom rises above distinct knowledge and grasps the perfections of God in an immediate fruition born of obscure mystical love. This is the basis of a supraconceptual judgment concerning God which is made not on the grounds of conceptual evidence but by the instinctive response of "connaturality." We "know" God because we have been identified with Him by love. But the one essential point to remember above all is, as Pope Pius XII points out in his encyclical *Humani Generis,* there is no opposition or contradiction between acquired and infused wisdom. Connatural knowledge of God helps us to perfect our concepts of Him, and dogmatic science serves as the guide for statements based on mystical experience. Theology is not made by mystics: mystics are formed by theology.

First of all, in approaching this question of concepts in mystical experience, let us define precisely what concepts interest us here. These concepts belong to a limited category: they are formulations of revealed truth which can serve as the object of theological faith. The Catholic cannot go through life making acts of faith in anything he pleases. Even though an ill-instructed Christian might imagine it to be divinely revealed that the sun spun on its axis at Fatima in 1917, this happening can never become the object of an act of theological faith. We can only elicit such an act of faith in some proposition which is known to have been revealed by God. The deposit of divine revelation was formally closed with the death of the last Apostle. Since then, nothing new has been publicly revealed. Dogmatic definitions made by the extraordinary teaching authority of the Church have had no other aim than to declare that various propositions do, in fact, form part of the original deposit of revelation. The Church does not manufacture articles of faith. She does not make revelations since she has nothing to reveal. But she is the custodian of divinely revealed Truth. Guided by the Holy Ghost, she is the only true and authoritative interpreter of that Truth. The treasury of faith to which she holds the key is a body of concepts about God. These are the statements which we believe. Believing them, we are able, with the help of our intelligence and the light of grace, to arrive at a certain measure of understanding concerning the things of God.

But now we face the question of mystical contemplation. What is this contemplation? It is simply the supernatural experience of the truths about God contained in the deposit of Christian faith. And since, in fact, all revealed Truth converges upon the Incarnate Word Who, by His death on the Cross, redeemed all mankind and united it to God mystically in His own Person, the consummation of mystical prayer is a fruition of God in which the mystic experiences in his own soul the fulfillment of the work Christ came to accomplish. This fulfillment is called transforming union. It is a perfect union of love with God, through Christ, in the Holy Spirit—a union which is designed, in its ultimate consummation, to embrace all the souls of the Blessed together in God. Of this union Jesus said, praying to His Father at the Last Supper: "May they all be one, as Thou Father in me and I in Thee, may they also be one in us. . . . The glory which Thou hast given me, I have given them, that they may be one as we also are one." [13]

So perfect is this union of Love that the soul actually lives and acts in its substance and in its faculties by the life and activity of God and feels itself as it were "transformed" into God so that there remains no apparent distinction between itself and God. This does not imply a destruction of the human substance or personality. But, on the other hand, it is a much closer union than a mere moral union of faculties. Although the expression would be philosophical nonsense, one may say that the saint "transformed" in God acts as though he were a "part" of God. My hand and my foot are parts of my body. Whatever my hand does, I do. Whatever my foot does, I do. What happens to them, happens to me. In this sense we are all said by Saint Paul to be members of the Mystical Body of Christ. Christ is God. One who is completely absorbed in the Christ-life which is his as a member of the Mystical Body will become, in fact, identified with Christ, and through Him with the Father, and in Him with all other members of Christ in such a way that they will be one with the same Unity that exists in

God between His Three Divine Persons. "I in them and thou in me, that they may be made perfect in one." The words of Christ allow of no looser interpretation. Jesus is saying that those who reach perfect union with God, in Himself, will be as much One with God by grace as He is One with the Father by Nature. This is the most tremendous and the central mystery of Christianity. It is into this abyss of blazing light, so infinitely bright as to be pure darkness to our intelligence, that the mystic enters not only with his eyes, his imagination, and his mind but with his whole soul and substance, in order to be transformed like a bar of iron in the white heat of a furnace. The iron turns into fire. The mystic is "transformed" in God.

# CHAPTER XVI

# A Dark Cloud
# Enlightening the Night

The safest way for us to advance on this part of our journey is to comment on two important passages, in which Saint John of the Cross talks about faith under these two aspects: as darkness and as certitude. From the point of view of our human intellect, these two qualities of faith seem to contradict each other. In the natural order, whatever is certain is clear to the intelligence that sees its certitude. In the supernatural order, things are, for the present, reversed: what is most certain is most obscure. For this reason, intellectual difficulties about the mysteries of faith cannot of themselves constitute doubts or temptations against faith. As Cardinal Newman said: "A thousand difficulties do not make one doubt." We cannot expect to understand with clear intrinsic evidence what is essentially obscure to our natural intelligence. Saint John of the Cross explains why. Faith makes us believe truths that are beyond all proportion to human understanding and are only known in so far as they are accepted on Divine Revelation.

Hence it follows that for the soul this excessive light of faith which is given to it is thick darkness, for it overwhelms that which is great and does away with that which is little, even as the light of the sun overwhelms all other lights whatsoever, so that when it shines and disables our powers of vision they appear not to be lights at all.[1]

It is only in this sense that faith is said to blind and darken the understanding. It is not that natural knowledge has no value in itself. But natural knowledge can no more serve to teach us the mysteries of God than a flashlight can help an owl to find its way about when it is dazzled by the light of high noon. The light of the sun blinds not only the owl but the flashlight, and he who wants to find his way to God must be led by the hand.

In the chapter we are considering,[2] Saint John of the Cross goes into psychological details which we have already talked about enough. It suffices for us to recall here that our natural knowledge depends on concepts abstracted from the images of things. Our intelligence is naturally disposed to arrive at truth with the help of the senses. However, Saint John of the Cross is careful to explain that it also "has a faculty for the supernatural, when Our Lord may be pleased to bring it to supernatural action." [3] In other words, the intelligence can know truths supernaturally without the medium of any sense image and without any concept. God can, if He so wills, illuminate the mind directly with His infinite light. And in fact He does so, in heaven. This "faculty" which the soul has for receiving such illumination is not, properly speaking, natural. But the intelligence is by nature in a state of passive or obediential potency to receive this light. This state of passive potency does not give the soul, strictly speaking, any "faculty" for supernatural illumination. That faculty comes with the active potency conferred by grace upon the soul proximately disposed and attuned to supernatural things.

Now, it is precisely by faith, hope, and charity that the soul develops this active potency for the supernatural which has been conferred upon it by grace. By this I mean that the practice of the theological virtues disposes the faculties of man to receive higher lights and inspirations from God, which reach our intelligence without passing through any sensible medium. In other words, the soul's growth in the infused virtues prepares it for a direct and supraconceptual experience of the reality of God and of His mysteries.

But is faith itself supraconceptual? Yes and no. It is on the borderline. It makes use of concepts in order to convey to our minds knowledge of a God Whose infinite perfections exceed the capacity of all concepts. Its concepts, as we have seen, really attain to Him. The statements made by faith about God are objectively true. Nevertheless the concepts used in these statements fall infinitely short of the actuality of God's perfections, so that in their mode of expression they can be said, in some sense, to hide Him as much as they reveal Him.

Saint John of the Cross explains the peculiar function of concepts in an act of faith by an interesting comparison:

If one should say to a man that on a certain island there is an animal which he has never seen, and give him no idea of the appearance of that animal, that he may compare it with others that he has seen, he will have no more knowledge or imagination of it than he had before, no matter how much is being said to him about it.[4]

In this example he assumes that the animal on the island really exists. Everything that is said about the animal is true. The man who hears about the animal discovers something he did not know before. If he believes its existence he has acquired a new truth. But unfortunately he has no means of knowing what kind of animal this is. Let us suppose that it resembles no other animal on earth. If our man sets out to imagine this strange creature under the same form as the animals he knows of, he will be misled by his own imagination. And Saint John concludes that the only thing this man would really know about the animal would be its name, which he had received "by hearing."

It is the same with the concepts of faith. The truths which faith proposes to our belief about God as He is in Himself have, as the saint says, "no relation to any sense of ours." We have never seen anything like them. And yet faith gives us possession of these truths in an obscure but certain manner, and it does so by means of the concepts and propositions to which we assent in an act of belief. How is this? Saint John of the Cross makes a distinction. The knowledge of God that is offered to us in the articles of our faith has *no proportion* to our senses or our natural understanding. Yet it is received through the senses *by our consent.*

For, as Saint Paul says, *fides ex auditu* (faith cometh by hearing). As though he were to say: Faith is not knowledge which enters by any of the senses but is only the consent given by the soul to that which enters through the hearing.[5]

Nevertheless, Saint John of the Cross goes on to insist on the second half of his paradox—the certitude of faith. Faith is not a mere blind assent of the will in defiance of the intellect. By its assent the understanding is blinded, yes, but it is also positively enlightened. Faith is an intellectual light. It enlightens the mind to supernatural things by depriving it of its natural light, not with respect to all knowledge but only with respect to supernatural mysteries which our intelligence alone could never penetrate. But while darkening our minds in this one particular way, faith simultaneously makes them capable of higher light by which they penetrate the mysteries of God. John of Saint Thomas would situate this higher light less in faith itself than in the illumination of the Gift of Understanding which perfects faith. Saint John of the Cross does not make that distinction. "Pure faith" for Him is faith enlightened and strengthened by all the power of the Gifts.

Faith is dark night to the soul, and it is in this way that it gives it light; and the more [the soul] is darkened, the greater light comes to it.[6]

It is here that the saint goes on to compare faith to the pillar of cloud that led the Children of Israel out of Egypt across the desert. This cloud was dark by day, and by night it was a pillar of fire. Yet, though it was a pillar of fire, it remained dark. *Erat nubes tenebrosa et illuminans noctem.* "That is to say the cloud was full of darkness and gave light by night." [7]

## 2

Man was made to know truth, and his salvation consists in loving the highest Truth, which cannot be loved unless it first be known. But there is only one kind of knowledge that effectively confers upon man the light without which he cannot reach this supernatural end. This knowledge comes to him in the obscurity of faith.

The prophet said, "unless you believe, you will not understand." [8] Faith alone can win us intelligence of the mysteries of God. But faith has something more. "Without faith," says Saint Paul, "it is impossible to please God." [9]

What does it mean to please God? God is said to be pleased with the soul which He finds filled with His own reality, His own love, His own truth. In a mysterious way, we please God by knowing Him, because we can only know Him by receiving His light into our hearts. Faith, then, is not only capable of penetrating the intimate substance of God's Truth, but it is an immediately redemptive knowledge of God. It "saves" us. Its light is more than a ray of speculation: it confers life. The awakening of faith not only gives light to the understanding and peace to the will: it transforms a man's whole moral being. He becomes a new creature. He is born again.

What is this new life? It is the substantial presence of God. Rather, it is a new and special presence of God Who, by His power, presence, and essence holds all things in being. This new presence is spiritual. What is it? We have already described it. God is present in His own light and His own love. By faith, hope, and charity, God becomes at once the potential object of an intimate spiritual experience, and confers upon the faculties of the soul the power and the vital desire to possess Him in that experience. He reveals Himself within the soul as the object of its deepest longing. He promises, by His obscure presence, clear vision. His promise makes us desire that vision. And by our desire, we already embrace the vision, though it remains obscure.

In a word, faith give us more than light, more than life: for the "light" it gives us is God Himself. The life it confers upon us is nothing else than the very being of God, Who created all life by breathing upon the waters of the

abyss, and Who becomes the principle of our new supernatural existence.

Now none of this flows purely and simply from the
conceptual content of faith. It comes directly from God.

What are we to conclude? In every act of faith, there
are two elements at work. First there is the formula, the
conceptual complex to which we assent. This presents itself to our mind like any other intentional knowledge:
in the form of a judgment. But it does not enlighten the
mind in the same way as ordinary knowledge. On the
natural plane, a conceptual judgment illuminates the mind
by the clear evidence which it contains. In an act of faith,
the conceptual content of the proposition throws no light,
of itself, upon the understanding. The difference between
belief and unbelief is not measured by our power to grasp
the *meaning* of the articles of faith. A man may acquire a
profound technical knowledge of the theology of the Holy
Trinity and never believe in the Trinity. Another who has
no grasp of the dogmatic problems involved in the mystery
may believe it. And he is the one who receives light. He
is the one who knows God. He is the one to whom God
has made Himself "present." He is the one who is "saved."
He is the one who can be raised to contemplation. Hence
in every act of faith there is a second and more important
element: an objective and supernatural light, penetrating
the depths of the soul and communicating to it the real
content of truth which cannot be fully grasped in the
terms of the proposition believed.

Each of these two elements is absolutely necessary for
an act of living faith, because there is an intimate relation between them. If the articles of faith were merely an
occasion for the infusion of supernatural light, then it

would not matter what God proposed to us for our belief. One concept would serve as well as another. But this would mean that the intentional content of our creed would be without value or meaning. Any creed would do as well. Hold anything you like! If you are sincere, God will infuse light into you, and you will know Him. But the God Who is Wisdom would not uselessly reveal a whole body of truths that had, in the end, no objective value. He Who is Truth would not complacently put His grace at the disposal of all, on the sole condition that they be ready to adhere to falsity on His account!

The relation between the conceptual content of faith and the infused light by which God actually gives us His Truth lies in this: that *the truth is actually contained, in a hidden manner, in the articles of faith themselves*. And it is by the light of faith that we find the truth in those articles.

This accounts for all the statements Saint John of the Cross has been making about the power of faith: that it is the only way to union with God: that it is essentially obscure and "hides" God, yet at the same time is pure truth, perfect in its certitude, and conveys God to us as it were under cover of a cloud.

Saint Thomas Aquinas also supports the distinction we have made by saying that faith consists principally in an infused light but that it receives accurate determination to a particular truth by the various articles proposed for our belief.[10]

## 3

Let us now turn the pages of Saint John of the Cross until we come to a classical passage in *The Spiritual*

*Canticle* [11] where he gives a full and beautiful explanation of the part played by the articles of Christian faith in mystical contemplation.

Here is the stanza which the saint proposes to explain:

> *O cristallina fuente,*
> *Si en esos tus semblantes plateados*
> *Formases de repente*
> *Los ojos deseados*
> *Que tengo en mis entrañas dibujados.*

The soul, in love with God, here addresses faith, not considered as an abstraction or as a mere allegorical figure, but as a living reality existing and working in the spirit of the believer. This fountain is what Christ called a spring of "living waters that springs up unto everlasting life." [12] I translate and paraphrase as follows; the soul says to faith: "O crystal fountain! I wish that you would suddenly form and display, in the reflection on your silvery surface, a clear picture of the eyes and visage of God which are now present in the depths of my being, not clearly seen but formless and obscure like a faint outline sketched in pencil." Like all the other stanzas of *The Spiritual Canticle*, this one is mysterious. Someone might easily quarrel with the explanation if it did not come to us from the poet himself, who might reasonably be expected to know better than anyone else what the stanza meant.

The soul here turns to faith with intense desire, says the saint, because it has just come from the consideration of all created things and is fully aware that God is not to be found in them as He is in Himself. Creatures are such faint reflections of His divine Being that they are no more than the footprints He has left behind Him as He went on

His way. They bear witness to His passing: but by that very fact their testimony is tinged with a special anguish. They only tell us that He has passed by. They cannot deliver to us the secret of where He has gone!

Faith, on the other hand, can tell us this secret. Much more, faith is actually His hiding place Who has "made darkness His covert, His pavilion round about Him." [13] As Saint John of the Cross already explained at the beginning of his *Canticle:* "He that has to find some hidden thing must enter very secretly into that same hidden place where it is, and when he finds it, he too is hidden like that which he has found." [14] And so Saint John repeats that faith will give the soul the "most vivid light from her Beloved" and will provide "the only means whereby the soul may come to true union and spiritual betrothal with God." [15] The thought comes from Scripture. *Sponsabo te mihi in fide,* "I will espouse thee to myself in faith." [16]

The soul is at once confronted by the paradox of faith. It is nailed to the Cross of anguish and darkness which is the crisis of true faith. It sees that faith, because it is at once certain and obscure, reveals God by hiding Him and by hiding reveals Him. However, this is no mere intellectual dilemma. It is not a problem, for a problem can be disposed of by reasonable solution. The soul is not looking for a solution. It is not proposing a question that faith must answer. Its anguish is of a different and far deeper nature. It is the agony of love that possesses God without seeing Him, which already rests in the possession of Him and is yet restless because it needs to rest in pure vision. Thus its rest is at best a suspension in the void.

Saint John of the Cross now comes out plainly and tells us the one great truth about faith which makes it the source at the same time of deepest anguish and of exalted peace. He tells us this truth in two ways. First he says, as he has said before, that faith communicates to the soul divine truth in "dark and unformed knowledge." Then finally he declares—and this is all-important—*"Faith gives and communicates to us God Himself."* [17] I quote the same idea from *The Dark Night of the Soul:*

This Dark Night [pure faith, perfected by the Gifts of the Holy Ghost] *is the inflowing of God into the soul,* which purges it of its ignorances and imperfections, natural and spiritual, and which is called by contemplatives infused contemplation. . . . Herein God secretly teaches the soul and instructs it in perfection of love without its doing anything or understanding of what manner is this infused contemplation.[18]

And now Saint John of the Cross explains how faith communicates God in a hidden manner. The articles of faith actually contain the truth of God. God is the formal object attained by our belief. He is the substance contained beneath the appearance which is constituted by a credible proposition about Him.

Articles of faith and truths revealed by God in Scripture or tradition can be compared to the Sacrament of the Most Holy Eucharist, in which Christ, God, is presented to our gaze under the species of bread and wine. There is no substance of bread in the consecrated Host. The only substance present is God Himself. The visible accidents of bread which strike our senses are maintained in being directly by His power, without inhering in any created thing or entering into metaphysical composition with the Divine Being. So too in the articles of faith. We begin the Creed with the words "I believe in God the Father Almighty." This proposition offers to our minds certain concepts based on images. The concepts and images suscitated in us by this article of belief contain the substantial truth of God, but in themselves they remain as it were created appearances or "species" through which faith must penetrate in order to arrive at Him. If the mind stops short at a subjective and imaginary notion of a human "Father" endowed with an indefinitely magnified human power, it does not reach God. This sterilizes our act of faith.

Saint John uses a different comparison. The articles of faith are like a precious vessel made of gold and plated over with silver. God is the gold overlaid by the silver of the formal propositions which we believe.

Faith is compared to silver with respect to the propositions it teaches us and the truth and substance which they contain in themselves is compared to gold; for that same substance which now we believe, clothed and covered with the silver of faith, we shall behold and enjoy in the life to come with the gold of the faith laid bare.[19]

# CHAPTER XVII

# The Loving Knowledge of God

Pure faith, perfected by the Gifts of the Holy Ghost and above all transfigured by charity, springs up in the depths of the soul and gives it to drink, in secret, the waters of divine truth. These waters are not only statements about God, but they are the very presence of God Himself. But from the moment our contemplation transcends concepts, from the moment the intelligence enters this divine darkness, our knowledge of God is dominated by love and flows from love. So true is this that many of the Fathers of the Church wrote, as did the Cistercian William of Saint Thierry, *Amor Dei ipsa est notitia* ("The love of God is our knowledge of Him"). This is, theologically speaking, a loose statement. Nevertheless it conveys a significant truth which is much emphasized by Saint John of the Cross and receives precise definition in the pages of Saint Thomas Aquinas.

Although contemplation consists, of course, in an act of the intelligence, not of the will, it is nevertheless true to say that in practice *the most important element in the contemplative life is not knowledge but love*. Here are some of the reasons why.

First of all, infused contemplation, though formally in

the intellect, flows from love and terminates in love. We
have seen that this contemplation consists in an experiential grasp of divine truth in a darkness that transcends
the limits of conceptual knowledge. *Such an experience
can only be valid and true if it be born of divine love.* Only
love can establish the vital contact in which the will outstrips the dazzled intellect and "touches" the very substance of the God Whom our minds are unable to see. Or
rather, to put it more accurately, the same divine action
which touches the depths of the soul, where the mind and
the will are one, simultaneously darkens the intelligence
with excessive light and sets the will on fire with love, filling the whole spirit with the cloud prefigured in Exodus
—the "dark cloud enlightening the night."

Hence, love is important first of all because it is the cause
of contemplation. Saint Thomas clearly distinguishes the
acquired wisdom, which arrives at intentional knowledge
by rational investigation, from the infused wisdom of mystical contemplation which makes a right judgment concerning the things of God by experience, *per modum in-
clinationis,* and by virtue of likeness or connaturality. This
wisdom, though it be formally an intellectual act, is rooted
in love, because it depends entirely on an experience of
union with God which can only be effected by love.[1]

In another place, Saint Thomas founds the same teaching on clear texts drawn from the Discourse of Christ to
His Disciples at the Last Supper. Jesus there told them:
*"If anyone love me* he will keep my word and my Father
will love him and we will come to him and make our
abode with him. . . . And I will ask the Father and He
will give you another Paraclete . . . the Spirit of Truth
whom the world cannot receive . . . *but you shall know*

*Him* because He shall abide with you and be in you." [2]
Commenting on this idea and speaking especially in reference to Saint John the Baptist, Saint Thomas remarks: "The
fire of love is the source of light, for by the burning of
love we arrive at knowledge of the Truth." [3] Now here it
must be well understood that love does not attain to some
different object from the one presented to our understanding by the articles of faith or the revealed words of Scripture. Love is not a source of knowledge in the sense that
it brings to the intelligence news of something it has never
heard of in any way. However, in the loving knowledge
of God which is obscure and mystical contemplation, love
penetrates the conceptual content of revelation in order
to know God experientially in a higher and more perfect
mode than is possible, as yet, to our intelligence.

To say, then, that love is the source of the contemplative's knowledge of God is not to say that mystical contemplation has no further use for concepts. A precise distinction must be made. It is true that concepts are no
longer the *formal means* by which we reach our higher,
experiential knowledge of God. Nevertheless they *condition* that knowledge, and mystical wisdom remains subject to specification by the definite conceptual propositions
of dogmatic theology. Jacques Maritain, whom I am here
following, compares the concepts in mystical contemplation to the disciples who fell asleep on the Mount of
Olives during the Agony in the Garden, and he explains
the function of this "loving knowledge" achieved by the
will, vigilant and agonizing in the darkness of faith. The
terms he uses recall the phrase I have just quoted from
Saint Thomas. Jacques Maritain says: "The proper light

of infused contemplation is the ardor of love which burns in the night." [4]

The exact teaching of modern Thomists, Garrigou-Lagrange, Gardeil, and Maritain, on this point, tells us that intense supernatural love for God, directed by the inspiration of the Holy Ghost through His Gifts, becomes a supraconceptual means of knowing God as He is in Himself. The precise distinction is important.

In any kind of love, human or divine, the soul can reflect on its own loving activity and thus become the object of its own knowledge. For this reason, the delight of human love can produce a state which resembles an inferior brand of contemplation, if the mind rests in this delightful experience and enjoys it for its own sake. In this case love is the object of a reflective intuition. The soul rests in fruition of its own experience. It is in love, and it knows it is in love, and knows that it is loved in return. This knowledge produces delight.

Now, in lower degrees of religious experience, the same thing can take place. The soul feels in itself an intense love for God, reflects upon that love, and adds to this reflection the thought that it is also loved, beyond measure by God Himself. Here too love itself is the object of knowledge. It is our love that we contemplate. We rest and rejoice in the knowledge that we love and are loved. This is not, strictly speaking, infused contemplation, at least in my opinion. It is rather what some writers call "acquired" contemplation, although the validity of such a term is disputed and I have no intention of discussing the question here.

The theologians I have cited above may or may not have different opinions about the nature of such contemplation. But in any case, they agree that contemplation which produces a real supraconceptual sense of the presence of God and which therefore most writers would agree in calling mystical, consists in something more than resting in the knowledge of our own love.

The distinction that must be clearly grasped is rather a subtle one. On one hand, the soul, moved by love, becomes the object of its own knowledge. On the other hand, the soul, touched and inflamed and transfigured by the illuminative flame of God's immediate presence, is no longer the object of knowledge but the actual medium in which God is known. Hence, God as He is in Himself is the object of the soul's contemplation. The medium in which He is seen is not charity considered as a habit or virtue, not the act of love reflected upon by the intelligence, but the soul itself burning and translucent in the flame of divine love.[5]

This divine love, which transfigures the soul and makes it the limpid medium in which God is known, is therefore remotely comparable to the Beatific Vision itself in which God's own divine light, filling and possessing and transforming the soul, takes the place of an idea or species in which the intelligence beholds Him.

To illustrate this distinction, let us make the following comparison. In the middle of the night, or on a rainy day, I can bring to mind the idea of a beautiful sunny afternoon and can re-create within myself the memory of sunshine and pleasure and warmth, flowers, trees, sky, clouds, and all the rest. As long as I reflect on them, these pictures and ideas are the object of my knowledge. So too when I reflect upon the idea of God's love, and upon the experience of love present within me. If, however, the sun is shining outside and I look out the window, without actually seeing the sun, I see its light everywhere in the sky. I know the sun in this atmosphere as in an actual medium.

I think I can do no better at this point than translate a passage from John of Saint Thomas which admirably sums up this connatural and mystical knowledge of God by love. This text is cited by Jacques Maritain in the chapter which I have been following. John of Saint Thomas says:

The Gift of Wisdom attains to the highest causes in a way that is mystical and affective [i.e. by way of love.] This means that it attains them in God's gift of Himself to us. It is true that all the supernatural habits are gifts of God. But it is one thing to receive an object by a gift, and another to attain to that object in the donation as such and by virtue of the donation, in such a way that the formal reason of the apprehension is found in the very Gift God makes of Himself to us, delivering Himself to us by His Spirit and His will. . . . Hence let us say that the formal reason by which the Gift of Wisdom attains the highest cause is the experiential knowledge of God in so far as He is united to us and enters into the most intimate depths of our being, and gives Himself to us. This knowledge is entirely spiritual and does not proceed only from light or from reasoning which shows us the nature of things. It proceeds from love and the experience of union.[6]

In order that John of Saint Thomas's remarks may not be misunderstood, we must remember that God is said to "give Himself" to us when we in fact give ourselves entirely to Him with a love that is in some sense comparable to His love for us because it is total, unquestioning, and absolutely pure. Such love of course can only be produced in us by a gift of God, and in making us love as He loves, God is said to take the soul entirely to Himself and to give Himself entirely to the soul. When He does this there is no longer any practical or experiential distinction between His activity and the activity of the soul united in one and the same perfect love. This love is God Himself.

## 2

In its highest perfection on earth, that is, in transforming union, this knowledge of God may be said to be immediate, though not in the sense that God is seen face to face by the intellect, for He is still known through love considered as an effect. However, since perfect love attains immediately to God and unites our substance with His Divine Being without any other medium, and since the soul of the mystic attains directly to God in the experience of this union, it is clear that mystical experience is the actual fruition of God as He is in Himself, beyond every created image or similitude or idea.

How is all this possible? It flows from the very nature of charity. All love tends to ecstasy, in the sense that it takes us out of ourselves and makes us live in the object of our love. In the case of human love, this ecstasy can never be more than a figure of speech, or a mere matter of moral and psychological agreement. But since our souls are spiritual substances and since God is pure Spirit, there is nothing to prevent a union between ourselves and Him that is ecstatic in the literal sense of the word. The only restriction placed upon this union is that a contingent and finite substance can never become one nature and substance with the infinite and Absolute Being of God in such a way that everything that belongs to Him by nature belongs to us by nature. The metaphysical impossibility of this is evident from the very notion of a substance being "changed into" what is, by nature, unchanging. We cannot "become God." God *is,* and His Being is infinitely above all becoming. But by His free gift He can make us participate by knowledge and love in everything that is His by nature.

All this brings us to the second reason why love is the most important thing in the contemplative life. It is the end and consummation of that life. In fact, as Saint Bernard says, to contemplate God without loving Him would be no contemplation at all. If we know God and do not love Him, what we know is not God.[7]

It must be quite evident that love is the end and perfection of all contemplation, since contemplation is not an end in itself. Contemplation is not sanctity. The full maturity of the Christian life, to which contemplation is only one of many means—though perhaps it is the most effective means—consists essentially in the perfect love of God and of other men. Hence, Saint Thomas Aquinas says:

Although the contemplative life consists especially in the activity of the intelligence, it has its beginning in the will. . . . And since the end must correspond to the beginning it follows that the term and end of the contemplative life is located in the will, so that while one rejoices in the vision of the God one loves, the very joy of the vision makes one's love grow stronger. . . . And so the ultimate perfection of the contemplative life consists in the fact that God's truth is not only seen but is also loved.[8]

This is all the more true because, as a matter of fact, love is perfection and sanctity in so far as it directly unites us to God and makes us live in Him Who is our life. God is, in fact, at once the sanctity of the saints and their contemplation and their life. They find all in Him. As Saint Augustine said: "Just as the soul is the life of the body, so God is the blessed life of man." *Ut vita carnis anima est, ita beata vita hominis Deus est.*[9] And Saint Thomas adds: "Charity makes man cleave to God for His own sake, uniting man's soul to God by the power of love. . . . Charity is what makes man tend directly to God, uniting the will of man to God in such a way that man lives for God and not for himself." [10]

However, a distinction must be made between contemplation in this life and in the next. In the Beatific Vision, God is formally and immediately attained and possessed by an act of the intellect. In this life, not so. But even in heaven, the purity and perfection of our vision of God depends entirely on how much we have loved Him in this life. Hence, even in heaven, love, though not the essence of beatitude, is intimately related to it. The greatest saints in heaven are those who can give God the most love there. Those who can give Him the most love are those who know Him best. And those who know Him best in heaven are those who have best loved Him on earth. Consequently, love is also the most important thing in the contemplative life in this third sense: it is the source of our merit.

Saint Thomas, contrasting the active and contemplative lives, says:

The root of all merit is charity. . . . The love of God is essentially more meritorious than the love of our neighbor. . . . The contemplative life immediately and directly pertains to the love of God . . . therefore of itself the contemplative life is more meritorious than the active life.[11]

But since we have brought up the question of knowledge and love in the contemplative life of heaven, let us pause for a moment to consider a most significant text from Saint John of the Cross. The doctrine here set down by the Spanish Carmelite might seem to be a modification of Thomist intellectualism. It is not in fact so. Here as everywhere Saint John of the Cross is a true Thomist. Describing the ardent longing of the mystical soul for heaven in *The Spiritual Canticle*,[12] he makes the soul cry out to God, asking Him for the perfect love of Him which the blessed have in heaven. And since the soul in *The Canticle* seems to be more anxious to possess this perfection of love, which is, technically speaking, accidental, than the vision which is the essence of beatitude, Saint John of the Cross feels that he must explain why this is. He proceeds to point out that even in heaven there is a sense in which love is more important than vision. It will be quite evident that his doctrine flows directly from the statements we have just quoted from Saint Thomas. Here are the words of Saint John:

Even as the end of all things is love, which resides in the will, whose property is to give and not to receive, and the property of the intellect, which is the subject of essential glory, is to receive and not to give, so the soul being here inebriated with love, puts not in the first place the glory which God is to give her, but rather the giving of herself to God, in surrender of true love, without any regard to her own advantage.

However, the saint immediately points out that this really creates no difficulty as far as the Thomist doctrine of beatitude is concerned since, as he says, "It is impossible to attain to the perfect love of God without the perfect vision of God."

Now, this passage of Saint John of the Cross is important for its undertones, which recall an often-disregarded aspect of Thomist intellectualism. In declaring that the intelligence is essentially superior to the will and is therefore man's highest faculty, Saint Thomas is careful to make certain qualifications which are extremely important for the practical guidance of Christian souls, especially in the ways of prayer. Saint Thomas reminds us that this superiority of the intellect over the will is primarily theoretical. It rests on the fact that the intelligence has a higher and purer object than the will. It is the function of the intellect to show man the very essence of goodness which the will seeks. However, in actual practice, the intelligence is not always superior to the will. This is because the will may often attain to a higher and more perfect object than the intelligence is capable of reaching. Saint Thomas is not here speaking of mere velleities, desires for things of which we have no certain knowledge. As Saint John of the Cross has just pointed out, following this doctrine of Saint Thomas, the intelligence acts upon what *it has received into itself,* but the will *goes out of itself into another.* As Aristotle says: truth and falsity, the objects of understanding, have only an abstract existence in the mind. But the will reaches out to good and evil *in their actual, concrete reality, in existing things.* From this distinction follow two most interesting consequences. A being below the human level exists more perfectly in man's intelligence than it does in itself—for in us its existence is spiritualized. Hence, when we deal with objects on our own level or below it, our intellect is superior to our will. On the other hand, when the good we seek is found above the human level, and especially in God Who transcends all creatures, *the will attains to Him more perfectly than the intelligence*. Saint Thomas concludes with three terse statements:

Hence, the love of God is better than the knowledge of God and, on the contrary, the knowledge of bodily things is better than the love of them. But in any case, the intellect is essentially nobler than the will.[13]

The first of these statements is reechoed everywhere in the teachings of the mystics. *Melior est amor Dei quam cognitio*. It is comforting to have such a plain and unmistakable formula from the pen of Saint Thomas Aquinas. It delivers us forever from the delusion that mystical contemplation is learned from books and that the contemplative life reaches its highest fulfillment in the stacks of a university library. But, at the same time, everything that has been said so far in this book should remind us to beware of contemplatives whose mysticism does not have a positive basis in theology. Saint Thomas himself is there to prove that there is no reason why God should not pour out His purest graces of mystical prayer even upon a professor, just as Saint Teresa remains as a monument to the truth that God can raise you to ecstasy while you are trying to fry eggs.

Saint Thomas's own master of theology, Saint Albert the Great, points out that love is the true mark of Christian contemplation. He says:

The contemplation of philosophers tends to the perfection of the one contemplating, and hence it ends in the intellect. Thus their aim, in all this, is intellectual light. [I here translate *cognitio intellectus* in a way that is supposed to include not only discursive knowledge but a purely intellectual intuition.] But [Saint Albert continues], the contemplation of the saints is fulfilled in the love of God Himself, Who is contemplated by them. Therefore its last end is not situated in the intellect or in thought, but it passes over to the will and becomes a matter of love.[14]

This loving knowledge of God is the closest approach to pure happiness that is granted to men in this mortal life. That is why those who are truly wise with the wisdom of the saints leave all things to follow Christ and seek to give themselves entirely, with all they have and all they are, to God. They consecrate their lives to Him alone and engage themselves in a ceaseless ascetic effort to attain perfection in the purity of their love for Him. The Spirit of God soon teaches them that contemplation is not something we get but something that is given to us. Therefore we must not try to acquire it by a vain effort of intelligence, but we must use our reason, in the service of faith, in order to direct every action and every desire of our body and soul to God and to His glory. This light that is in us has been given us for the service of love. That is not to say that the intelligence is inferior to the will, but only that the purest thing that is in us, the mind, is what enables us to make a total gift of ourselves to God. If we did not have intelligence, we would not be free, and if we were not free our love could not be disinterested; and if our love were not disinterested it would not be pure. And without pure love we cannot see God. Since it is written: "Blessed are the clean of heart, for they shall see God!" [15]

The greatest sorrow of the saints lies in the fact that this purity and their freedom of love, which are themselves God's greatest gifts to us because they enable us to reach Him, quickly fall out of our grasp. We are never clean for long. We always have to wash our souls as well

as our hands. We are always falling back into darkness
and selfishness and thoughtlessness and imperfection. That
is why contemplation on earth is only a faint foretaste of
beatitude: it is so inconstant. Nevertheless, Saint Thomas
shows us how the life of the contemplative can always be
at least virtually ordered to union with God. It is consoling
to hear him say that even necessary and seemingly un-
spiritual bodily operations like eating and sleeping, which
may sometimes interrupt our contemplation, nevertheless
form part of the contemplative life on earth because without them we would not be able to go on praying and
loving and contemplating God.[16]

# CHAPTER XVIII

# To the Mountain
# and the Hill

We are getting to the end of our long journey. It is now possible to formulate in precise terms the function of love in mystical contemplation and to discuss a few more passages in which Saint John of the Cross sketches out for us something of the reality of mystical experience. Before we do so, let us look back over the road we have traveled.

First, however, let us realize that the end of our own road is only the beginning of a far longer voyage: for it has only been the purpose of this book to bring us to the frontier of the Promised Land and to view its landscape from the wrong side of Jordan. Our only task has been to give a clear and concrete idea of the prelude to mysticism and to lay down a few fundamental principles without which infused contemplation cannot be thoroughly understood.

In the present rather widespread revival of interest in Christian contemplation, we may come upon many books which give the impression that the mere beginning of infused contemplation is the end of the journey and that the Prayer of Quiet is the culminating point of the unitive way. This is a serious error for, as Saint John of the Cross says, the Night of Sense and the period of consoling quietude are only a preparation for the real mysticism of the Spiritual Night, Betrothal, and Transforming Union. In the Night of Sense and the Prayer of Quiet the contemplative is still in his infancy, and the tragedy is that in most cases mystical prayer does not get beyond this cradle stage. The cause of this arrested development is to be found in subtle forms of attachment to which the spirit clings perhaps without ever realizing its own imperfections.

The growth of mystical prayer depends on the purity of our love, and there can be many reasons why our love never gets purified. Some of these factors may be entirely beyond our control. Lack of proper spiritual guidance is one of the most common causes of the stunting of contemplative souls. Others who might possibly arrive at a higher degree of self-abnegation in more favorable surroundings are forced, by factors beyond their own control, to remain in an atmosphere of activity and confusion. For some inscrutable reason God may leave a potential contemplative in a situation where contemplation is all but out of the question. Such a one can be sure that Divine Providence will not, for all that, deprive him of one degree of sanctity and of glory in heaven. But the way to that consummation will be dark and winding and full of confusion and delay.

## 2

What are the stages of the journey from unformed faith to contemplative prayer?

To begin with, there can exist a kind of faith which is essentially supernatural and which is nevertheless not capable of establishing any vital contact between the soul and God. Such faith is an assent to revealed truth, but it has no life and no soul because it is not prompted by charity. It accepts the truth without any desire for God. Its submission is completely servile, as though it would have the unavoidable truth to be somehow other than it is. It receives the Gift of God's light without gratitude. It seeks to avoid all the consequences of this acceptance. It produces no fruit, no virtue, no evidence of love. This is faith born dead—and it might, perhaps, have been better for such faith never to have been born at all. Yet it can live. A movement of will, in correspondence to God's grace, can enkindle the breath of life in this belief and give it a soul, a "form."

So from the very beginning there is an especially intimate connection between our knowledge of God and our love for Him.

As soon as a soul is enlivened by grace, charity must work in it. God's love cannot be idle. Nor can any love. And there are other loves working in the soul besides the love of God. From the beginning, there is war between these different kinds of love. The love of God, which is selfless, declares war on the other love which is centered on ourselves. These two loves fight for possession of the soul. They have two main objectives. The ultimate objective is possession of the depths and substance of man's spirit: his whole being. In order to do this, they fight for his intelligence. And in order to gain the intelligence they work with diplomatic arts upon his will, because the will can give the whole soul away in one decision, either to one love or to the other.

There are many men in whom this conflict never takes

a decisive turn. Their life is a constant evasion and compromise. They fluctuate in a no-man's land between God and Mammon, which is as good as belonging to Mammon because Christ said, "He that is not with me is against me and he that gathereth not with me, scattereth." [1]

But when the love of God gains possession of a man's soul, it makes him want to know God, to know how to please God and to discover every possible way of serving Him and giving Him glory. Therefore, one of the first effects of charity is an intense hunger for the truth. Under the impulsion of this love man applies his mind to the conceptual knowledge of God. He seeks to find out as much as can be learned both from reason and from revelation about God and about the way to union with Him. Not all temperaments will seek God in the same way. Some will try above all to satisfy their minds with precise reasoning and clear speculative thought, by which, to some small extent, the truths of faith can be explained. Others will become engrossed in the vital organism of liturgical prayer in which God is at the same time known, loved, and served in a way that brings into play all the faculties of man's being and elevates his soul to God by easy and simple means. Still others will be drawn to seek God, almost from the first, by interior recollection and affective union within their own souls, and they will strive to effect this union by works of prayer, of self-denial, and of love. But in every case the concepts and propositions taught by faith are a kind of needle's eye. The virtue of faith itself is the needle. Our intellect and will, like a double thread, must be threaded into the needle and drawn by the needle through the veil of obscurity that separates us from God. Without the needle of faith the veil can never be penetrated.

In the first stages of the interior life, the mind and affections are easily absorbed in all the concepts which faith and reason have to offer us about God. Our love takes pleasure in the work of discovery—finding out new ideas, new levels of thought and of affective experience, and coming unexpectedly upon vast fields of activity that satisfy the cravings of a soul that has suffered a long spiritual confinement. Even though, from the beginning, the sure instinct of faith reminds such souls that all these affirmations about God are hedged in with a negative limitation, this presents no problem. They find a double delight in the positive and negative aspects of our intentional knowledge of God. They rejoice in the positive knowledge of His perfections as they are reflected by analogy in His creation, and then they multiply their joy beyond measure with the thought that God Himself is infinitely beyond every created perfection.

How long can love go on being satisfied with this play of concepts and affections? That depends on temperament and grace. It is a matter of individual vocation. In some saints, "light" and "darkness" bring alternate joy and anguish and yet never offer a serious theological problem. To some of the mystics, no matter how much they may have suffered, God was always Light, and when He came they always had something positive to say about Him. For others—as for Saint John of the Cross— God descends upon the soul in the "inflowing" of deep night and empties it of everything, reducing all thought and language to silence.

There is no essential difference between the mysticism

of "light" and the mysticism of "darkness." In either case, the experience of God in contemplation is one in which love outstrips the intelligence and attains to Him immediately in the darkness which lies beyond all our ideas. The difference between the two schools, if we can call them such, lies in the language in which they try to express what is essentially the same experience. The mystics of "light" come down out of the cloud and clothe their knowledge of God in positive images and concepts. They know well enough that no imagery can perfectly communicate what they have experienced, but they are bent on making as good a use of concepts as they can. The mystics of night are just as eager to use concepts for that purpose. But they insist on the transcendent character of the mystical experience. That is why they keep emphasizing the fact that mystical knowledge is attained in a "cloud of unknowing."

Saint Bernard of Clairvaux is a mystic of "light." His writings emphasize the delight rather than the anguish of the ascent to God. There is in him very little of the apophatic tradition. Yet a close study of his writings proves that mystical experience as he describes it is the same as that which we find in Saint John of the Cross.

## 3

How can love be said to "enlighten" the soul in the experience of that mystical Wisdom which is a Gift of the Holy Ghost and which properly constitutes Christian contemplation?

Christian theologians in general agree with Saint Thomas in saying that mystical wisdom knows God not "quidditatively" or in a clear concept of His essence but by a kind of secret affinity based on love. This mode of knowing is called "connatural" because, as we have seen, love unites the soul with God, and we can hardly help knowing something of One with Whom we have become identified!

Theologians offer different explanations of the precise way in which love illuminates the soul. The problem lies in the fact that the will is blind. Love is not knowledge.

Suarez solves the problem by saying that since the soul is one with God by love, it is an easy matter for the will to keep the intellect fixed on God. Hence, according to this view contemplation could sufficiently be described as gazing into the darkness where the will is held by love. This would not really be an illumination at all, since the intellect would see nothing. At best, the action of the will would keep the intelligence concentrated upon its invisible object—or, to put it in more practical terms, love would hold the mind suspended above concepts between earth and heaven, leaving it satisfied to take in, with a sweeping intuition, all the truth it has acquired by concepts, while realizing that God is infinitely more than thought can tell. The chief difficulty of this conception is that it suggests a kind of contemplation in which nothing ever happens. Such contemplation is only possible in theory. In practice, if the soul has nothing to do either on its own account or under the passive guidance of the Holy Spirit, the faculties fall asleep. And this sleep has nothing mystical or figurative about it. It is plain, ordinary sleep.

According to the spokesman of the Thomist school, John of Saint Thomas, love does more than merely direct the mind to an invisible object. Love makes a positive contribution to our knowledge of God in contemplative prayer. How? Not by attaining any other object than that which has already been presented to the intelligence and accepted by it in the conceptual formulas of faith. This object is God Himself. But while faith and hope only reach God at a distance—seeking Him as the Revealer of Truth and the Rewarder of our love—love goes straight to the depths of the Divine Substance and rests in God for His own sake alone, taking us, so to speak, out of ourselves and making us live entirely in Him. Such is the teaching of Saint Thomas Aquinas,[2] and theologians agree.

It follows from this that love gives the soul concrete possession of everything that is contained in the truths of faith. Love gives us an experience, a taste of what we have not seen and are not yet able to see. Faith gives us full title to this treasure which is ours to possess in darkness. Love enters the darkness and lays hands upon what is our own!

The precise point of the Thomist opinion is therefore that love gives us *a positive experience of the superabundant perfections which concepts can only express in a negative way*. Faith tells us: "God is good in a way that infinitely transcends any of our ideas of goodness." But when the flame of the Spirit of Love visits the soul in the darkness of wisdom and enkindles in it the Divine Fire, this experience of love gives us a direct and positive realization of that abundant goodness which concepts could only declare to be beyond their knowledge. Faith tells us of the infinite power of God, which is so great that no word of ours can contain its meaning. But love, which

transports the soul into the darkness beyond faith, unites
our being to the Being of God in such a way that we seem
to be annihilated and to vanish out of existence, so that
nothing remains but the power and the glory of God. It
is in this way that love astounds the intelligence with
vivid reports of a transcendent Actuality which minds
can only know, on earth, by a confession of ignorance.
And so, when the mind admits that God is too great for
our knowledge, Love replies: "I know Him!"

Nevertheless, Love is the first to admit that her own
experience of God is not, strictly speaking, knowledge.
It is here that the real anguish of the mystical night
begins. The problems and sufferings of the soul that has
had to abandon the evidence of sense and imagination
and to transcend the level of reason in order to find God,
are only the foretaste of the struggle that is to follow.
For now the soul must go forth unarmed and stripped of
every natural resource to enter that terrible purgation
which is the Night of the Spirit.

It may have seemed, to the contemplative, that when
he first entered the regions of mystical prayer the problem
of knowing God had solved itself by love. In one sense,
love does indeed provide a solution to a problem. It does
give us some experience of the God Who eludes our intentional knowledge of Him. But sooner or later it will
become quite evident to the mystic himself that this
apparent solution was merely the prelude to the statement
of the only problem that has any ultimate meaning for
any Christian, whether he be a contemplative or not.

Knowledge was not enough. Love is better than knowledge. But even then, love is not enough either. For the
action of God upon the soul that loves Him enlarges the

capacities of that soul until its faculties seem to acquire an infinite depth. But their indigence is as great as their capacity. They are as hungry as they are empty, and they have been made infinitely empty by the ravening fire of God's love. This emptiness, this huge agonizing void in which the soul is turned inside out by its own nothingness and by the emptiness of all things: this is the true problem.

The full, perfect, unlimited, untrammeled possession and fruition of God is only had in the Beatific Vision. The Beatific Vision does not exist outside heaven. The fleeting raptures of this earth, which are a prelude to heaven, can never turn the eyes of the contemplative from his true destiny. His whole life is consumed in this desire for God as He can only be seen in heaven.

In the beginning of the contemplative life, it is possible for the soul to rest for long periods absorbed in the consolation of divine love. The spirit is in a certain sense satisfied by that love. Contemplation can even appear to become an end in itself, as if the intimate embrace of God's love were already as good as heaven. But this is an illusion. Sooner or later, like all created things, this joy must end. God takes care to see that it ends sooner in some souls than in others. The love that was sweet and consoling becomes a purgatorial flame. The repose that was our friend becomes a terrible adversary. It devours our bones. Contemplation descends upon us now no longer like dew but like a desert wind, smothering our whole being in fire and sand. The faculties begin to turn upon themselves like paper blistering at the approach of flame. The will shrivels and twists and the mind disintegrates into ashes consumed by thirst for the vision of God.

If love, which seemed to be heaven itself, suddenly

turns into hell, how can it be the solution to a problem? Love is no solution. Love is the problem.

If love alone were heaven, there would be no anguish on earth for those who love God. Yet it is those who love God who must suffer the greatest anguish on earth. This is absolutely necessary. For just as conceptual knowledge creates anguish in the contemplative by reminding him how little he can know of God, so the possession of God by love, on earth, fills him with still greater agony because it tells him, even more clearly, that he can only rest in vision.

If neither the mind nor the will can solve our problem, who can? The answer is to be found in God alone. We cannot see Him with our own intelligence, because no intelligence that is not God can see God. God Himself must become our vision of God. And so, as Saint John of the Cross says:

The soul then desires to see herself possessed by this great God, by whose love the heart feels itself to be stolen away and wounded; and being unable to suffer any longer she begs Him to reveal and show His beauty, which is His divine essence and to slay her with the vision thereof and thus to loose her from the flesh since she cannot see Him in the flesh and have fruition of Him as she desires.[3]

The whole mystical ascent of the soul is a purification by infused love. When the soul is completely purified, it will see God. In proportion as it is purified, it comes to know Him better and better. For He reveals Himself to the soul, as we have said, by the action of His love. The contemplative is repeatedly made aware of this tremendous stranger dwelling within him. Every movement of the Spirit of God within us increases our love for Him and our desire to see Him clearly. In the words of Saint John of the Cross:

This special presence of God in the soul by love is so lofty that it seems to the soul that there is an immense hidden being there, of which she is conscious, and out of which God has communicated to her certain obscure glimpses of His divine beauty; and these produce such an effect upon the soul that they cause her to conceive a great aspiration and to faint in desire for that which she feels to be hidden there in that presence. . . . At this time the soul faints with the desire to immerse itself in that supreme good which it feels to be present and hidden; although it be hidden, the soul is very deeply conscious of the good and delight that are therein. And therefore the soul is attracted by this good and carried away by it with greater violence than that wherewith the natural object is attracted to its center.[4]

The verse of *The Spiritual Canticle* on which the saint is here commenting repeats exactly what we have been saying about love. Love does not heal our ignorance: mystical love is a sickness which vision alone can cure.

> *Mira que la dolencia*
> *De amor, que no se cura*
> *Sino con la presencia y la figura.*

*The Spiritual Canticle* contains the most complete exposition of the highest degrees of the mystical life—spiritual betrothal and transforming union. In transforming union the soul is almost as completely united to God as it will be in heaven. It sometimes sees the three Divine Persons within itself, and itself in them, with a clarity so great that some theologians think it is an immediate intuition of God as He is in Himself, differing only from the Beatific Vision by its transient character and by its comparative obscurity.

But in his description of mystical experience on the level of transforming union, Saint John of the Cross emphasizes the fact that here in this state the soul is filled with a more intense and ardent desire for the clear and permanent vision of God than it ever knew before. True, the soul is now almost perfectly pure and the only thing that stands between it and God is the thin veil of mortal and bodily existence. True, also, its desire can no longer cause it any suffering. The flame of love has burned every imperfection out of the soul and there remains nothing to be destroyed. Therefore the fire of the Holy Ghost consumes the soul no longer with agony but with joy. The flames of this fire entirely envelop the spirit and transform it into fire like itself, and together, in the exultation of divine liberty, they celebrate the feast of their nuptials.

Yet even here, at the climax of mystical perfection, which is the consummation of perfect charity in so far as it can be attained on this earth, love cries out with a more and more ardent hunger and sweetly demands the satiation of perfect vision. The last four stanzas of *The Spiritual Canticle* are the most perfect hymn ever written in the praise of that supreme theology which is the contemplation of God in heaven. Here there is no darkness. The dawn has come. The first rays of the morning sun, the Divine Word, have penetrated the pure depths of the soul transformed in His Light.

The soul stands on the bank of another Jordan—the bright calm river of death. It looks across the river and sees clear light upon the mountains of the true promised land. It begins to be ravished to the depths of its being by the clean scent of forests full of spice and balsam. It stands upon the river bank with the wonderful soft wind of the New World playing upon its cheeks and upon its eyelids and in its hair. And now it knows that the country it once took to be Canaan, the poor indigent earth of early contemplation, was nothing more than a desert—a waste of dry rock to which it had escaped, at great cost, from the vain wisdom that is Egypt.

But here is God. He is the Promised Land. Nothing is lost in Him. The whole world shines in His bosom. Creatures of all kinds spring forth without end from the bright abyss of His Wisdom. The soul itself sees itself in Him, and Him in itself, and in them both, the whole world. It sees all things, all men living and dead, the great souls and the little souls, the saints, the glorious Mother of God, and it is one with them all for they are all One, and Christ, God, is this One. He is the Promised Land, He is the Word, He is the Beloved.

Here, in Him, all the articles of faith have converged their rays and have burst open and showered the mind with fire. From Him they came, through Him they came, to Him they return, bringing with them the minds they have raised up in radiance from the sepulcher of vain learning. In Him the articles of faith have disappeared. He is their substance. There is no further need for them to prophesy in part, for when that which is perfect is come, that which is in part shall be done away. The whole *Spiritual Canticle* can be summed up in a sentence from Saint Paul: "We see now, through a glass, in a dark manner: but then, face to face. Now I know in part; but then I shall know even as I am known." [5]

And so the soul, transformed in God and waiting at the threshold of heaven, sings its desire for His theology.

Let us rejoice, Beloved,
Let us go to see ourselves in Thy beauty,
To the mountain and the hill
Whence the pure water flows.
Let us enter deeper into the thick woods

And then we shall go on
To the high caverns on the crag
To the well-hidden caverns!
And we shall go inside
And taste new pomegranate wine!

You would show me there
My soul's desire.
And there, soon, You, my Love, my Life
Would give me what you let me have the other day:

The breathing of the air,
The song of the sweet Philomel,
The grove and its beauty,
In the serene night,
The flame that burns me up but gives no pain

For no one looked upon it.
Neither did Aminadab appear.
The siege calmed down.
And the long train of horses
Went winding down to look upon the waters.[6]

# 4

Having come this far and being so near the end of the road,
our minds and hearts, swifter than the tortuous development of thought on paper, run forward to their goal. They
already fly to rest in Him Who is the end of all our search.
It becomes burdensome to write longer, and even the reader
finds no further use in reading. Nevertheless it would do
less honor to our saint and give less glory to God if we

omitted to round out the logical development of our theme. For there is much contained in these few stanzas. A brief explanation will make that content our possession.

These verses contain the essence of Catholic theology. They are a summary of the most perfect contemplation. They give us, once again, the conclusions we have already discovered to be those of Saint Thomas Aquinas on the ultimate relations of knowledge and love in divine union.

Saint Paul says that in heaven "I shall know even as I am known." The perfect contemplation of God on earth in transforming union and in heaven in the Beatific Vision is the mutual vision of the Word and the soul united in God's own vision of Himself. They see one another "in His beauty" according to the words of the poem. Saint John of the Cross paraphrases the statement of the soul:

May I be so transformed in thy beauty that, being alike in beauty, we may both see ourselves in Thy beauty, since I shall have Thine own beauty; so that when one of us looks at the other each may see in the other his beauty, the beauty of both being thy beauty alone, and I being absorbed in Thy beauty.[7]

This vision is the highest perfection of the intellect. It is the most perfect theology. It is the consummation of wisdom. In what does it consist?

The lines that follow show us that Saint John of the Cross is here completing the doctrine which He has taught us all along. It is nothing else but the doctrine of the Catholic Church. The perfect vision of God is a clear intuition which in one glance takes in and, in a certain measure, comprehends everything that is obscurely revealed, in fragmentary fashion, by all the separate articles of faith, by all the truths revealed by God and even by those truths about God and His creation which reason can grasp, analogically, through philosophy. "The Mountain and the Hill" are, says Saint John of the Cross, symbols for all knowledge. They stand for the two kinds of knowledge of God of which the Fathers spoke. The "mountain" is what is traditionally called the "morning knowledge" (*cognitio matutina*) of God: the vision of the divine perfections in the Word. The "hill" is the lesser, "evening knowledge" (*cognitio vespertina*) of God's perfections reflected through His creatures. But make no mistake about these two kinds of knowledge: they are both clear, face-to-face visions of God. The "evening knowledge" is not our sorry analogical and deductive reasoning about God. It sees Him resplendent in His creation because, like Saint Benedict, it sees the world and all things gathered together in one ray of His light.

From this mountain and this hill flows the "pure water" of understanding without images, without phantasms, and without the slightest taint of ignorance.

As for the "thick woods," what are they? Saint John of the Cross tells us that he meant them to symbolize all the judgments and works of God, all the mysteries of His manifestation of Himself in history, in the action of His Divine Providence which shapes all things in all lives in order to make everything converge toward the working out of His divine plan.

The soul desires to enter this thicket and incomprehensibility of judgments and ways, because she is dying with the desire to enter very far into the knowledge of them; for to have that knowledge is a priceless delight, exceeding all that can be felt. Wherefore David, speaking of their sweetness, said thus: The judgments of the Lord are true and have justice in themselves; they are more to be desired and more coveted than gold and than the precious stone of great worth; and they are sweet above honey and the honeycomb. So much so that thy servant loved and kept them. Wherefore the soul greatly desires to be immersed in these judgments and to have a deeper knowledge of them and to that end it would be a great consolation and joy to her to pass through all the afflictions and trials of the world, and through all else that might be a means to her thereto, howsoever difficult and grievous it might be; and through the agonies and perils of death, that she might enter more deeply into her God.[8]

It would require pages to exhaust the deep beauty of the thought contained in this passage. Let it serve, if God so wills, for other reflections at some other time. Sufficient, at this point, is the observation that this knowledge of God in "His judgments" is one of the great prerogatives of obedient faith and of a submission that discovers the highest good when good is apparently overwhelmed by evil. This, and this alone, is the wisdom which penetrates that mystery of iniquity which is the scandal of the world. This is the only wisdom which has eyes to discover that evil has no power against God because even the wills of those who hate Him serve only as the instruments of His love and shape the destinies of His elect and polish the stones of His eternal City.

I said explicitly that this vision of God in His judgments implied a kind of mystical intuition of God's action in human history. That thought was not explicit in Saint John of the Cross. It nevertheless flows necessarily from what he says, because every new development in human history is the expression of some mysterious and divine judgment. This is also true of the smallest events in the life of every individual. The wisdom and mercy of God shape our whole lives, "rough hew them though we may." The only means by which we can surely learn to find God in our lives is by the identification of His mercy with His justice. We do not learn, in all truth, that justice and mercy are ultimately one, unless we experience God's mercy in His justice. That means that we must learn, by faith, first of all, and then by supernatural science and fortitude and counsel and piety, to recognize God's love in things that cause us suffering. And so Saint John of the Cross can say:

Suffering is a means, to the soul, of entering farther into the thicket of the delectable wisdom of God; for the purest suffering brings with it the most intimate and purest knowledge, and, in consequence, the purest and loftiest joy which comes from having penetrated into the deepest knowledge.[9]

We are here breathing the pure, rarefied atmosphere of great heights, for we are walking along a ridge where even strong climbers grow dizzy with mountain sickness. How much more we of little faith! Yet we are the ones in some sense best equipped to understand the mystery of His mercy because we are so constantly and so totally its object. Saint Thérèse of Lisieux had entered as deep into these deep woods as ever did her Father and Master, Saint John of the Cross.

# CHAPTER XIX

# The Giant
# Moves in His Sleep

God, Who is infinite intelligence, contemplates His Truth in the Mirror of an Idea which is at the same time identical with His Substance and Nature and yet a Person in His own right. The Person, this Image which is in every way identical with the Father except for a special relation of Sonship, since He proceeds from the Father, is the Word. He is the Splendor of the Father's Glory, as the liturgy sings. *Splendor paternae gloriae de luce lucem proferens.*[1] In order to reveal all His Divine Perfections to the world, God was not content to speak to the patriarchs and prophets. The Word assumed a Human Nature which subsisted in His Divine Person in such a way that the Man, Jesus Christ, was in all literal truth God and the Word of God. He and the Father were one, not in the moral or mystical union by which holy persons become one with God, but consubstantially identified in one Divine Nature. Therefore Jesus could say, "He that sees me, sees the Father also. The Father and I are One." [2] And Saint Paul tells us that God has "spoken to the world in His Son." *Locutus est nobis in Filio.*[3]

The Divine Purpose in all this was not simply that the Word should be made flesh and dwell among us for a while, giving us a glimpse of the Divine Perfections hidden in what the Fathers called the "Cloud" of His Sacred Humanity. He would not linger in the world for a brief moment and then withdraw, leaving only a faint and transitory memory of His passage. The Apostle John tells us the true purpose of the Incarnation. Jesus came to unite all mankind to God in Himself, in what Saint Paul calls "one Body." "To as many as received Him He gave the power to be made the sons of God, to them that believe in His Name." [4] Christ is the Living Bread of divine Truth, sent to nourish the supernatural life which begins with faith. We enter into the Mystery of Christ most fully by partaking of His Body and His Blood in the Blessed Eucharist and by carrying out in our lives the commandments and counsels which He gave us. This life of the Christian in Christ, by the Sacraments and by the practice of Christian virtue, makes him share in the very life by which Christ Himself lives in the Father. Therefore the whole Christian economy is ordered to this: that men should be drawn, by the Holy Spirit of love, through Christ, to God the Father, and should live immersed in the abyss of divine contemplation of which the pure, flaming center is the Divine Word. Jesus clearly told us this when He said: "As the living Father hath sent me, and I live by the Father, so he that eateth me the same shall live by me." [5]

Just as all the infinite Light, Life, and Goodness which are in the Word are generated by the Father, with whom He is one, so too the divine wisdom and contemplation, the supernatural life and love and peace which fill the heart of the Christian proceed from Christ with the Holy Ghost and the Father dwelling in the depths of his being.

Saint John of the Cross has just told us something of this mystical presence of Christ within us. The mystic begins to discover something of Christ dwelling within him by grace "like an immense hidden being . . . out of which God has communicated certain obscure glimpses of His Divine Beauty." [6]

In a word, there is no contemplation of God save in Christ, for Christ is the Word of God and the Beauty of God and the Truth of God, in Whom God beholds His own Divine Splendor.

In *The Ascent of Mount Carmel,* after rejecting all spurious forms of mysticism and even all genuine forms of mystical experience that were less pure than perfect faith, Saint John of the Cross devotes a powerful chapter to the truth that in Christ, as He is presented to us by the deposit of Revelation entrusted by Him to His Church, we find all that can possibly be known of God. And now, in *The Spiritual Canticle,* he is about to tell us also that even in heaven the saints behold God in the mysteries of Christ.

First, let us consider the passage from *The Ascent:*

He that would now enquire of God or seek any vision or reve-lation would not only be acting foolishly but would be commit-ting an offence against God by not setting his eyes entirely on Christ and seeking no new thing or aught beside. . . .

If anyone, says Saint John of the Cross, were to ask God for some new revelation that was outside the deposit of faith, God might answer him in these terms:

If thou desirest me to answer thee with any word of consolation, consider my Son who is subject to Me brought into subjection [to men] for love of me, and afflicted [by them] and thou shalt see how fully He answers thee. If thou desirest me to expound to thee secret things or happenings, set thine eyes on Him alone

and thou shalt find the most secret mysteries and the wisdom
and wondrous things of God which are hidden in Him, even as
My Apostle says: *In quo sunt omnes thesauri sapientiae et
scientiae Dei absconditi.* That is: In this Son of God are hidden
all the treasures of wisdom and knowledge of God. These treasures
of wisdom shall be very much loftier and more delectable and
more profitable for thee than the things that thou desirest to
know.[7]

And now, the soul sings in *The Spiritual Canticle* of a
mysterious ascent with the Beloved into the "caverns on
the crag." These caverns, says Saint John of the Cross,
are the mysteries of Christ, and the crag itself is Christ.
The language in which the saint describes this wisdom
is everywhere superlative. The contemplation of God in
the mysteries of the Incarnate Word is "the loftiest and
most delectable wisdom of all His works." [8] He insists, of
course, that the soul is here talking about contemplation of these mysteries not on earth but in the Beatific
Vision of heaven. In fact, one of the reasons for the ardent
desire of the soul to attain to this perfect vision is that it
longs to know "the lofty mysteries of God and Man (that
is: of the Incarnate Word, the Man-God) which are loftiest in wisdom and are hidden in God." [9]

What is more, Saint John of the Cross makes a most
powerful statement which has altogether been overlooked
by some of his commentators. He not only says that the
mystical penetration of the mysteries of Christ is the highest of all the graces of prayer, but he even declares that all
the graces, all the mystical favors, all the passive purifications and all the manifold preparations which the soul has
had to pass through in its ascent to transforming union,
and even transforming union itself, have no other function
than to dispose it for this supereminent knowledge of God

in Christ. We seem to be hearing an echo of the great Saint Paul:

To me, the least of all the saints, is given the grace to preach among the Gentiles the unsearchable riches of Christ and to enlighten all men that they may see what is the dispensation of the mystery which has been hidden from eternity in God Who created all things: that the manifold wisdom of God may be made known to the principalities and powers in heavenly places, through the Church according to the eternal purpose which He made, in Christ Jesus our Lord.[10]

Here are the words of Saint John of the Cross:

All these favors are inferior to the wisdom of the mysteries of Christ for all are, as it were, preparations for coming thereto.[11]

How does he describe this wisdom? I quote his explanation of the line about the "caverns on the crag."

The rock of which she here speaks is Christ. The lofty caverns of this rock are the lofty and high and deep mysteries of the wisdom of God which are in Christ, concerning the hypostatic union of human nature with the Divine Word and the correspondence to this, which is the union of men in God, and in the agreement which there is between the justice and mercy of God as to the salvation of the human race in the manifestation of His judgments. . . .[12]

The emphasis placed by Saint John of the Cross on the knowledge of the mysteries of Christ might arouse a question in the mind of a theologian. But if he has paid attention to the words we have just quoted, the question will already have been answered. Or at least Saint John of the Cross will have given some suggestion of what will presently be his answer. If Saint John of the Cross meant that the highest wisdom and the loftiest contemplation of the blessed in heaven terminated in the Sacred Humanity of Christ, considered precisely as a Human Nature, the statement would be most incorrect and would fall far short of the truth. But in any case, Saint John has made it quite clear that for Him the "mysteries of Christ" mean not merely the exterior events in the historical life of Christ—which were nevertheless all manifestations of the infinite wisdom and goodness of God—but especially the union of two Natures in One Person and the union of all men in the Mystical Body of Christ.

But even taking the "mysteries of Christ" in their deepest possible sense, it would be incorrect to say that the mystery of the Incarnation, the Hypostatic Union, and the mysteries of our Redemption intimately connected with it formed, together, the "loftiest of all mysteries" and were therefore the highest object of the contemplation of the blessed in heaven. Such a statement would be plainly false and contrary to the whole teaching of the Church. It would be an unwarranted exaggeration and a distortion of Catholic Truth.

But Saint John of the Cross has made no such exaggeration. He situated the Incarnation in its proper place when he said that it contained "the loftiest and most delectable wisdom *of all God's works*." [13] This is of course absolutely unquestioned, when the Incarnation is taken, as it is by Saint John of the Cross, to include also the whole economy of Redemption which flowed from it.

In actual fact, however, the first and greatest of all mysteries, which exceeds all others by its infinite dignity and depth, is the mystery of the Inner Life of God Himself, Whose One Nature subsists in three really distinct Persons. Considered in relation to this Mystery, the Incarnation is only a means to an end: the Word made flesh manifests the Truth of God to men, makes His Life theirs to share by right of adoption. But if He does so, it is only because the only worthy end of all is the glory of the Most Holy Trinity of Persons in One Nature. This, and this above all, is the highest and most perfect object of the contemplation of the blessed in Heaven. And it is precisely this that Saint John of the Cross will explain when he unveils the hidden meaning of his stanza:

> The breathing of the air,
> The song of the sweet Philomel,
> The grove and its beauty,
> In the serene night,
> The flame that burns me up but gives no pain . . .[14]

When we read his profound, though brief, reflections on the life of the three Divine Persons in the beatified soul, we can see that in some manner this mystery was already contained in the whole complex of mysteries surrounding the Incarnation. This "breathing of the air" which is the Spiration of the Third Person of the Blessed Trinity in the soul, is communicated to the soul by the Father, through the mysteries of Christ. It is therefore given to it in the "high caverns on the crag." And therefore, in this sense, the Incarnation can once again be said to be pre-eminent: for although like all other mysteries it flows from the highest of all, the mystery of the Trinity, yet with regard to us the Incarnation is the most important of all because it is through Christ that we are incorporated into the life of the three Divine Persons and receive into our souls the Holy Spirit, the "bond of perfection," Who unites us to God with the same Love which unites the Father and the Son.

Let us glance at the beautiful paragraph Saint John of

the Cross devotes to this action of the Holy Spirit in *The Spiritual Canticle,* leaving the reader to study, at his own leisure, the more extended treatment of the same idea which is the theme of *The Living Flame of Love.*

It would not be a true and total transformation if the soul were not transformed in the three Persons of the Holy Trinity in a revealed and manifest degree. . . . The soul united and transformed in God breathes into God the same divine breath that God, when she is transformed in Him, breathes into her in Himself. . . . And there is no need to consider it impossible that the soul should be capable of aught so high as to breathe in God as God breathes in her after a mode of participation. For since God grants her the favor of uniting her in the most Holy Trinity, wherein she becomes deiform and God by participation, how is it a thing incredible that she should also perform her work of understanding knowledge and love—or rather should have it performed in the Trinity, together with it, like the Trinity itself? This however comes to pass by a mode of communication and participation which God effects in the soul herself; for this is to be transformed in the three Persons in power and wisdom and love, and herein the soul is like to God, for it was to the end that she might come to this that He created her in His image and likeness.[15]

Saint John of the Cross leaves us no doubt as to the supereminent dignity of this great mystery when he closes his description of the union of the soul with the three Divine Persons by explicitly saying that this is the final end for which we were all created. This, therefore, is the very substance of the Beatific Vision, which flows from love because it depends entirely on a transformation of the soul in God by love.

But now, we have already insisted on the doctrine of Saint Thomas who, while declaring that the Beatific Vision is essentially an act of the intellect, and that it

flowed from love, also completed his statement by the conclusion that the vision also had its end and perfection in
love. This brings us, at last, to the final convolution of
our spiral ascent to God through the mystical dialectic of
knowledge and love.

Love of God first led reason to seek Him in faith. Faith
gave reason light to seek Him in greater love. This greater
and more sacrificial love raised the intelligence above the
concepts of reason and took it beyond the intentional
knowledge of theology. But it was not the solution of the
problem of knowledge and love, even though it did give
the soul a quasi-experience of God as He is in Himself.
This intimate union of love with God in obscurity kindled
in the soul a dark and consuming flame of desire for perfect vision. Progressively purified by this flame, the soul
has grown in vision and reached the highest knowledge of
God possible to it in this life. There remains the Beatific
Vision alone, which gives the soul perfect possession of
God. We have already seen Saint John of the Cross's
explanation that the soul does not seek this vision merely
for the sake of seeing. It wants to see in order to love.

Love, then, is to be the end of all. Perfect praise and
adoration of God clearly seen and possessed in the light
of glory—these will be the final and the eternal delight of
the soul transfigured in God and overflowing with His
own delight.

Saint John of the Cross describes the joy of the soul,
entering with Christ into the knowledge of His mysteries,
in order, with Christ, to give perfect praise to the Most
Holy Trinity Whose wisdom and mercy they manifest in
full measure. This jubilation, this *laus gloriae* or praise of
glory, in the words of Saint Paul, is what the mysterious

poem of the Carmelite mystic offers to us under the symbol of new "pomegranate wine."

The new wine of these pomegranates [the mysteries of Christ] which the Bride says here that she and the Spouse will taste is the fruition and delight of the love of God that in the knowledge and understanding of them overflows the soul. For even as from many pomegranate seeds there comes but one new wine when they are pressed, even so from all these wonders and grandeurs of God which are infused into the soul there overflows for her one fruition of delight of love alone, which is the drink of the Holy Spirit; the which she offers at once to her God, the Word-Spouse, with great tenderness of love.[16]

With the taste of this wine on our tongue and the longing of love in our hearts, with the divine thirst beginning to burn even in our own poor tongues spoiled by the taste for this world and for its many sins, we can at last conclude this introduction to Christian mysticism. And we do so, after all, with the reflection that silence is better than speech, even though speech is necessary, because faith cometh by hearing, and the seed of contemplation, which is nothing else but the seed of the word of God, is only sown in the hearts of men by the speech of other men.

The Blessed Virgin Mary was the wisest theologian. She was the Mother of the Word Who is at once the Theology of God and of Men. God's Truth entered so deeply into her life as to become Incarnate in her virginal flesh. All Wisdom was centered in her Immaculate Heart, *sedes Sapientiae*. When the angel came to her at the Annunciation he found her in deepest silence. Few words are recorded of her who gave us the Word. And when she had given Him to the world, what should she do but listen to Him? "She kept all these words, treasuring them in her heart?" [17] And so, in every way, Our Lady is the model of contemplatives and the mirror of mystics. Those who love the pure Truth of God instinctively love the simplicity of the Immaculate Mother of God. She draws them into the heart of her silence and of her humility. She is the Virgin of Solitude, Whom God called His hermit—*una est columba mea in foraminibus petrae*. She hid in the caverns of the rock Saint John of the Cross was just talking about. She lived as a hermit in the lofty mysteries of her Son. She lived all the time in the sky, though she walked on the earth and swept floors and made beds and made supper for the Carpenters. What was happening in her unimaginably clean soul, in the stainless mirror of her being which God had made to receive His perfect likeness?

When the angel spoke, God awoke in the heart of this girl of Nazareth and moved within her like a giant. He stirred and opened His eyes and her soul saw that in containing Him she contained the world besides. The Annunciation was not so much a vision as an earthquake in which God moved the universe and unsettled the spheres, and the beginning and end of all things came before her in her deepest heart. And far beneath the movement of this silent cataclysm she slept in the infinite tranquillity of God, and God was a child curled up who slept in her and her veins were flooded with His wisdom which is night, which is starlight, which is silence. And her whole being was embraced in Him whom she embraced and they became tremendous silence.

It is the mission of Our Lady in the world to form this Christ of hers, this Giant, in the souls of men much as He formed Himself in her. She brings them His grace, and

His grace is His own life-giving presence. He is born in every man by Baptism, but we do not know it. He casts His shadow over the soul that first senses Him in the peace of contemplation: but that is not enough. At the summit of the mystical life, God must move and reveal Himself and shake the world within the soul and rise from His sleep like a giant.

That is what Saint John of the Cross tells us in *The Living Flame of Love*. It is my last quotation:

This awakening is a movement of the Word in the substance of the soul, of such greatness and dominion and glory, and of such intimate sweetness, that it seems to the soul that all the balms and perfumed spices and flowers in the world are mingled and shaken and revolved together to give their sweetness; and that all the kingdoms and dominions of the world and all the powers and virtues of heaven are moved. And not only so, but all the virtues and substances and perfections and graces of all created things shine forth and make the same movement together and in unison. . . . Hence it comes to pass that when this great Emperor moves in the soul, Whose Kingdom, as Isaias says, is borne on His shoulder . . . then all seem to move together. . . . Even so, when a palace is thrown open a man may see at one and the same time the eminence of the Person who is within the palace and also what he is doing. . . . Though the soul is substantially in God, as is every creature, He draws back from before it some of the veils and curtains which are in front of it so that it may see of what nature He is; and then there is revealed to it and it is able to see (though somewhat darkly, since not all the veils are drawn back) that Face of His that is full of grace. And since it is moving all things by its power, there appears together with it that which it is doing and it appears to move in them, and they in it, with continual movement; and for this reason the soul believes that God has moved and awakened, whereas that which has moved and awakened is in reality the soul itself.[18]

# Biographical Notes

(The theological writers named and quoted in the course of this volume are, for the most part, still unknown to the average American reader. The works of some of them have never been translated into English. Even their strange names resemble one another—for example, Saint John of the Cross, John of Saint Thomas, and Saint Thomas Aquinas. Without trying to identify every name mentioned in the book, I can at least give a brief sketch of the principal writers I have followed and show where they belong in the history of Christian thought.)

## Saint Gregory of Nyssa
### [ASIA MINOR, 4TH CENTURY, A.D.]

Gregory, Bishop of Nyssa (in Asia Minor), is at once the most important and the most neglected of the early Christian mystical theologians. He was the brother of Saint Basil the Great, who introduced monasticism into Asia Minor, whence it was to pass to Europe. The two brothers, together with another Gregory, Bishop of Nazianz, formed a powerful triad. They saved the Church in the age of its greatest peril—for theirs was the century of Arianism. And since Arianism denied the Divinity of Christ, its triumph would have meant the extinction of Christian mysticism. For Christian mysticism would be impossible without the Incarnate Word, and without a Trinity of Persons in the unity of Divine Nature. Both these doctrines were denied by the Arians. The consequence of such a denial, in mysticism, reduces contemplation to the level of poetry or, at best, of pantheism.

Gregory of Nyssa was born in Cappadocia (part of modern Turkey) about 335 A.D., when the fervor of the Desert Fathers

was at its height. A man of literary tastes, he first married and
settled in the world, but later he entered the monastery founded
by his brother, Saint Basil, on the banks of the river Iris. There
he gave himself to prayer, asceticism, and the contemplative
study of theology. In 371 Saint Basil, who had meanwhile become Bishop of Caesarea, consecrated Gregory bishop of a nearby
city called Nyssa. Although Gregory did not come up to his
brother's expectations as an administrator, he distinguished himself by his theological writings and by his preaching against the
prevalent Arian heresy. His was certainly not an age in which
contemplatives were tempted to imagine that questions of dogma
were mere matters of speculation and therefore had no essential
role to play in an "affective" monastic spirituality. It was, in
fact, contemplatives—Saint Athanasius, Saint Basil, the two
Gregorys—and the monastic order as a whole who saved Christian theology in the fourth century.

Saint Gregory is the true Father of Christian apophatic mysticism, but this distinction of his has been forgotten since the
appearance of a certain Christian Platonist of the fifth century,
whose works were falsely ascribed to Denis (Dionysius the
Areopagite, converted by Saint Paul at Athens in the Apostolic
Age [1]). This *Pseudo-Dionysius,* as he is called, was a follower of
Proclus, the last of the great Neo-Platonists (fifth century, A.D.),
but in his reconciliation of Platonic ideas with Christian faith
he was also following in the footsteps of Saint Gregory of Nyssa,
who had died at the end of the fourth century. Since they were
supposed to spring from the Apostolic Age, the works of Pseudo-
Dionysius acquired such prestige that all subsequent apophatic
Christian mysticism has rested on him. In actual fact, Gregory
of Nyssa was not only the true fountainhead of this mystical
tradition but was also perhaps a greater philosopher and theologian than Pseudo-Dionysius. Two great followers of Saint Gregory of Nyssa share with him the honor of laying the foundations
of mystical theology. They were both hermits at Nitria, in the
Egyptian Desert. One was *Saint Macarius* of Alexandria, the
other *Evagrius Ponticus.*

Saint Gregory of Nyssa played such an important part in the
Second General Council of Constantinople that communion with

him was henceforth a proof of strict orthodoxy. His greatness as a dogmatic theologian has never been forgotten. His mystical and ascetical works have always been well known in the Oriental Church. Only in our own day have they have rediscovered by the West.

## Saint Bernard of Clairvaux
### [FRANCE, 12TH CENTURY]

Although he does not belong to the Patristic Age, Saint Bernard is sometimes called the "last of the Church Fathers." The title is justified by his loyalty to the spirit of Patristic theology in a period of intellectual ferment that preceded the great development of medieval scholasticism. Bernard of Clairvaux is one of the greatest and most characteristic figures of the Middle Ages. The son of a Burgundian nobleman, Bernard entered the newly-founded monastery of Citeaux, near Dijon, in 1112. In doing so, he believed that he was leaving behind everything that attracted the attention of the world. Yet within a few years he covered the face of Europe with Cistercian monasteries. In turning the Order into a world movement, he made his time keenly conscious of the contemplative and penitential character of the monastic vocation.

The vast diffusion of Saint Bernard's writings—especially of his Sermons on the *Canticle of Canticles*—contributed more than any other single influence to form the mysticism of the Middle Ages. The spirit of Saint Bernard, strongly colored by his own temperament and personality, is one of ardent lyricism combined with seriousness and strength. We do not find in him the tenderness of Saint Francis, and yet he is not quite as tough as some of his descendants make him out to be, since one of the principal traits of his spirituality is his keen awareness of the goodness of God. The mystical writings of Saint Bernard are hymns that celebrate the sweetness of Transforming Union. They have earned him the title of "the mellifluous Doctor." Yet there is nothing mellifluous about some of the letters Bernard wrote to noblemen and members of the clergy who did not seem to him to be living up to their obligations. Indeed there is in them a certain note of violence; but we must not exaggerate either his sweetness or his strength.

Saint Bernard was a man of contrasts, almost a man of contradictions. He was keenly aware of this himself, since he called himself the "chimera of the age," burdened as he was by the distress of being the most important public figure in Europe when he wanted to remain hidden in the cloister. Not only did Bernard settle the destinies of nations, heal the wounds of religious dissidence and schism, and send Europe off on a Crusade, but his disciple was Pope Eugene III, who had once stoked the furnace in the warming-room at Clairvaux. Saint Bernard contributed more than inspiration, example, and advice to the society of his time. Although he frequently expressed his contempt for the philosophical speculation of the new schools that were growing up everywhere, he played a crucially important part in the theological developments of his age. In fact, he did theology a service which no other technical theologian was capable of doing when he brought about the condemnation of Abelard and Gilbert de la Porrée. His condemnation prepared the way for the sane intellectualism of the scholastics and it was perhaps partly due to the action of Saint Bernard that a thinker like Saint Thomas Aquinas was able, in the end, to set decadent Patristic theology free from its preoccupation with accidentals. After all, Saint Thomas adopted the same critical approach as Abelard, although he used it in an entirely different spirit and with altogether different results. The condemnation of Abelard also saved true Christian mysticism, and it was indeed the instinct of the contemplative that showed Saint Bernard the dangers inherent in Abelard's false notion of faith. The same instinct led the Abbot of Clairvaux to point out the error of Gilbert de la Porée's distinction between "God" and the "Divinity" which would have ended by reducing God to the level of any other being and would have disposed of His transcendence by narrowing it down to the limitations of a philosopher's concept. The greatest service Saint Bernard did for Christian mysticism, in his detection of singularly dangerous errors, was precisely the work of a technical theologian.

*Saint Thomas Aquinas*
[ITALY, 13TH CENTURY]

The greatest of all theologians surely needs no introduction. The vast scope of his theological and philosophic synthesis, the logic and serene clarity of his thought, and above all the combination of order, simplicity, and depth which characterize his *Summa Theologica* are a monument to his genius and to his sanctity. The power of Saint Thomas's speculative thought should not make us forget that he was also a mystic. His mystical theology fits into the apophatic tradition (for Saint Thomas commented on the works of Pseudo-Dionysius) but is not confined to it. Nor is his mystical doctrine formally separated from his dogma and moral theology. Since for Saint Thomas theology was an organic whole, his mysticism is not merely centered in the questions of the *Summa* devoted to the contemplative life [2] but in all his discussions of the relations of men with their God.

One might imagine, from the dispassionate objectivity of Saint Thomas, that the *Summa* was composed in years of silent and unruffled tranquillity. Yet Saint Thomas lived and fought in the thick of a tremendous intellectual crisis. The lucid order of the *Summa* was, in actual fact, not the fruit of cloistered rest but of an intense conflict amid the agitation of the Schools. Few people realize that Saint Thomas's contemporaries did not all receive his statements with wholehearted approval. Many of his characteristic doctrines were formulated in the hour of battle and defended at the risk of condemnation for heresy.

Born in 1225 in a castle of southern Italy, the young Aquinas was educated by the Benedictines at Monte Cassino. He later passed to the University of Naples, where he made his first acquaintance with the wave of skeptical rationalism which was flooding Christian universities under the influence of the Spanish Moor, Averroes. Thomas, whose ardent faith and love of God were united with a brilliant intelligence, entered the newly founded Order of Friars Preachers in order to lead a life of prayer, study, and defense of the truth. His brothers did not approve of his vocation and threw him in prison. There he spent a profitable year meditating on the Bible and on Aristotle. After recovering his freedom he went to Paris, then to Cologne, studying in both universities under the Dominican Master, Saint Albert the Great, who prepared him for his great work.

The intellectual world of the mid-thirteenth century was divided among three powerful forces. The future of Christian thought and, therefore, of the Christian religion depended on the struggle among these forces. At one extreme was the rationalism of Averroes. At the other was the strong traditionalist group which followed Saint Augustine and the Arab Neo-Platonist Avicenna. In the center were the Christian Aristotelians, Albert the Great and Thomas Aquinas.. The issues at stake were completely fundamental to Christianity. Averroism demanded the rejection of theology, placed man's highest happiness in the exercise of reason. The activity of knowing for its own sake completely fulfilled man's aspirations because, in fact, it was simply the manifestation of a Universal Intelligence working in him. The Augustinians, recognizing the implicit atheism of this philosophy, reacted powerfully against it. In reaffirming the transcendence of God and man's absolute dependence on Him, they ended by saying that even man's natural knowledge demanded the direct action of God upon his soul. This led them to deprecate reason in favor of faith and mystical intuition.

The greatest of the Augustinian school was *Saint Bonaventure,* Minister General of the Order of Friars Minor, who was Saint Thomas's contemporary, opponent, and friend. They died in the same year (1274). Close to Saint Thomas on many fundamental questions, Saint Bonaventure differed from him on others, especially on the relations of faith and reason in our approach to God, on the primacy of the intelligence over the will, on the unity of man's substantial form, and on the source of man's knowledge of transcendentals.

Saint Thomas entered the lists with one supremely important ideal: to defend the autonomy of man's intelligence and of the human personality against the extremists on both sides who threatened to submerge man in God, on the one hand, and in a universal active intellect on the other. The eagerness of the Augustinians to safeguard Christian mysticism and to bring the soul to divine union by the paths of faith and charity had,

Saint Thomas thought, actually jeopardized Christian mysticism by an unwise fideism and an unbalanced emphasis on love. Saint Thomas was an intellectualist, but it cannot be too often repeated that his insistence on the primacy of the intelligence was intended as the only safe guarantee of perfect charity and of mystical union. Saint Thomas, like all Christian theologians, knows perfectly well that the consummation of man's destiny is love and that the way to divine union is the way of the theological virtues, through the night of faith. Hence the paradox that the intellectualism of Thomas Aquinas turns out, after all, to be the supreme criterion of true mysticism, because there is no such thing as a sanctity that is not intelligent.

## Blessed John Ruysbroeck
### [BELGIUM, 14TH CENTURY]

One of the greatest of Christian mystics and the author of magnificent books on contemplation, John Ruysbroeck dominated the golden age of German and Flemish mysticism—the age of Tauler, Suso, and Thomas à Kempis. He was born in 1293 in a little village outside Brussels. Educated in the city, he grew up under the shadow of the Cathedral of Saint Gudule, where he became a chaplain after his priestly ordination in 1318. He spent some twenty-five years in the active life, but his preaching was already based on a deep interior life of contemplative prayer. Ruysbroeck devoted most of his gifts and energies to expounding the true nature of contemplation. It was a most important work. In 1308, the greatest theologian of the time, *John Duns Scotus,* had been sent to Cologne to refute the errors of the Beghards and Brothers of the Free Spirit. But Scotus died before his work was begun. The pantheism of the Beghards held that man was by nature identified with the Divine Essence and that, as soon as the "spiritual man" had acquired the proper techniques of recollection, he could achieve a perfect realization of his essential identity with God. This made him henceforth unable to sin and delivered him from all obedience to Church authority. It also enabled him to enjoy the Beatific Vision even on earth. Although Ruysbroeck sometimes attacked the Beghards with direct refutation, he concentrated above all on the positive statement of true doctrine rather than on the denial of what was false. In any case, Ruysbroeck was first of all a contemplative himself. Finding the busy life of Brussels too much of a distraction and wearied by the manner in which the liturgical offices were chanted by the canons of Saint Gudule, Ruysbroeck retired in 1343 to a forest hermitage at Groenendael, where he subsequently founded a small contemplative community under the Rule of Saint Augustine. Here Ruysbroeck led a simple retired life, frequently withdrawing into the forest to be alone with God. Yet he did not neglect to return to share with others, by writing and by the spoken word, the fruits of his contemplation. Groenendael became a center of Christian spirituality, attracting visitors from all parts of Germany and the Netherlands, so that the influence of Ruysbroeck was as widespread as it was to be lasting. The greatest of his books are *The Adornment of the Spiritual Marriage* and *The Sparkling Stone,* translated into English but now out of print. His *Seven Steps of the Ladder of Love* was also translated (London, 1943). The Benedictine monks of Saint Paul de Wisques, who translated Ruysbroeck from his original Flemish into French, assert that "no one has equaled Ruysbroeck in his ability to establish the structure of the contemplative life on firm philosophical foundations." [3]

It is quite true that Ruysbroeck's doctrine rests on firm philosophical and theological foundations, but he certainly does not deserve the unqualified praise which his learned translators have accorded him in this respect. Ruysbroeck's terminology is often extremely confusing, and it is not difficult to understand why he was bitterly attacked by theologians who, like Gerson, chancellor of the University of Paris, accused him of falling into the same pantheism which had misled the Beghards. This accusation was false, but the confusion which inspired it flows from the fact that Ruysbroeck's theology is at the same time eclectic and independent. He sometimes agrees with Saint Thomas Aquinas but most of the time falls within the Augustinian tradition. In any case, writing of mystical experience in poetic terms, he can justly claim the right to a certain independence.

Nevertheless, Saint John of the Cross, who was a far greater poet than Ruysbroeck and perhaps a greater mystic as well, is able to fit his mystical doctrine into a simple and powerful theological structure which is greatly superior to anything we find in Ruysbroeck. Saint John of the Cross has not lacked critics either, for severe criticism is the professional hazard of all who write about mystical experience. Nevertheless, the fact that Saint John of the Cross was faithful to a clear, well-established, and universally recognized set of principles, far from obstructing his freedom, only increased the power and the scope of a theology which is characteristically his own. The mystic of Groenendael, long venerated, was never formally beatified, but his *cultus* was sanctioned by the Holy See. His feast is celebrated locally in the diocese of Mechlin with a proper Mass and Office.

## Saint Teresa of Ávila
[SPAIN, 16TH CENTURY]

Since sanctity and contemplation perfect the whole human person, it is not surprising that some of the greatest mystics have been characterized by their warm human tenderness, their vivacious humor, and their simple common sense. All these natural qualities were transfigured by grace in the soul of Teresa de Ahumada to make her one of the most attractive personalities in the annals of the Church. As reformer of the Carmelite nuns she combined with her contemplative life a level-headed talent for administration and seemingly tireless resources of energy. Her story has come down to us in an autobiography which is considered one of the greatest productions of Spanish literature, although her other works are no less wonderful.

Born at Ávila on March 28, 1515, Teresa entered the Carmelite convent of the Incarnation, in her native city, when she was twenty-one. Far from becoming a saint in her novitiate, she drifted through some twenty years of religious mediocrity, neglecting the graces of interior prayer and living aimlessly from month to month without serious ideals with no one to direct her along the paths of religious perfection.

Only when Teresa was forty did she suddenly wake up to the seriousness of her position. Guided by the light of grace, she applied herself seriously to mental prayer and began to bring order into her life. Her progress was very rapid, especially under the influence of some of the great saints and theologians who providentially entered her life at this time. Her meeting with the Jesuit Saint Francis Borgia, her friendship with the Franciscan reformer Saint Peter of Alcantara, the direction of such men as the Dominican Bañez and the Jesuit Balthasar Álvarez contributed immensely to her spiritual growth.

The chief characteristic of Saint Teresa's spirituality is her realization of the importance of mental prayer. It was this that inspired her plans for the Carmelite reform. Her whole aim in returning to the original Carmelite Rule was to enable persons like herself to find the solitude and spiritual liberty upon which the contemplative life depends.

Teresa herself had a clearly apostolic notion of the contemplative life. She believed that her nuns, by their lives of prayer and sacrifice, would do much to atone for the religious confusion of sixteenth-century Europe, to save souls, and to preserve the unity of the Catholic Church. It is extremely significant that one of the finest fruits of the Catholic counterreformation should have been an order in which contemplative prayer in the strict sense was not only emphasized but adopted as an end.

When Saint John of the Cross joined Saint Teresa in 1568 and began, in his turn, to lay the foundations for a reform of the Carmelite Friars, a new note was added: the priests of the order would not only practice contemplation, they would also preach the ways of interior prayer and enable souls, by their direction, to arrive at a certain degree of contemplation, not only in convents but even in the world.

After a life of high contemplation, prodigious activity, and unbelievable suffering, Saint Teresa died on October 4, 1582. By that time there was scarcely an important town in Spain that did not have a convent of Discalced Carmelites.

*Saint John of the Cross*
[SPAIN, 16TH CENTURY]

Juan de Yepes was twenty-six when he first met Saint Teresa
in 1568. He had been five years in the Carmelite Order, but
because his hopes of a solitary and contemplative life could
not be fulfilled under the mitigated rule, he was preparing to
pass over to the Carthusians. Saint Teresa persuaded him that
God had other plans for him: he was not to join one of the
monastic orders for whom contemplation was largely a matter
of vocal prayer. He had not done wrong in becoming a Carmelite: all he needed to do was return to the original Carmelite
ideal and he would find plenty of opportunity for solitary communion with God, along with the mortification which protects
the "purity of heart" without which no man can "see" God.

At first sight, the young Carmelite friar was not the sort of
material on which you would expect to build a whole new
order. He was only five feet two. He had a shy, silent, sensitive
disposition and, far from being talkative, was sometimes so abstracted that he was often unaware that others were talking to
him. Nevertheless Saint Teresa soon found that he had profound wisdom born of experience. He was just as level-headed
as she was, and what is more, he was something of a theologian.
Besides all this, he had her energy and her courage, although he
did not share her colorful temperament. Finally, as it turned out,
he was a poet, one of the most interesting poets in an age of
genius. This, however, did not transpire until later.

The winter of 1568-1569 found the first three Carmelite friars
living in a little farmhouse outside a village called Duruelo.
They had tiny cells in the attic, and the snow blew in upon
them through the cracks in the tiles during their hours of
contemplation. In the daytime they preached all over the coun-
tryside. Foundations soon began to be made, and the reform
grew. But before long it had to stand the test of serious conflict.
The inevitable jealousy of the unreformed members of an order
undergoing reformation found numerous pretexts for hindering
the work of Saint Teresa. As a sequel to a stormy convent elec-
tion, John of the Cross was imprisoned in Toledo, where he was

very badly treated for about nine months. During this time, however, he wrote three of his greatest poems, which contained the doctrine which would later fill three books on mystical prayer.

After an escape from prison which was, to say the least, sensational, Saint John of the Cross rejoined his reform for a short but fruitful period of work and writing, during which he presided over several new foundations. By this time, the reform had become well established. In 1585 a new system of government was adopted by the Discalced Carmelites, and John of the Cross was named as a consultor on the new administrative council. The new system was none of Saint John's devising. Since the death of Saint Teresa in 1582 a new generation had sprung up and started to run the reform on new lines. The guiding spirit of this new development was a converted Genoese banker, Nicholas Doria. He was simply a man of action. He was a rigid, domineering ascetic with little relish for contemplation, and Saint Teresa had once drily remarked concerning him: "There are some kinds of sanctity that I do not understand."

Doria had already disposed of one of Saint Teresa's favorites, Jerome Gracian. The turn of John of the Cross was soon to come. After five years as a consultor, the saint was suddenly deprived of office and ordered to Mexico. He never left Spain, however. His health broke down completely in the summer of 1591. He was hospitalized in a convent, where the Prior disapproved of him and did not fail to remind him daily of the fact. There he died late in the year. He was canonized in 1726 and declared a Doctor of the Church two hundred years later.

Saint John of the Cross has never been a very popular saint, outside his native Spain. His doctrine is considered "difficult," and he demands of others the same uncompromising austerity which he practiced in his own life. Nevertheless, a close study of his doctrine, such as we have attempted in the present book, should prove that Saint John of the Cross had all the balance and prudence and "discretion" which mark the highest sanctity. He is not a fanatic, bent upon loading his subjects with insupportable burdens which will end by reducing them to moral and physical wrecks. The demands he makes are uncompromising in their essentials but flexible in all their accidental aspects. His only purpose is to bring the whole man, body and soul, under the guidance of the Spirit of God. In actual practice, Saint John of the Cross was relentlessly opposed to the formalism and inhumanity of those whom he compared to "spiritual black-smiths," violently hammering the souls of their victims to make them fit some conventional model of ascetic perfection. He well knew that this kind of asceticism was itself one of the most serious of defects, because it was often a manifestation of incorrigible spiritual pride. The clarity and logic of this Spanish Carmelite, added to his unsurpassed experiential knowledge of the things of God, make him by far the greatest as well as the surest of all mystical theologians.

### Blaise Pascal
[FRANCE, 17TH CENTURY]

Blaise Pascal was born at Clermont Ferrand, in central France, in 1623. His first "conversion" to Jansenism took place in 1646 and he retired to Port Royal after his vision in 1654. It was then that he began the *Lettres Provinciales*. He later left Port Royal and died in Paris on August 15, 1662.

Few Catholic writers have been the subject of as much discussion as Pascal. He has found enemies everywhere, inside the Church as well as among the greatest enemies of the Church. He still has friends, Catholic and otherwise. If he has enemies, it is largely his own fault. His brilliant intelligence and his keen observation of human nature still demand our admiration. His tortured life deserves a sympathy which he is often denied. Everything about him has been called in question, from his sanity to his loyalty to the Church. Perhaps he was a neurotic. Certainly he defended some erroneous theological opinions. He could have chosen a more healthy spiritual atmosphere to live in than the Jansenism of Port Royal. Nevertheless, it would be folly to question his fundamental sincerity, and his wisdom is still able to speak for itself. Pascal has never been condemned as a heretic, he never contumaciously resisted Church authority, and he died, as he sincerely believed he had lived, a loyal Catholic. How-

ever, the fact remains that he was for a great part of his life
associated with the Jansenist heresy, and he defended it by a
series of anonymous and surreptitiously printed pamphlets. Yet
his defense of Port Royal was not strictly a defense of condemned
doctrine. He merely tried to argue that the doctrine that had
been condemned had never, in fact, been held by Port Royal.

Nevertheless, it is useless to deny that even in Pascal the
odiousness of Jansenism is not mitigated by style, perspicacity,
or literary skill. The *Lettres Provinciales,* as Pascal himself seems
to have realized later on, remain a blot on his reputation. These
pamphlets are most famous for their bitter excoriation of the
Society of Jesus. It is here that Pascal's theology, as well as his
Catholicity, went wrong. His exaggerated and false picture of
Jesuit moral theology brought odium upon the whole Church.
It was Pascal who, more than any other, made "casuistry" a
term of opprobrium in the mouths of the Church's enemies.
He did as much as any "anti-Papist" to popularize the legend
that moral theology is fundamentally dishonest and that many
Catholic priests and religious are nothing but political oppor-
tunists, seeking to dominate the world by means of the confes-
sional! Cardinal Newman wrote his *Apologia* to defend the
Church and himself against this very charge. Yet the accusation remains the principal weapon in the hands of the Church's
enemies today. If Pascal alone had been responsible for its forg-
ing, he would indeed have something to answer for. He certainly
intended no such harm. When he later realized what might
eventually be the consequences of his statements, he seems to
have undergone a change of heart. He devoted his later years
to a book in defense of the Catholic faith against the rationalism
which was already prevalent in his time. The book was never
finished. Yet the notes alone form one of the most interesting volumes in all literature. This is the famous book of his
"thoughts," *Les Pensées.* In the *Pensées* we see much less of
Pascal the Jansenist and much more of the true Catholic that
was in him. Here Pascal prepares a brilliant defense for the
rationality of Catholic faith and in doing so attacks the pseudo-
Catholic philosophizing of thinkers like Descartes who, in their
anxiety to meet rationalism halfway, were actually emptying

faith of all its content and reducing religion to a matter of form, a superficial accident in a society of mathematicians.

Actually, Pascal was well equipped to undertake such a task because he was himself a scientist. He had grown up in the most advanced circles of mathematical and physical empiricism. Yet at the same time he had been trained in the Catholic faith. The problem of living as a Catholic in a century that was essentially skeptical and mundane involved Pascal in a certain ambivalence which did him no good. His series of "conversions," his celebrated vision, the "miracle of the thorn," his association with Port Royal, the ill-balanced moralism reflected in the *Lettres Provinciales* seem to manifest something of the dark unhappiness of a soul that has not found true spiritual rest. The unfinished book of *Pensées* remains, then, a true witness to his spirit, as well as a monument to an unsettled genius.

No doubt Pascal would have been scandalized to think that the "probabilism" which seemed to him to be so odious in moral theology would one day be universally adopted, in practice, by theologians. And yet the spiritual life is best developed where souls are allowed freedom of choice in doubtful cases. The strictness of the Jansenists, who believed that a truly "spiritual" man would always, in case of doubt, be prompted by a special interior attraction to choose what was harder and more repugnant to human nature, was in actual fact the kind of thing that hampers the action of the Holy Spirit. It narrows and contracts the soul, confining it to hairsplitting considerations of detail like those which preoccupied the Pharisees in the time of Christ. But what is worse, this asceticism is dangerous because it is explicitly irrational. Pascal, who defended reason in the *Pensées,* attacked it, in a different context, in the *Lettres Provinciales.* And it was this, perhaps, that lay at the root of all his errors. This one fact is very important and it must never be overlooked by anyone who wishes to understand the difference between the asceticism of Saint John of the Cross, on the one hand, and the false asceticism of the Jansenists on the other.

*John of Saint Thomas*
[SPAIN, 17TH CENTURY]

No more striking contrast could be found than that which exists between Pascal and John of Saint Thomas, though these two men were contemporaries, intellectuals, mystics. John of Saint Thomas found his place and his vocation without difficulty and spent long, fruitful years in study, teaching, and writing. But he is very little read. His work is, in many ways, much more significant than Pascal's, but it has never attracted the interest of any but specialists in theology. John of Saint Thomas is one of those speculative theologians who cannot reach the average educated man except through a mediator who is willing to translate his thought into ordinary terms. The issues which concern such theologians are generally matters of such minute detail that this work of mediation is scarcely ever worth while. The treatise of John of Saint Thomas on the Gifts of the Holy Ghost is an important exception to this general rule.

Although his life was uneventful, John of Saint Thomas has an interesting background. Born at Lisbon in 1589, he was the son of an Austrian diplomat who soon moved, with his family, to the Spanish Netherlands. John received a cosmopolitan education from various universities, including Louvain, Belgium, and Coimbra, Portugal. In 1623, some years after his ordination to the priesthood, he entered the Dominican Order at Madrid. From then on he devoted himself to the special vocation which is reflected in his religious name: all his gifts were consecrated to the study and interpretation of Saint Thomas Aquinas.

In the age following the great Thomist revival of the sixteenth century, it might seem that there was nothing wonderful in such a vocation. No doubt John of Saint Thomas never stopped to ask himself whether what he was doing happened to be remarkable. On the contrary, his most admirable characteristic is the completeness with which he proposed to submerge his own talents and personality in the thought of the Angelic Doctor. And it is here that we find him in such marked contrast to Pascal. For John of Saint Thomas, like Pascal, found himself in controversy with the Jesuits. But what a difference! Here we find no acrimony, no editions confiscated by the police, no bitter accusations of heresy on both sides, no public clamor and disturbance of souls. John of Saint Thomas was the seventeenth-century Dominican opponent to the great Suarez. Both commented on Saint Thomas. Both deserve their share of honor in the schools. Suarez was perhaps the greater theological genius of the two. John of Saint Thomas sought only the pure doctrine of Saint Thomas Aquinas, which he opposed to the "eclectic" Thomism of those who, though they may have acquired great names for themselves, never came anywhere near the Angelic Doctor. One tract of John of Saint Thomas stands out above all the rest. His study of the Gifts of the Holy Ghost is of capital importance. It contains the solution to some of the problems that have most exercised mystical theologians in our day. The claims of modern writers like Father Garrigou-Lagrange, Father Gardeil, and others who hold that the mystical life is the normal fulfillment of the Christian life of grace, rest almost entirely on the teaching of Saint Thomas about the Gifts of the Holy Ghost as it has been developed by John of Saint Thomas. There can be no question that the seventeenth-century Dominican has given us, with absolute clarity and fidelity, the true doctrine of Saint Thomas Aquinas.

After teaching for seventeen years at Alcalá, John of Saint Thomas was named, much against his will, confessor to Philip IV. In 1644, soon after the appointment, he died.

# Sources

PROLOGUE

1. C. G. Jung, *Modern Man in Search of a Soul* (New York, Harcourt, Brace and Company), p. 264.
2. *Menti Nostrae,* Sept. 23, 1950.
3. I Pet. 3:15.
4. John 17:22-23.
5. *Sancti Thomae huc omnis theologia spectat ut ad intime vivendum in Deo nos adducat.* Pius XI, *Studiorum Ducem,* June 29, 1927.
6. *Apostolic Letter,* August 24, 1926, declaring Saint John of the Cross a Doctor of the Universal Church.

I: VISION AND ILLUSION

1. Blaise Pascal, *Les Pensées* (Paris, Ed. Giraud, 1928), p. 66.
2. Saint Gregory of Nyssa, *Commentary on the Psalms,* P.G. 44: 464-465. Cf. Daniélou, *Platonisme et Théologie Mystique,* p. 133.
3. *Homily 1 on Ecclesiastes,* P.G. 44:628. Cf. Daniélou, *op. cit.,* p. 136.
4. I am not insisting that Pascal had read Saint Gregory of Nyssa. His thoughts on *divertissement* may have been drawn from a reading of Saint Bernard's *De Gradibus Humilitatis.* It is in any case in the full tradition of Saint Augustine's *De Trinitate,* Bk. xii (on the fall of Adam).
5. Pascal, *op. cit.,* p. 67.
6. *Ibid.,* n. 171, p. 75.
7. Saint Gregory of Nyssa, *Commentary on the Psalms,* C. 5. P.G. 44:450-451.

II: PROBLEM OF UNBELIEF

1. *Commentarium in Epistolam ad Romanos,* cap. 10, lectio ii.

III: ON A DARK NIGHT

1. Saint Gregory of Nyssa, *In cantica canticorum,* Hom. 11, P.G. 44:999.
2. Saint Gregory of Nyssa, Hom. 7 on Ecclesiastes, P.G. 44:729. Cf. Daniélou, *op. cit.,* p. 139.
3. It is generally forgotten that at the beginning of *The Ascent of Mount Carmel* (which for convenience I shall hereafter list in references as *Ascent*), Saint John of the Cross makes this threefold division of his night into a night of sense, night of faith, and night of pure contemplation or mystical union with God. We generally think of a twofold division. In reality, the second and third of the three nights above both belong to the "Night of the Spirit."

See *Ascent,* i, 1 and ii, 1 and 2. Peers tr., vol. i, pp. 20-21, 66-69.

4. *Ascent,* Bk. i, c. 13, n. 11. Peers, vol. i, p. 62.

5. Cf. *Ascent,* Bk. iii, c. 16, n. 5. Peers, vol. i, p. 260.

6. *Ascent,* Bk. iii, c. 16, n. 1. Peers, vol. i, p. 259.

7. *Ascent,* Bk. i, c. 13, n. 4. Peers, vol. i, p. 60.

8. *Ascent,* Bk. i, c. 8, n. 1. Peers, vol. i, p. 41.

9. *Ascent,* Bk. iii, c. 20, n. 2. Peers, vol. i, pp. 272-273.

IV: FALSE MYSTICISM

1. The statements appeared in front-page article in the official Vatican newspaper, *Osservatore Romano,* February 3, 1951.

V: KNOWLEDGE—UNKNOWING

1. *Ascent,* Bk. i, c. 4, n. 5. Peers, vol. i, pp. 26-27.

2. *The Dark Night of the Soul,* Bk. i, c. 1, n. 1. Peers, vol. i, p. 350.

3. *Ascent,* Bk. i, c. 4, n. 1. Peers, vol. i, p. 24.

4. John 14:6.

5. *Ascent,* Bk. ii, c. 7, n. 8. Peers, vol. i, p. 91.

6. *Ascent,* Bk. ii, c. 7, n. 12. Peers, vol. i, p. 93.

7. *Life,* 13. Peers, vol. i, p. 81.

8. *Life,* 13. Peers, vol. i, p. 82.

9. *Living Flame of Love,* 1st redaction, iii, n. 29. I have translated the passage differently from Professor Peers, who does not bring out with full force Saint John's contrast between knowledge and discretion, on the one hand, and experience on the other. Cf. Peers, vol. iii, p. 75.

10. *Life,* 13. Peers, vol. i, p. 78.

11. See, for instance, *Ascent,* Bk. iii, c. 21, n. 2. "The spiritual man must purge his will . . . *bearing in mind* that beauty and all other natural gifts are but earth," etc. Peers, vol. i, p. 275.

12. *Ibid.,* Bk. i, c. 13, n. 3. "*First* let him have a habitual desire to imitate Christ in everything that he does, conforming himself to His life: upon which *he must meditate* so that he may know how to imitate it, and to behave in all things as Christ would behave." Peers, vol. i, p. 60.

13. *Ascent,* Bk. ii, c. 8, nos. 1 and 7. Peers, vol. i, pp. 94 and 98.

14. *Ascent,* Bk. ii, c. 15, n. 3. Peers, vol. i, p. 128.

15. *Ascent,* Bk. ii, c. 11, nos. 2 and 3. Peers, vol. i, pp. 102-103.

16. *Ascent,* Bk. ii, c. 15. Peers, vol. i, p. 128.

17. *Ibid.*

VI: CONCEPTS—CONTEMPLATION

1. *Summa Theologica,* i, 13, a. 5.

2. *Summa, loc. cit.*

3. Cf. Saint Bernard, *De Consideratione,* v, 13. Saint Thomas, *Summa,* i, 13, a. 4.

4. II, Sent. D. 33, a. 2, q. 3.

5. Collatio ii in Hexaemeron, n. 32.

6. See Jacques Maritain, *Degrees of Knowledge* (New York, 1938), p. 278.

7. *De Potentia,* vii, 5, ad. 14.

8. *In Boetium de Trinitate,* i, 2, ad. 2.

VII: DARK KNOWLEDGE

1. Saint Teresa of Ávila, *Way of Perfection:* 10, Peers, vol. ii, p. 45.

2. *Ad rationem summi boni pertinet quod summo modo se creaturae*

*communicet: quod maxime fit per hoc quod naturam creatam sic sibi conjungit, et una persona fiat ex tribus, Verbo, anima et carne.* Summa Theologica, III, i, 1. Saint Thomas is referring to a text of Saint Augustine's *De Trinitate*, xiii, 17.

3. Cf. Søren Kierkegaard, *Fear and Trembling*.

4. Baptism is the sacrament by which a full and living faith is formally conferred upon the soul. In the case of adult conversions, however, it is highly probable that living faith is usually present in the soul before the baptism of water.

VIII: THEOLOGICAL BACKGROUND

1. *Ascent*, Prologue. Peers, vol. i, p. 11.

2. *Spiritual Canticle*, Prologue, n. 4. Peers, vol. ii, p. 25.

3. *Ibid*.

4. *Spiritual Canticle*, Prologue, n. 3. Peers, vol. ii, p. 25.

5. He was then still a member of the Calced Carmelites, whose habit he had taken under the name of John of Saint Mathias.

6. Three years of philosophy and one of theology would be unthinkable in a Catholic seminary today. However, though Saint John of the Cross did not get a "survey" of the whole field of theology in a dogmatic digest like that of Tanquerey, his intense application to particular tracts in theology certainly ended up by giving him a sure knowledge of theology as a whole.

7. *Spiritual Canticle*, i, 1. Peers, vol. ii, p. 31.

8. See I IIae. Q. i, a. 8; Q. ii, a. 8; Q. iii, a. 3; Q. iii, a. 8; Q. iv, a. 3.

9. *Summa*, I IIae. Q. ii, a. 1-6. Cf. *Ascent*, Bk. iii, c. 18-26.

10. *Summa*, I IIae. Q. ii, a. 7.

11. *Ascent*, Bk. iii, c. 27 *ff*.

12. Cf. *Ibid.*, Bk. ii, n. 8.

13. *Summa*, I IIae. Q. 6, a. 7. See also the two previous articles.

14. *Spiritual Canticle*, xxiv, n. 5. Peers, vol. ii, p. 162. The question of the essence of beatitude still divides Catholic theologians. Those who follow Saint Thomas hold that the soul is united to God in an act of the intelligence, or vision, and that love follows from this as an accidental consequence. The Scotists hold that the union is actually effected in an operation of the will, an act of love, for which the way is prepared by vision.

15. *Summa*, I IIae. Q. 3, a. 6.

16. *Ascent*, Bk. i, n. 4. Peers, vol. i, p. 26.

17. *Summa*, I IIae. Q. 5, a. 5.

18. *Ascent*, Bk. ii, n. 8. Peers, vol. i, p. 94.

19. He was a professor at the Collège de France. The commentary was in fact a piece of piracy. Robert Estienne had first printed it from the lecture notes of one of Vatable's students, and against the vigorous protest of Vatable himself, in 1545. Cf. Vilnet, *Bible et Mystique chez Saint Jean de la Croix*. Etudes Carmelitaines, 1949, p. 22. All through this section I am following Vilnet.

20. See Vilnet, *op. cit.*, c. iv.

IX: FAITH AND REASON

1. Bruno de J-M., *Saint Jean de la Croix* (Paris, 1932), c. 10, p. 115.

2. "A man of prayer and a man of study:

   But primarily a man of prayer."

   Cf. Bruno, *op. cit.*, c. 10, p. 122.

3. Bruno, *op. cit.*, p. 221.

4. Luke 10:16.

5. *Maxims*, n. 7. Peers, vol. iii, p. 241.

6. See Herbert, Jean, *Spiritualité Hindoue* (Paris, 1947), p. 356.

7. *The Cautions*, n. 12. Peers, vol. iii, p. 224.

8. *Ascent*, Bk. ii, c. 22, n. 11. Peers, vol. i, p. 179.

9. *Ibid.*

10. *Ascent*, Bk. ii, c. 22, n. 11. Peers, vol. i, p. 179.

X: REASON IN CONT. LIFE

1. *Ascent*, Bk. ii, c. 22, Peers, vol. i, p. 181.

2. *Ascent*, Bk. ii, c. 21 and 22.

3. See the frontispiece to *The Ascent*.

4. *Ascent*, Bk. ii, c. 21, n. 1. Peers, vol. i, p. 163.

5. *Ascent*, Bk. ii, c. 22, n. 13. Peers, vol. i, p. 181.

6. *Ex toto posse suo homo debet diligere Deum et quidquid habet ad Dei amorem ordinare. Summa,* II IIae. Q. 27, a. 5.

7. *Spiritual Canticle*, xxvii.

8. *Ascent*, Bk. ii, c. 15, n. 1. Peers, vol. i, p. 259.

9. *Dark Night*, Bk. ii, c. 10, Peers, vol. i, p. 434.

10. Saint John of the Cross, *Living Flame of Love*, II, n. 23. Peers, vol. iii, p. 51.

11. *Ascent*, Bk. iii, c. 16, n. 2. Peers, vol. i, p. 259.

12. *Ibid.*, Peers, vol. i, p. 260.

13. *Ascent*, Bk. iii, c. 16, n. 2. Peers, vol. i, p. 261.

14. Luke 11:34-35.

15. *Ascent*, Bk. iii, c. 23. Peers, vol. i, p. 281.

16. *Ascent*, Bk. iii, c. 34, Peers, vol. i, p. 283.

17. *Ascent*, Bk. iii, c. 24, n. 4. Peers, vol. i, p. 285.

18. *Ascent*, Bk. iii, c. 24, n. 5.

19. *Ascent*, Bk. iii, n. 6, Peers, vol. i, p. 285.

20. *Ibid.*, Bk. i, c. 13, nos. 3-4. Peers, vol. i, p. 60.

21. *Ascent*, Bk. i, c. 13, n. 4. Peers, vol. i, pp. 60-61.

XI: REASONABLE SERVICE

1. Rom. 8:13-14.

2. *Ibid.*, 12:1.

3. I Cor. 14: last verse.

4. *In Epist. Pauli ad Romanos, Cap.* xii, Lect. i.

5. *Dark Night*, Bk. i, c. 6, n. 2. Peers, vol. i, p. 365.

6. I Cor. 2:14-15.

7. *Ascent*, Bk. ii, c. 19, n. 11. Peers, vol. i, p. 156.

8. *Dark Night*, Bk. i, c. 6, n. 1. Peers, vol. i, p. 364.

9. *Dark Night*, Bk. i, c. 6, n. 1. Peers, vol. i, p. 364.

10. *Dark Night*, Peers, vol. i, p. 364.

11. Maxims, nos. 41, 42, 43. Peers, vol. iii, p. 246.

12. Maxims, n. 34. Peers, vol. iii, p. 245.

XII: INSTINCT—INSPIRATION

1. *Ascent*, Bk. i, c. 9, n. 3. Peers, vol. i, p. 52.

2. Cf. *Dark Night*, Bk. ii, c. 2. Peers, vol. I, p. 400.

3. *Dark Night*, Bk. ii, c. 2. Peers, vol I, p. 400.

4. St. Teresa of Ávila, *Life,* c. 18 and c. 22, especially Peers, vol. i, p. 140.
5. *Summa,* I. Q. 82, A. 23.

XIII: REASON—REASONING
1. *Ascent,* Bk. ii, c. 29, nos. 4-5. Peers, vol. i, p. 210.
2. *Ascent, ibid.,* p. 211.
3. *Ibid.,* p. 212.
4. *Summa,* II IIae. Q. 180, a. 3, ad. 1.
5. *Summa,* II IIae. Q. 1, a. 7.
6. Hebrews 11:6.
7. See Saint Thomas, *Summa,* I IIae, Q. 89, a. 6, and Pope Pius IX, Denzinger Bannwart, *Enchiridium Symbolorum,* n. 1677.
8. Jean de Saint Thomas, *Les Dons du Saint-Esprit,* trad. de Raïssa Maritain (Juvisy, 1930), p. 13. (From John of Saint Thomas's *Commentary on Saint Thomas, Summa Theologica,* I II, Q. 68.)
9. Jean de Saint Thomas, *op. cit.,* p. 81.

XIV: PRAYER OF QUIET
1. *Life,* c. 15. Peers, vol. i, pp. 88 *f.*
2. *Life,* c. 22. Peers, vol. i, p. 142. Saint Teresa does not mean that mystical contemplation was ever natural to man in the strict sense of the word, but that it was included among the gifts super-added to man's nature by God in the creation of Adam, so that it was historically part of the spiritual make-up of the first man, and would have been transmitted by him to all his descendants but for original sin.
3. *Life,* c. 15. Peers, vol. i, p. 89.
4. *Ibid.,* p. 91.
5. J. Ruysbroeck, *"L'Ornement des Noces Spirituelles,"* Bk. ii, c. 74, Wisques tr., p. 195.

6. J. de Guibert, S.J., *Etudes de Théologie Mystique* (Toulouse, 1930), quoted in Jules Lebreton, S.J., *Tu Solus Sanctus* (Paris, 1948), pp. 135-136.
7. *Ascent,* Bk. ii, c. 13. Peers, vol. i, pp. 114 *f.*
8. *Ascent,* Peers, *loc. cit.,* p. 116.
9. *Ascent,* Bk. ii, c. 29. Peers, vol. i, p. 213.
10. *Living Flame,* Bk. iii. Peers, vol. iii, p. 195.
11. *Spiritual Canticle,* Bk. xxvi, n. 15. Peers, vol. ii, p. 334.
12. *Living Flame,* Bk. iii, n. 27. Peers, vol. iii, p. 74.
13. Peers, vol. iii, p. 77.
14. *Ibid.,* p. 80.
15. *Ibid.,* p. 74.
16. *Living Flame, ibid.,* p. 78.
17. *Living Flame, ibid.,* p. 78.

XV: MIRROR OF WATERS
1. Eph. 2:6.
2. John 20:29.
3. *Ascent,* Bk. ii, c. 22, n. 7. Peers, vol. ii, p. 176. I have rendered *Cristo hombre* as Christ the Man-God. Prof. Peers translates it as "Christ made man," but that is theologically incorrect. The Word-made-flesh is Christ. Christ is Man and God, but Christ is not "made man." Note, however, that the expression *Cristo hombre* puts emphasis on the Humanity of the Redeemer.
4. *Ascent,* Bk. ii, n. 27. Peers, vol. i, p. 205.
5. Cf. Garrigou-Lagrange, *Christian Perfection and Contemplation* (St. Louis, 1937), p. 57 *f.*
6. *Ascent,* Bk. ii, c. 24, n. 3. I do not agree with Prof. Peers's translation (vol. i, p. 189), "those that are spiritually most strong in the

Church," as a rendering of *Aquellos que son muy fuertes del espiritu de la Iglesia.* (Silverio, vol. ii, p. 200.)

7. Cf. *Definitions of the Council of Orange,* Denzinger Bannwart, 178-180.
8. *Ascent,* Bk. ii, n. 9. Peers, vol. i, p. 98.
9. *Ascent,* Bk. ii, n. 24. Peers, vol. i, p. 189.
10. *Catech. Trid.* Pt. i, c. ii, Q. 6.
11. *Ascent,* Bk. ii, n. 9. Peers, vol. i, p. 98.
12. *Ascent,* Bk. i, n. 2. Peers, vol. i, p. 20.
13. John 17:21-22.

## XVI: A DARK CLOUD

1. *Ascent,* Bk. ii, c. 3. Peers, vol. i, p. 70.
2. *Ibid.*
3. *Ascent, loc. cit.,* pp. 70-71.
4. *Loc. cit.,* p. 71.
5. *Loc. cit.,* p. 72.
6. *Ibid.*
7. *Ibid.*
8. Isaias, 7:9 was quoted in this sense by many of the Fathers of the Church.
9. Hebrews, 11:6.
10. *Fides principaliter est ex infusione . . . sed quantum ad determinationem est ex auditu.* IV *Sent.,* D. 4, Q. 2, A. 2; Sol. 3, ad. 1.
11. Stanza xii. Peers, vol. ii, pp. 245 *ff.*
12. John 4:14.
13. Psalm 17:12.
14. *Spiritual Canticle,* I, Peers, vol. ii, p. 198.
15. *Spiritual Canticle, loc. cit.*
16. Osee 2:20.
17. *Spiritual Canticle, loc. cit.,* p. 247.

18. *Dark Night,* Bk. ii, n. 5. Peers, vol. i.
19. *Spiritual Canticle, loc. cit.,* p. 246.

## XVII: LOVING KNOWLEDGE

1. *Sapientia quae est donum causam habet in voluntate; sed essentiam habet in intellectu cujus actus est recte judicare.* II II, Q. 45, A. 2.
2. John 14:23-16-17.
3. *Commentarium in Evangelium Joannis,* V.
4. *Degrees of Knowledge,* p. 326.
5. See Maritain, *op. cit.,* p. 322.
6. John of Saint Thomas, *Cursus Theologicus,* I II, Q. 68-70, Disp. 18, a. 4. In Raïssa Maritain's French translation, pp. 138-139.
7. Sermon VIII in *Cantica,* n. 5.
8. *Summa,* II II, Q. 180, A. 7, ad. 1.
9. *De Civitate Dei,* xix, c. 27.
10. *Caritas facit hominem Deo inhaerere propter seipsum, mentem hominis uniens Deo per affectum amoris . . . Caritas proprie facit tendere in Deum, uniendo affectum hominis Deo ut homo non sibi vivat sed Deo.* II II, Q. 17, a. 6.
11. This quotation must be understood in the light of Saint Thomas's full teaching on the active and contemplative lives. Also it must be noted that, in distinguishing the love of God from that of our neighbor, Saint Thomas does not deny that in loving our neighbor we are also loving God. II II, Q. 188, A. 6.
12. Stanza 38. Peers, vol. ii, p. 391.
13. *Summa,* I, Q. 82, A. 23.
14. *De Adhaerendo Deo,* IX. Cf. Maritain, *op. cit.,* p. 330.

15. Matthew, 5:8.
16. *Summa,* I II, Q. 3, A. 2, ad. 4.

XVIII: MOUNTAIN AND HILL
1. Luke 11:23.
2. *Caritas attingit ipsum Deum ut in ipso sistat, non ut ex eo aliquid nobis proveniat.* II II, Q. 23, A. 6. Cf. II II, Q. 17, A. 6, quoted above, chapter xvii, note 10.
3. *Spiritual Canticle,* Stanza xi.
4. *Ibid.,* II. Peers, vol. ii, p. 240.
5. I Cor. 13:12.
6. *Cantico Espiritual,* Stanzas 36-40. I have only used a few lines from Prof. Peers's translation; *op. cit.,* vol. ii, p. 191.
7. *Spiritual Canticle,* Stanza 36. Peers, vol. ii, p. 380.
8. *Spiritual Canticle,* Stanza 36. Peers, vol. ii, p. 383.
9. *Ibid.*

XIX: GIANT MOVES IN SLEEP
1. Hymn at Lauds, Cistercian Breviary.
2. John 14:9; 10:30.
3. Hebrews 1:2.
4. John 1:12.
5. John 6:58.

6. *Spiritual Canticle,* II. Peers, vol. ii, p. 240. See above, p. 299.
7. *Ascent,* Bk. ii, n. 22. Peers, vol. i, pp. 174-175.
8. *Spiritual Canticle,* Stanza 37. Peers, vol. ii, p. 385.
9. *Spiritual Canticle, loc. cit.*
10. Ephesians 3:8-10.
11. *Spiritual Canticle,* Stanza 37. Peers, vol. ii, p. 386.
12. *Spiritual Canticle,* Stanza 37. Peers, vol. ii, pp. 385-386.
13. *Spiritual Canticle,* Stanza 37. Peers, vol. ii, p. 385.
14. *Spiritual Canticle,* Stanza 39.
15. *Spiritual Canticle,* Stanza 39. Peers, vol. ii, p. 396.
16. *Spiritual Canticle,* Stanza 38. Peers, vol. ii, p. 388.
17. Luke, 2:51.
18. *Living Flame of Love,* IV. Peers, vol. iii, pp. 208-211.

BIOGRAPHICAL NOTES
1. Acts, 17:34.
2. *Summa,* II IIae, Q. 179-182.
3. *Oeuvres de Ruysbroeck l'Admirable* (3rd edition, Brussels, 1935), vol. ii, p. 16.